THE DOGS OF MARIUPOL

TOM MUTCH

THE DOGS OF MARIUPOL

RUSSIA'S INVASION AND THE FORGING OF UKRAINE'S IRON GENERATION

Biteback Publishing

First published in Great Britain in 2025 by
Biteback Publishing Ltd, London
Copyright © Tom Mutch 2025

Tom Mutch has asserted his right under the Copyright, Designs and Patents Act 1988
to be identified as the author of this work.

All rights reserved. No part of this publication may be reproduced, stored in a retrieval system or transmitted, in any form or by any means, without the publisher's prior permission in writing.

This book is sold subject to the condition that it shall not, by way of trade or otherwise, be lent, resold, hired out or otherwise circulated without the publisher's prior consent in any form of binding or cover other than that in which it is published and without a similar condition, including this condition, being imposed on the subsequent purchaser.

Excerpts from *I Will Show You How It Was* by Illia Ponomarenko reproduced
by kind permission of Illia Ponomarenko and Bloomsbury Publishing.

Excerpts from Tom Mutch's articles in the *Evening Standard* reproduced
by kind permission of the *Evening Standard*.

Excerpts from Tom Mutch's articles in the *Daily Beast*
reproduced by kind permission of the *Daily Beast*.

Excerpts from Tom Mutch's articles in the *New Zealand Herald*
reproduced by kind permission of the *New Zealand Herald*.

Every reasonable effort has been made to trace copyright holders of material reproduced in this book, but if any have been inadvertently overlooked the publisher would be glad to hear from them.

ISBN 978-1-78590-973-3

10 9 8 7 6 5 4 3 2 1

A CIP catalogue record for this book is available from the British Library.

Set in Minion Pro and Trade Gothic

Printed and bound in Great Britain by
CPI Group (UK) Ltd, Croydon CR0 4YY

For Arman Soldin and the other countless dead heroes

'We have shared the incommunicable experience of war. We have felt, we still feel, the passion of life to its top. In our youths, our hearts were touched with fire.'
– OLIVER WENDELL HOLMES JR

'The good book does indeed count war an evil, said Irving. Yet there's many a bloody tale of war inside it.'
– CORMAC MCCARTHY, *BLOOD MERIDIAN: OR, THE EVENING REDNESS IN THE WEST*

CONTENTS

Maps	xi
Glossary	xv
Author's Stylistic Note	xix
Prologue *Ruskiy Mir*	xxi

Chapter One	The Dogs of War: Ukraine's Turbulent History and the Build-Up to Russia's Invasion	1
Chapter Two	Cry Havoc: The Battle for Kyiv and the Invasion of Northern Ukraine	31
Chapter Three	The Empire Strikes Back: The Conquest of the South and the First Battle of Donbas	69
Chapter Four	Hero City: The First Ukraine Counteroffensive and the Unbreakable Defiance of Kharkiv	103
Chapter Five	The Wrath of the River: Occupation, Liberation and Agony in Kherson	137
Chapter Six	Fortress of Regrets: The Merciless Meat Grinder of Bakhmut	167
Chapter Seven	In the Mood for Love: Kyiv in the Blur Between Peace and War	191
Chapter Eight	See No Evil, Hear No Evil, Speak No Evil: The Russians and How They Rule	215

Chapter Nine	The Longest Days: Ukraine's Failed Counteroffensive	245
Chapter Ten	The Doldrums: Ukraine's War of Attrition and the Rise of the Deadly Drone	275
Epilogue	Tragedy Then Farce: The Second Munich Betrayal	299
Acknowledgements and the Writing of This Book		311
Select Bibliography and Notes on Sources		317

MAPS

Control of Ukraine as of March 2025

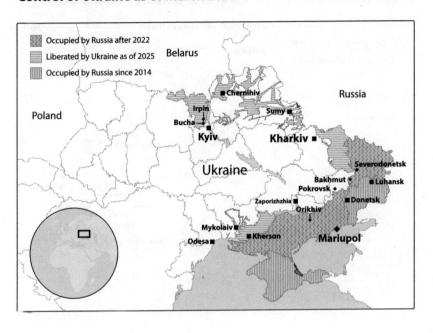

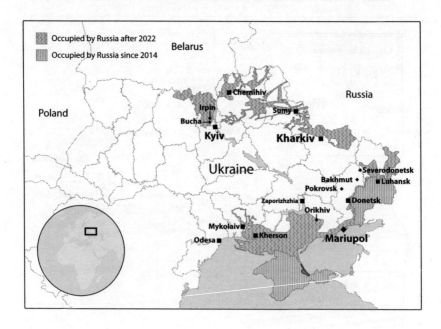

Greatest Extent of Russian Control of Ukraine in March 2022

MAPS

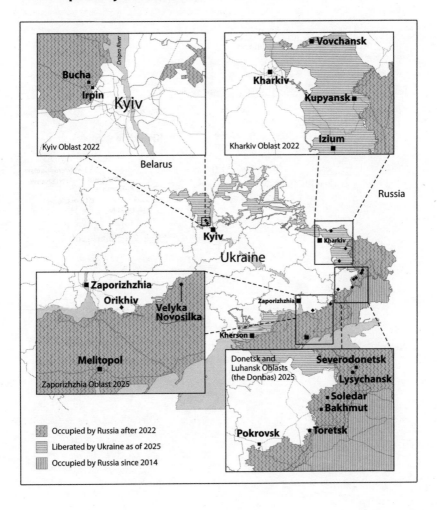

GLOSSARY

AFU: Armed Forces of Ukraine, the umbrella term for the Ukrainian military.

APC: Armoured personnel carrier, commonly confused with a tank. A tank has tracks, an APC has wheels.

ATACMS: Army Tactical Missile System, a long-range US missile system, fired from a HIMARS rocket launcher.

Banderite: A derogatory term used by Russians for supporters of Ukrainian independence. Refers to followers of Stepan Bandera, a nationalist leader from the Second World War era.

FPV: First-person view, usually used in the context of a drone which the pilot directs through goggles linked to a camera on the machine itself.

Grad: From the Russian/Ukrainian word for 'hail', it is a truck that fires up to twenty unguided rockets at a single time. To be caught under it is utterly terrifying.

HIMARS: M142 High Mobility Artillery Rocket System, a ground-based mobile missile system mounted on the back of a truck with high range and accuracy.

Holodomor: A devastating famine caused by Soviet state policy in the early 1930s that killed as many as 4 million Ukrainians. Widely considered a genocide.

Hryvnia: The Ukrainian unit of currency – 100 hryvnia is roughly £2.

JFO: Joint Forces Operation. This was the name for the parts of Donbas, still controlled by Ukraine, that the Ukrainian Army controlled between 2015 and 2022. It was home to the most experienced Ukrainian soldiers, and destroying it was a key early objective of the Russian Army.

LDPR (LPR/DPR): Luhansk/Donetsk People's Republics. The two self-declared states in the parts of Luhansk and Donetsk Oblasts controlled by Russian separatists in 2014.

Left bank/right bank: Refers to which side of the Dnipro River a particular place is. Confusingly, this follows the river downstream, so it is the opposite of what it looks like on a traditional northwards-facing map of Ukraine. Left bank is east, right bank is west.

Oblast: Ukrainian/Russian word for 'region'.

Orc: A deformed evil creature from *The Lord of the Rings*, used by Ukrainians to refer to Russian soldiers.

GLOSSARY

OUN: Organisation of Ukrainian Nationalists, a movement that fought for Ukrainian independence in the Second World War. Still lionised in Ukraine, it is controversial abroad due to its participation in the ethnic cleansing of Poles and Jews.

Palianytsia: A type of flatbread, and a difficult word to pronounce for non-native Ukrainian speakers. Used as a password to root out Russian-born spies.

Ruskiy Mir: A phrase that can be literally translated as either 'Russian World' or 'Russian Peace'. Used by Russians and pro-Russian Ukrainians to refer to a Russian cultural world and by most Ukrainians to refer ironically to the damage done by Russia.

Separ: Short for a 'separatist', a supporter, either Russian or Ukrainian, of Donbas secession from Ukraine or joining with Russia.

Surzhyk: A mixture of Ukrainian and Russian, spoken in a variety of dialects throughout Ukraine and in small parts of Russia. From a word for a mix of rye and other grain.

USSR: Union of Soviet Socialist Republics, the Moscow-dominated communist state that Russia and Ukraine were members of until 1991.

Zhdun: From the Russian word 'waiting', a *zhdun* is a pro-Russian Ukrainian, mostly in the Donbas, who stays in war-torn cities waiting for the Russians to come.

AUTHOR'S STYLISTIC NOTE

I have used Ukrainian, rather than Russian, spelling in most cases for people and place names. This means Kyiv instead of Kiev, Odesa instead of Odessa, Mykolaiv instead of Nikolaev, Kharkiv instead of Kharkov and so on. The exception is where I am quoting an original source that uses the now out-of-favour Russian spelling, particularly in Chapter Eight. The same applies to the name 'Ukraine'. Some Russian sources refer to 'the Ukraine', which is a designation Ukrainians find offensive, as it implies that Ukraine is a region rather than its own country.

Ukrainians prefer to call the war that broke out on 24 February 2022 the 'full-scale invasion', to remind observers that Russia's aggression against Ukraine began in 2014, and thus to distinguish between the smaller war and the larger one. For the sake of brevity, when I refer to the war or invasion, I am talking about events from 2022 onwards, except when otherwise specified.

Where possible, I have used people's full names. However, there are several important exceptions. Generally, when writing about members of the Ukrainian military, the custom is to use only their first name or a callsign for security reasons. Some people in Ukraine have family in Russian-occupied territories who could face retaliation if their relatives were identified speaking to the western press. In some cases, their names have also been redacted either in full or in part.

PROLOGUE

RUSKIY MIR

NOVOPETRIVKA, KHERSON OBLAST, NOVEMBER 2022

On closer inspection, the body was filled with sand and straw, not blood and bone. Clad in dark green and brown soldier's fatigues, he reclined lazily against a tree, head slightly askew.

The mannequin was staring at the twisted wreck of a Russian armoured vehicle whose remaining metal tracks and spokes were scattered around the clearing I was standing in. Whatever arrow from the varied quiver of Ukrainian artillery that had struck this trespasser scored a direct hit. Ukrainian locals here cheerfully admitted they would give their army the coordinates of any Russian military equipment nearby, and the results were clear as day.

Since I'd grasped the cold, clammy hand of my grandfather as a child, the first body I had seen was six months ago, a soldier lying prostrate, his face in the dirt, on a highway leading to Bucha, a portent of the horrors that we would find littering that town's streets. The dead were a routine sight in this most violent of wars. They were wrapped in bags and stacked in warehouses waiting for burial; they floated down the streets turned canals of Kherson after the flooding of the Dnipro; they were dug up after months of putrefying in the ground in a mass grave near Kharkiv. Yet somehow the neatness of the figure's dress and his tidy placement against a tree caught my eye as a quaint contrast to the surrounding carnage.

The occupants of these trenches had left in a hurry. Full belts of ammunition were lying on the ground, and there were a few army uniforms still hanging on clotheslines pegged between the deciduous trees, stripped of their leaves by the freshly arrived winds of a mild winter. Anti-tank mines were neatly stacked next to the wooden slats that held up the entrance to a dugout in which the occupiers had lived. The six-month Russian tyranny over Novopetrivka, a tiny town in the Kherson region of southern Ukraine, had been presented to its inhabitants as a 'liberation'. At first, the Russians had an uneasy peace with the locals, but as their military situation deteriorated, it devolved into an orgy of bloodletting and robbery.

It was a figure in miniature of events all across Ukraine. During that time, this series of muddy ditches just metres in front of the village had been the front line. After months of vicious fighting, the nearby Ukrainian Army had finally broken through Russian defences. They were threatening to squeeze the Russians here in the Kherson region against the right bank of the Dnipro, cut off their supply routes and ultimately slaughter them. Before departing, they had left decoys like the mannequin beside me all over their positions to fool the drone teams scouting from the sky into thinking that there were still soldiers present. That way, they could slip back over the river unnoticed. Overnight, the villagers said, they had vanished like smoke in the wind.

Novopetrivka is probably not a name you've heard before. It wasn't the location of a headline-grabbing massacre or grungy attritional battle. After nine months of war, the sight of atrocities in Ukraine had become routine. They were blurring together, and people outside the country were tuning out the stacks of broken bodies and minds as footnotes to be filed in a human rights report or as colour to spice up a short news story. Mostly, they mattered only to the victims and their loved ones. As Joaquin Phoenix's cynical journalist in *Hotel Rwanda* says of the genocide he's filming: 'People will say, "Oh my God, that's horrible" and go on eating their dinner.'

There are dozens of these devastated towns scattered across the steppes of Ukraine. Bilohorivka, Posad-Pokrovske, Borohodychne, Kamianka, Selydove. These specks on a map used to be homes and communities for hundreds or even thousands of peaceful people before the Russian invasion reduced them to cinders. When I'd previously been to Bucha, the site of the Russians' most infamous murders, I'd been in a large press bus full of forty or so other reporters and escorted by Ukrainian Army minders. We'd been herded around like cattle from grave to grave. The scenes of murdered bodies hastily thrown into shallow pits had shocked us and the world. But when my colleagues and I had turned up, we knew in advance what to expect. The people in these towns also quickly tired of telling their personal stories of grief to the endless queues of reporters, most of whom came in for a few hours to grab a heartfelt quote or a gruesome photo and then left. I realised why the loose community of war reporters I had joined called themselves the 'Vulture Club', as they swarmed over carcasses, devouring every morsel of suffering, before moving on to the next story. These trips had an uncomfortable air of spectacle, as if we were paparazzi gatecrashing a funeral.

Novopetrivka was different. Our small team had stumbled upon these trenches and the village neatly tucked behind them by chance while looking for a back road to recently liberated Kherson. The Ukrainian Army itself had not been here yet, so the rough country roads were still strewn with metallic debris, unexploded ammunition and unspent rifle bullets. The Russians had pulled out less than two days ago and the once-terrified population were just beginning to realise their freedom. Here was the raw, unfiltered emotion of people who were telling their stories for the first time.

Viktor Afanov, a spirited and affable elderly farmer, ushered us into his house, poured generously from a jug of homemade wine and told his tale. 'We had just held a funeral for two young men the Russians had taken,' he said, his eyes shuddering, gesticulating firmly to emphasise each point. 'They were found drowned in the swamp; hands tied behind their backs,' he continued, describing a telltale sign of abduction and murder. 'The faces of the dead were blue, and it was clear to see they had been tortured.' Nobody knew for sure why. The Russians often suspected that young men here could be spies, giving the Ukrainian Army information on their positions, or saboteurs ready to stick bombs under their cars or knife them in the streets. But the Russians didn't have to give a reason: they were fickle and drunken masters, a law unto themselves. Viktor continued, swilling his wine, a thick, sickly sweet burgundy, while making sure our cups stayed topped up. He explained that some of the soldiers were incredulous at their living standards, having come from poor regions of Russia, seeing that the village had Wi-Fi. 'You have internet here?' they asked in shock. They then looted the whole town, he said. 'They took fridges, toilets, washing machines. It was total lawlessness!'

Viktor spat and exclaimed, 'That is the *Ruskiy Mir!*'

I'd first heard this phrase nearly a year ago in Borodyanka, a city in the Kyiv region that was nearly destroyed in the early days of fighting. 'Look!' my Ukrainian companions would say as we walked around, pointing at another patch of rubble that had once been a

PROLOGUE

cherished home or centre of a community, 'That is the *Ruskiy Mir!*' *Ruskiy Mir* is a curious phrase that can be translated as either 'Russian World' or 'Russian Peace'.

This concept was used by the Kremlin and its nationalist allies to refer to a shared cultural space encompassing literature, religion and language that they believed stretched through every part of the world that spoke Russian, including most of Ukraine. Their propagandists had justified their invasions, first in 2014 and now in 2022, by saying that the people living in these places were under threat from 'Nazis' and they needed to be 'liberated', brought back into the bosom of Mother Russia by force. When Russian troops hadn't been welcomed with the flowers they expected, they had lashed out like jilted lovers, taking their rage out on civilians and soldiers alike wherever they had managed to take control. This is what had happened in Novopetrivka. Now, '*Ruskiy Mir*' was used ironically to refer to the mass aerial and artillery bombing of cities, the levelling of schools and hospitals, the torture chambers and mass graves the invaders left in their wake.

Further down the road, we were invited into the farmhouse of an exhausted, pale-faced woman in her thirties I'll call Tatiana. After her family had run out of bread, she had sent her teenage son to walk to a neighbouring town to buy more. On the way back, he had been accosted by a group of Russian soldiers, drunk as usual, in the middle of the day. They demanded money from the boy, but he had spent the last of his money on his family's rations. So they beat him, then demanded at gunpoint he take them to his home, where they proceeded to threaten Tatiana to show them where they were hiding the money. She protested they had none. 'Well,' one of the soldiers had told her with a crazed smile, 'if you can't pay with money, you can pay with your body' to a burst of laughter from his comrades. Her face went blank, and she stopped speaking. The welling of tears in her eyes and shaking of her hands told the rest.

Yet the villagers in Novopetrivka told us all these tales of woe while speaking in Russian, or to be precise 'Surzhyk', that colloquial mix of Russian and Ukrainian that varies by region. As recently as ten years ago, many in Ukraine had still believed in the *Ruskiy Mir*. They spoke the Russian language, read the works of Chekhov, Tolstoy and Dostoevsky, worshipped following the rites of the Russian Orthodox Church. Near this town, as all over Ukraine, was a monument commemorating the Second World War, or what the Soviets called the Great Patriotic War, when both nations sacrificed millions of their young men and women to free the continent of the Nazis. Many Ukrainians had family and friends in Russia, travelled between the two countries and spoke Russian as fluently as anyone from Moscow. The concept of 'brotherly nations' was not just a figment of Russian propaganda. But Cain and Abel were also brothers. Now the Ukrainians called Russians 'orcs', because their behaviour seemed to mark them out as beasts, incapable of kindness, rationality or anything except brutish destruction.

When we followed the trench lines, moving slowly to check for mines or booby traps, what we found in the sleeping quarters showed a few wrinkles in this narrative. Among the scattered ration packs, discarded cigarette butts and muddy jackets, one soldier had left a journal behind. It describes the make-up of his unit, the Russian 2nd Motor Rifle Company, and the daily tasks and routine of the fifty-seven men in his unit. But it also reveals the soldier's growing disgust and anger towards their fighting conditions and their far-off superiors. 'Fuck you, I fought hard,' the soldier writes,

PROLOGUE

slamming the 'civilian guys on their fancy motorcycles' who had stayed in Russia and not come to war but nevertheless 'got buckets of unearned medals'. This was a possible reference to the widely despised Defence Minister, Sergei Shoigu, who was notorious for pinning his uniform with dozens of awards for gallantry despite never having seen a day of action in his life.

I was fascinated and frustrated in equal measure with these finds. Lying next to the journal was a page ripped from a Russian edition of Paulo Coelho's mystical novella of self-discovery, *The Alchemist*. 'Whoever interferes with the destiny of another will never discover his own!' reads one line on the page. I wondered if the soldier reading that had taken a moment to reflect on what that said about him being here. I longed to talk to the young man who'd left these scattered pages, who was clearly literate and intelligent. Did you really think you'd be welcomed as liberators? Were you motivated by patriotism, coercion or something as banal as cash? What did you think about the atrocities you witnessed or participated in? But I never even discovered his name.

INTRODUCTION

In the days before 24 February 2022, most inhabitants of Ukraine lived lives anyone in the west would recognise. The seed that grew into this book was planted by the woman in the red dress I met in a cafe just before the Russians invaded. Her name was Kateryna. She was a blogger and looked to be in a rut, swilling a glass of wine while she tapped on a laptop, a look of boredom and ennui etched on her face. I remember clearly her painted nails. She'd still have them when I saw her again just over a year later in the trenches, on the front line near the embattled city of Bakhmut and standing next to an artillery cannon, now a proud officer in the Armed Forces of Ukraine.

My subject is war, but it is not, as Wilfred Owen put it, just the pity of war. Owen was the great poet of the First World War, which he recognised as a pointless slaughter that cost the continent millions of lives for nothing. Posterity has largely agreed with him. There is much that connects these wars, especially in imagery. Muddy, murky trenches stretching for hundreds of miles, huge artillery barrages followed by infantry charges towards almost certain death. Shellshock, wastelands, despair. There is a great deal of pity in these pages, but I also highlight the life, happiness, determination, inventiveness, heroism and bravery in the story of Ukraine's resistance.

I grew up, like many young men of my generation, playing first-person shooter (FPS) video games, set in a variety of historical and futuristic battlefields. They seemed at the time to be escapist fantasies, but the battlefield looks scarily similar to those games, down to the men with controllers, their eyes fixed on screens or into goggles, piloting deadly drones into men and machines thousands of times per day. When I crept down the stairs of a farmhouse in eastern Ukraine, I saw a group of young men who looked just like me and my childhood friends did, controllers in hands, snacks and energy drinks on their tables, killing pixelated figures on their screens. But the men they were killing were real. None of the players in this game would respawn.

One old role-playing game, *Planescape: Torment* (from which the name of Chapter Six is taken), posed the question: 'What can change the nature of a man?' My answer is war. In these pages, I cover much of the politics and military history of the invasion, but above all, this book is about what war does to ordinary people thrust into

PROLOGUE

extraordinary circumstances. Hundreds of thousands of Ukrainians like you or I slammed shut laptops, downed construction tools and swapped suits and dresses for combat armour to defend their country. I tell the stories of such people over the book's ten chapters, which are arranged thematically but in a roughly chronological order.

The first covers Ukraine's turbulent history and its relationship with Russia, as well as the weeks-long build-up to the war, focusing on two key cities, Kyiv and Mariupol, which suffered wildly different fates. Although it is not a comprehensive account, it provides crucial context for the events of the invasion itself.

The next two cover the shock of the initial invasion and the disaster of the Russian campaign of northern Ukraine that attempted to capture the capital, Kyiv. Then, I explain the Russians' significantly greater success in the south and east, in the Battle of the Donbas. They shed light on some lesser-known battles in the war, such as those for Chernihiv, Sumy and Lysychansk. These stories are forgotten outside of Ukraine but contained as much heroism as the more famous encounters.

The next three chapters cover the story from the perspective of three Ukrainian cities that were the sites of some of the crucial encounters of the war, namely Kharkiv, Kherson and Bakhmut, each possessing cultural and geographic differences that affected the outcome of the fighting. They show how Ukraine and its partners scored great victories but failed to capitalise on this success and got bogged down in a grinding war of attrition.

The seventh and eighth chapters cover civilian life both in war and in peace and contrast the experience of those living in Kyiv after the battle with those in Russia and under Russian occupation.

The final two cover the most difficult periods of the war for Ukraine – the failed counteroffensive of 2023 and the grinding war of attrition in 2024, when, more than once, it seemed all was lost. An epilogue brings the story through 2025 at time of publication, examining the extraordinary political changes that have occurred after the election of Donald Trump and locating the war in a wider historical context.

I will also draw attention to some of the more uncomfortable aspects of life in Ukraine that reflect the flawed reality of a poor and often unstable country. Examples include the rampant corruption at many levels of officialdom and the brutality with which young men were forcibly enlisted off the street or their lives sacrificed in pointless battles. When the tide of the war slowly shifted against Ukraine, there was a reluctance to criticise Ukrainian command or their strategy. This book will try to correct that balance, while still making the case that Ukraine is one of the most important moral and political causes of our time.

The leadership and cohesion of Ukraine's western allies was initially essential to Ukraine's survival but became gradually overshadowed by the cowardice and naivety of world leaders who failed to grasp the nature of the Kremlin's threat to the world outside of Ukraine. But even as the United States seems content to sell out an ally it had promised to stand behind 'as long as it takes', Ukraine continues to stand strong, taking advantage of a huge drone production industry and a wealth of talented people that are determined to keep resisting. As I write this, air raid sirens ring out in the streets of cities and the bright orange flashes of missiles and air defence cover the sky. 'Ukraine has not yet perished,' says the national anthem. God willing, it never will.

Tom Mutch
Kyiv, March 2025

CHAPTER ONE

THE DOGS OF WAR: UKRAINE'S TURBULENT HISTORY AND THE BUILD-UP TO RUSSIA'S INVASION

'Only God prepares in this country.'
– Oleg Budnikov, Donbas villager

A MONUMENT TO ALL OUR SINS
POBUZKE, KIROVOHRAD OBLAST, AUGUST 2021

'Stretched out huge in length the Archfiend lay,' John Milton says of the defeated Devil in *Paradise Lost*. Milton's great villain was God's creation, but the Devil in front of me was manmade, an eighty-foot behemoth of steel and electrical wire built to hold rocket fuel and nuclear explosive. The 'Satan II' intercontinental ballistic missile was given its terrifying name because it could carry the highest yield nuclear warhead humanity's best scientific minds had devised. Travelling faster than the speed of sound, this missile and thousands like it would have streaked through the atmosphere and when they detonated over their targets in the United States, they each would have become towers of flame with temperatures as hot as the sun. The Satan II infernos would release more explosive energy in a second than all the weapons dropped in the Second World War combined. If the command to fire from Moscow had been given, most people on earth would have had about twenty-three minutes to live.

For nearly fifty years, the United States and the Soviet Union engaged in a Mexican standoff, and here was the bullet in the gun pointed at the head of the world, kept on hair-trigger notice, to be fired from a forty-metre-deep chasm nearby. The firing protocol was not based on the ominous big red button from Cold War fiction but a small, rectangular grey piece of plastic that could have easily been the control panel of an industrial waste disposal system. 'Go on, press the button!' Olena Smerychevska, our smiling black-haired Ukrainian guide, urged after taking us in through the huge steel doors guarding the silo and into a cramped and creaking elevator that slowly dropped us eleven floors down. This facility had been converted into the Ukrainian Strategic Missile Forces Museum, the only one of its kind in the world, and its main attraction was to let groups of adventure tourists pretend to be the commander to start the Third World War. Sitting so far underground, you would likely survive the nuclear holocaust. In the living quarters below were bunkbeds and forty-five days of provisions, intended for survival until radiation levels outside dropped to something safer. If you couldn't live with the guilt of having participated in the end of humanity or simply found life in the post-apocalyptic wasteland on the surface not to your liking, there was a loaded pistol left in your personal safe to take care of that.

If the missiles had ever been fired, Major General Valeriy Kuznetsov could have been the one to do it. Nestled in the bunker, he would have been one of the last people alive. An officer in the 46th Division of the Soviet Strategic Rocket Forces, he was stationed here decades ago, where he and two other officers prepared to receive orders. 'It would have been my duty,' he smiles. 'What would have happened to my family, my relatives, my country, all that was a secondary thing. We had to be there in that bunker till the end of life on earth.'

Protected by six-foot-thick metal walls, the capsule was fitted with shock absorbers and seatbelts, enabling those inside to survive the impact of a direct western nuclear strike. It would then have been Kuznetsov's duty to type a set of codes into a keyboard, then push a button marked 'Start Up'. They had regular drills on how to fire the missiles, and several times in their careers they were told it was the real thing. It was a test from their superior officers, to see whether they would still push the button for real – each time, they did just that.

Milton's Satan ends 'chained on the burning Lake, nor ever thence Had risen or heaved his head'. The Satan missile is now equally useless; today, it lies harmless, neutered, on a grassy field in the steppes of central Ukraine. The apocalypse that was feared for decades is yet to arrive. But this is where the rules-based international order died – and with it, the possibility of these missiles rising from their resting place. In exchange for security 'assurances', which turned out to be worthless when Russia invaded, Ukraine signed the Budapest Memorandum in 1994, which gave over the vast nuclear arsenal it had inherited from the Soviet Union to the tender care of the Russians.

'We are glad we have a museum; it is unique,' Olena said. 'But we are not pleased to have such pain in our history. It saddens me because Ukraine has a lot more to show to foreigners.' Ukraine developed a reputation for grungy 'dark tourism', based on reliving the horrors of the twentieth century. Most famous was the Chernobyl exclusion zone, another monument to the perils of the nuclear era. She hoped that as these events faded from view, the country would welcome tourists to the stunning cave monasteries in Kyiv and Sviatohirsk, the ski resorts and hot springs of the Carpathian Mountains or the cobbled streets and church domes of Lviv and Chernivtsi.

The history of the twenty-first century has been just as cruel to Ukraine.

MEMORY LANE

KYIV, AUGUST 2017

I first touched down in Ukraine in 2017 with Alex, an old friend from school in New Zealand. My first impression was of the sway that the dour Soviet-era bureaucracy still held. An inexplicably exasperated border guard refused to accept my visa form until I camped outside his office door for half an hour and finally thrust it on his desk. An Uber driver charged me triple the local price for a taxi from the airport, clocking me as a gullible foreigner. But after I'd got used to Ukraine's rough edges, it began to sink its claws into me. The city had a frenetic, vibrant and grungy energy. The people, men and women, were beautiful and stylishly dressed. Some visitors have described Khreshchatyk, Kyiv's wide Soviet-era central boulevard, as oppressive and grey. I thought it imposingly grand, especially as a short walk over a hill would take you down to the charming old town of Podil, with its winding medieval alleyways, hipster cafes and electronic music clubs. I thought much of Kyiv's appeal came from its clash of architectural styles, where turning a corner could take you straight to a new period of Ukraine's history. I was surprised that Kyiv did not have the recognition of Kraków, Budapest or Prague. I was fascinated by this country, which I'd previously written off as a backwater, and began to delve into books on its rich and tragic history.

Serhii Plokhy's *The Gates of Europe*, the most thorough account of Ukraine's past, begins with Herodotus, the father of history. Herodotus wrote extensively on the land of Scythia, an ancient precursor of Ukraine. He described the Dnipro River that flows through Ukraine as providing 'the finest and most abundant pasture, by far the richest supply of the best sorts of fish ... No better crops grow anywhere than along its banks ... The grass is the most luxuriant in the world.' This is no mere historical footnote; international officials stress about how best to ensure the safe passage of Ukrainian grain from the country's Black Sea ports, fearing widespread famine in developing countries if the Russians blockade them.

This wealth of resources gave rise to a great kingdom, known to history as 'Kyivan Rus'. In the eleventh century, Kyiv was for a time the grandest city in Europe, while Moscow was still a patch of arid and uninhabited swampland. Anna Yaroslavna, a princess from Kyiv who ruled France as Queen Regent, was reported to have introduced advances such as cutlery and private bathhouses and invested heavily in schools and libraries in Paris; she was literate at a time when the King of France could not sign his name.

Yet the kingdom disintegrated due to factional squabbles over succession, and what civilisation remained here was almost destroyed by the Mongols. Borders would shift back and forth significantly over the centuries, and a truly sovereign, independent Ukraine in its modern form would not be established until 1991. Ukraine's turbulent relationship with Russia began in the seventeenth century. At this time, most of these lands were dominated by the Cossacks, a proud, self-governing and warlike people who are now revered as the founding fathers of Ukraine. The Cossacks had a brutal side, including penchants for raiding, slave-taking and pogroms. After a series of military defeats against Polish nobles, the most powerful Cossack, Hetman Bohdan Khmelnitsky, swore fealty to the Tsar of Russia. Khmelnitsky had wanted protection from the west but believed that his treaty with the tsar, signed in 1654 at the town of Perieslav, would preserve Cossack rights and freedoms.

Moscow instead saw any subject under the tsar as owing him total and unquestioning obedience. In the coming centuries, the Ukrainian lands would be gradually 'Russified'. The Russians enforced the use of their language in public life, and ethnic Ukrainians and Crimean Tatars would be killed or deported to make way for Russian settlers. At the end of his life, Khmelnitsky was said to have broken into tears and cried, 'This is not what I wished,' but by then, it was too late. Most of Ukraine would remain under Russian domination, as part of the Russian Empire or the Soviet Union, until 1991.

In 1954, commenting on the 300th anniversary of the signing of this treaty, historian Isaac Deutscher wrote that 'the image of the weeping Hetman has haunted Russo-Ukrainian relations ever since'. Dominated by a much larger and richer neighbour, Ukrainians for the next hundreds of years 'hired themselves to the Polish gentry, to the Turkish Sultan ... to Austro-Hungary and Germany; and each time they were disillusioned with their new masters, vanquished by Russia and forced back into dependence'. Foreign powers sought access to Ukraine's vast resources, and Ukrainians would then use these resources as a bargaining chip for military support. When Volodymyr Zelensky thrashes out a deal with Donald Trump that would give the US access to Ukraine's rare earth mineral resources in exchange for security aid, he is drawing on a long historical tradition.

The most notorious of these alliances was a brief one in 1941, when the Organisation of Ukrainian Nationalists (OUN) led by Stepan Bandera declared an independent state in the western city of Lviv. He originally wanted an alliance with Nazi Germany against the Soviet Union. Considered horrific now, it makes more sense in historical context. Stalin and his underlings launched a genocidal famine against Ukraine in the 1930s, the Holodomor, killing around 4 million Ukrainians. The Allied victory in the Second World War ensured Russian domination of Ukraine, which would spend most of the next fifty years as part of the Soviet Union.

In 1986, a meltdown at the Chernobyl nuclear power plant caused the world's most serious nuclear incident in history. The Moscow-directed cover-up helped reawaken a nascent Ukrainian nationalist movement. Within four years, masses of students poured onto the streets and the Maidan Square in Kyiv demanding autonomy for Ukraine, which soon morphed into wider political demands for complete independence. It became known as the 'Revolution on Granite', and it was the first of several popular protest movements here to wield significant political power in Ukraine. The heads of the Russian, Belarusian and Ukrainian republics met in a prototypical smoke-filled room in the Belovezha Hunting Ground in December 1991, where they plotted to dissolve the Soviet Union and strengthen their own power. But when the Ukrainian parliament voted to secede, they had made a fateful decision. They would give the final decision to the Ukrainian people in a democratic referendum.

On 1 December 1991, nine in ten Ukrainians of the 84 per cent of eligible voters opted to declare independence. The results in the traditional nationalist heartland of Galicia – the western cities of Lviv, Ternopil and Ivano-Frankivsk – were no surprise. These places had only come under the Russian thumb after the Second World

War and had experienced a flowering Ukrainian cultural movement when they were part of the Austro-Hungarian Empire. But the capital of Kyiv, as well as the Russian-speaking cities of Kharkiv, Donetsk and Luhansk, and the Crimean Peninsula also voted in favour of leaving. The break-up of the Soviet Union in Ukraine was therefore a curious mix of secretive elite scheming and popular democratic mobilisation. This tension between elite and popular politics is one of the themes that recurs in Ukrainian history. Others include a general rebelliousness and scepticism towards centralised authority and a respect for the participation of ordinary people in the politics and culture of everyday life, which is almost entirely absent in Russia. These circumstances set independent Ukraine on a very different course from that of its larger neighbour.

A TROUBLED INHERITANCE

After the fall of the Soviet Union in 1991, the newly independent nation of Ukraine inherited the world's third largest nuclear arsenal. Sitting in silos and hangars like the one Olena had shown me were hundreds of nuclear warheads, now the property of a fragile state suffering an economic crisis. While many in the west celebrated the end of the Soviet Union, bloody conflicts such as those in Nagorno-Karabakh and the former Yugoslavia were a warning of how fragile peace in this region could be. A potential conflict between countries with nuclear weapons would raise the stakes dramatically.

Ukraine wanted to enter the world as a forward-looking nation, a good global citizen with friendly relations with all its neighbours, and it was willing to work towards a diplomatic solution. There were more prosaic motives as well. The Ukrainian economy was collapsing after the end of the Soviet Union, and the government allowed its short-term priority of needing quick cash to win out over its long-term national security interests. Experts still debate over whether Ukraine could have kept these weapons working or refashioned its existing stocks into a working nuclear deterrent – the launch codes were stored in Moscow – but their presence was a concern to world leaders.

At a summit in Hungary in 1994, the leaders of Russia, Ukraine, the UK and the US signed the Budapest Memorandum. In this document, Ukraine agreed to hand its nuclear weapons over to the care of the Russian Federation – the Soviet Union's successor state and therefore one of the five states allowed by the Non-Proliferation of Nuclear Weapons Treaty to possess an atomic arsenal. In return – alongside an injection of ready cash – the powers agreed in the text of the memorandum 'to respect the independence and sovereignty and the existing borders of Ukraine'. Bill Clinton thanked the Ukrainians, saying, 'Ukraine's decision will allow the United States, Russia and the United Kingdom to extend formal security assurances to Ukraine ... People around the world admire you for your wisdom in leading your country towards a non-nuclear future.' The country had given up its missiles because it wanted to become part of the west and be a responsible global actor. Now Ukrainians bitterly regret their naivety. It was, UK Prime Minister Boris Johnson said, the most useless piece of paper signed since the one Chamberlain had waved at Munich. Ukraine put its faith in international order rather than brute power and was betrayed.

In a 1993 *Foreign Affairs* article titled 'The Case for a Ukrainian Nuclear Deterrent', John Mearsheimer warned that the decision was folly, saying, 'Ukrainian nuclear weapons are the only reliable deterrent to Russian aggression.' He predicted, with alarming clarity, that a conventional war between Russia and Ukraine would entail vast military casualties and the possible murder of many thousands of civilians ... [They] have a history of mutual enmity; this hostility ... could entail Bosnian style ethnic cleansing and mass murder. This war could produce millions of refugees clamoring at the borders of Western Europe.

Looking back now, it is as if he had a crystal ball.

But this danger was far in the future. In the 1990s, Ukrainians were simply trying to get through one day at a time. After the end of the Soviet Union, the economy collapsed, with GDP falling by nearly 40 per cent by the end of the millennium. Two political poles emerged in response to this crisis, one pushing for greater European integration, the other wanting to resurrect ties with Russia that resembled the former Soviet Union. Ukrainian politics was beset by all manner of ills that we associate with dictatorships or banana republics – the attempted killing of political opponents, threats against and murders of journalists, blatant ballot rigging and mass demonstrations, both peaceful and violent. Yet somehow, democratic politics survived. Elections were often neither free nor fair, and transfers of power could be far from peaceful. Yet whereas Russia has now had a single leader for twenty-five years, Ukraine cycled through five Presidents and countless Prime Ministers in this time.

Russians speak about Ukrainian politics with incredulity. Their popular revolutions are said to instead be CIA coups, and they called the Zelensky government a 'proxy' or 'puppet' of the US. Plenty of Ukrainians, especially oligarchs and politicians, played negative roles, but they were genuinely independent actors, which meant that politics was never consolidated in a particular person or faction. The Kremlin became scared that the Ukrainian example was a threat to the centralisation of power under Putin in Russia. It was a kind of violent democratic anarchy of which the Cossacks would have approved.

The 2004 election was particularly chaotic. The leading pro-western candidate, Viktor Yushchenko, barely survived a disfiguring poisoning attempt, likely on the orders of Moscow, and the winning pro-Russian candidate Viktor Yanukovych was found to have committed electoral fraud, which caused the Ukrainian Constitutional Court to order a rerun of the election. Hundreds of thousands of Ukrainians protested in what became known as the 'Orange Revolution' after the Yushchenko team's colours. The defiant Yushchenko won handily. But his administration failed to tackle major issues in Ukrainian society, such as the corruption that has devastated the economy and public affairs since 1991. Yanukovych rehabilitated his image, rose from the political ashes and went on to win the 2010 election fair and square.

Ukrainians of this period generally had a positive view of Russia. This did not mean that they wanted Ukraine to be ruled again from Moscow, let alone be invaded. Taya Shchuruk, a Ukrainian actress, explained: 'People in most major cities, overwhelmingly spoke Russian in daily life. They watched Russian movies, read Russian books (even by Ukrainian authors) and had friends and family in Russia.' But on a personal level, most of them truly didn't care all that much about Russia. 'There was no deep fascination with Russian politics, in the way that Russia was obsessed with everything in Ukraine.'

'LIKES' DON'T COUNT

TORETSK, DONETSK OBLAST, APRIL 2018

The crack of rifle fire sounded out in the distance, and the nearby trees were beginning to blossom. The trenches near the Donetsk Oblast town of Toretsk seemed flimsy, and Vitali Krasovsky, our Ukrainian special forces escort, told us to get down immediately. The trenches were barely a metre and a half high, reinforced with a few planks of wood, which seemed unlikely to survive an artillery hit from the forces of the Donetsk People's Republic less than a kilometre away. I was with Lord Michael Ashcroft and Isabel Oakeshott, researching a book about the future of the British military. We had decided to take a trip to visit a potential conflict that could draw in British troops. The UK's training mission out here, Operation Orbital, was helping bring Ukraine's Army into the twenty-first century.

By now, a frozen conflict had dragged out on the plains of Ukraine's eastern regions, the Donbas, for nearly four years. A few lives were regularly lost to sniper fire or small calibre mortars. Occasionally, one side would send saboteurs to destroy an enemy dugout or even try to capture a farmhouse here, a treeline there. But there were no serious attempts at changing the facts on the ground. By 2018, the fighting showed no signs of ending, but nor was it escalating. It was becoming background noise, slowly fading from the minds and priorities of the Ukrainian people.

During Ukraine's early years of independence, many cultural elements of Russification remained. But politically and economically, Moscow became steadily less attractive. Barely 10 per cent said they wanted a union of the two countries, a similar proportion of Canadians who would favour becoming the fifty-first state of the US. Throughout Ukraine, Moscow's increasingly authoritarian dictatorship and corrupt oligarchy were losing their appeal. Walking through Kyiv's main streets, you could see posters for club nights with famous Berlin DJs, and across the road the great Opera House was advertising for Italian operas like *Rigoletto* and *Madame Butterfly*. The economic, cultural and social opportunities of European Union membership were undeniable. The countries that had stayed in the Russian orbit – Belarus, Moldova, Georgia, Armenia – had stagnated, their economies controlled by oligarchs, their politics ranging from corrupt to authoritarian. This made many people, especially the young, turn towards Europe for a better future.

Alexander Pushkin, Russia's most famous poet, once wrote in horror about the suggestion that 'Kiev, decrepit, golden dome, this ancestor of Russian towns, will it conjoin its sainted groves, with reckless Warsaw?' Having looked at both Moscow and Warsaw, this is exactly what a young generation of Ukrainians decided to do. The Polish capital is another city that impresses visitors with its spotlessly clean streets, its profusion of new skyscrapers and shopping centres full of posh western brands. Young people speak impressive English, at a level better than countries like Spain or France. The country has had one of the fastest growing economies in the world since the end of the Communist era. Ukrainians often travelled and worked in Poland, sending back remittances and earning qualifications, exposing them to the benefits of integration with Europe.

When the Soviet Union ended, the economies of Ukraine and Poland were nearly equal in size. By 2014, the Polish economy was three times as large and, along with the Baltic states, Romania and Hungary, was growing steadily richer and more prosperous as citizens travelled and worked freely throughout Europe. All these countries had joined NATO and the European Union. As their integration with the west grew, their democratic institutions strengthened.

Yanukovych was so corrupt that Ukrainians maintain a museum to his greed. Around an hour's drive outside Kyiv, I visited his old private residence, a modern Versailles called Mezhyhirya. His greed shocked even Transparency International, whose staff are usually inured to corruption. They called it 'a palace of cartoonish opulence' with a cryotherapy chamber, a private zoo with animals as exotic as bears and peacocks, an $11 million gem-studded chandelier and a personal lake where he had a model pirate ship to entertain guests for lavish parties. This all cost a fraction of the $37 billion his clan is believed to have stolen from the coffers of the Ukrainian people. In late 2013, when President Yanukovych pulled out of an integration agreement with the EU after an offer of a bribe from Moscow, Mustafa Nayyem, a young journalist, the son of refugees from Afghanistan, made a Facebook post calling for a mass demonstration on Maidan Square. 'Well, let's get serious,' he wrote. 'Who today is ready to come to Maidan before midnight? "Likes" don't count. Only comments under this post with the words, "I am ready."' Thousands gathered, but Yanukovych was terrified of a repeat of the Orange Revolution in 2004. So, he cracked down hard, sending in Ukraine's feared riot police, the Berkut. For many Ukrainians, the Maidan defined their national consciousness and political awakening. This was a revolution against corruption and for democracy. As Illia Ponomarenko, a young Ukrainian journalist, described it:

> We were a generation open to the world around us as never before, unlike so many of our parents, whose lifetime's greatest journey was the Soviet Army conscription service in Central Asia and maybe even the 1980 Olympics in Moscow. We wanted clean streets, polite police, and government officials that resign because of petty corruption scandals. We wanted to be able to start a business without passing money under the table and to trust that the courts of law would render justice. We did not want irremovable,

lifetime dictators who packed their governments at every level with corrupt cronies flush with ill-gotten cash.

Yanukovych tried to suppress the protests with deadly force but fled the country after the Maidan massacre threatened to trigger his violent overthrow. He tried to call in the army to put down the citizen rebellion, but they were stymied by popular resistance. A soldier at the time, codenamed 'Yakut', remembered: 'The government had decided to call in the army, not just the police. However, we never made it to Kyiv because unarmed civilians blocked the train tracks and cut the brakes to stop us from moving forward.' Many of the men and women of this brave and patriotic generation would join the armed forces when Russia invaded in full eight years later, and thousands would die.

Nayyem looks back on the Maidan with pride, but his expression and tone betray a wistful sadness: 'The country was pregnant and ready for change,' he told me in Kyiv more than ten years after the uprising. 'Our aspiration was the European Union, and the values shared with these countries, their level of life, prosperity and democracy. I was just the trigger, but it came from the people.' Russia wasn't the focal point of these protests, but the demonstrators were pushing against laws based on the Russian model of repression. In the end, just over a hundred protestors were killed, a fact Nayyem reminded me of.

'It is important to know that today, we are meeting on the anniversary of the Maidan massacre.'

These events were not popular everywhere in Ukraine. There were large-scale protests against the Maidan in 2014 in majority Russian-speaking cities throughout Ukraine, including Kharkiv, Odesa, Donetsk and Luhansk. Putin saw an opportunity in the chaos and used unmarked Russian troops to annex Crimea. This was done almost bloodlessly and was the first seizure of territory by military means on the European continent since the Second World War and a brazen repudiation of international norms, not to mention international agreements like the Budapest Memorandum that Russia had signed with Ukraine.

Russian proxy forces and local rebels then captured large swathes of territory in the east, including the regional capitals of Donetsk and Luhansk. They declared independent states, the 'Donetsk People's Republic' and the 'Luhansk People's Republic', which remained unrecognised by any country until the eve of the February 2022 invasion. The Ukrainian Army was parlous, hollowed out from years of corruption and underfunding. Its regular troops were in a poor position. Leonid Ostaltsev, a veteran of the Donbas war, told me:

> Our soldiers were cleaners and painters, not soldiers. In my country, our government had sold almost everything we had after the fall of the Soviet Union. I was in the regular army for one year, and I know the army was fighting against Russians in 2014. We didn't know anything. It was men and women in very bad uniforms without any combat experience or useful skills that could help in a battle. When I went to fight for the army in July 2014, I bought my own uniform and wore New Balance shoes. My friends all pitched in to buy me body armour, which was in terrible condition. In one whole year of military training before the war, I shot only six bullets, two times. The training was so poor that I had to Google 'how to set up a checkpoint' so that our friends wouldn't get killed if we had to fire at the enemy. Funny, but not funny. It is a big difference now.

Yakut said that for years, Russia had waged a propaganda war in Ukraine, particularly targeting Donbas and Crimea, and said it was most shocking to see his fellow citizens suddenly treat him as if he were the enemy – 'blocking roads with their cars, shouting curses and throwing stones'. He explains that both they and the separatist forces were poorly equipped. When he and other Ukrainian troops tried to recapture the eastern city of Slovyansk, in the war's first major battle, the Russians and their separatists resorted to desperate measures to fight back, including stealing a Second World War-era T-34 tank that had been put on a plinth as a monument and firing it at the Ukrainians. 'I don't know how they managed it, but they somehow got it to work and shot at us – it was very surreal.'

Eventually, the Russians sent regular forces in to reinforce the rebels, who trapped many of the best Ukrainian troops near a city called Debaltseve. 'The battle was brutal,' Yakut recalls, 'especially when we were surrounded. The Russians shelled us almost constantly, and we couldn't escape. All our vehicles were destroyed, and we barely managed to flee on foot.' In February 2015, with Ukraine losing militarily, it was forced to sign an agreement in Minsk, intended to secure a ceasefire in the region, but it never fully took hold. NATO began supplying equipment and training soldiers. Since then, the agreement has been a cornerstone of Russian propaganda, which has claimed that Ukraine never respected the agreement, although neither side honoured their obligations.

But while it didn't bring lasting peace, it did calm the situation down. By the time I visited in 2018, the sounds of war were faint. In the capital, the war was far from the average person's mind. People were still talking mainly about the economy and ongoing problems with corruption. We can see what people's concerns were by looking at one of the most popular TV shows of the era, a product of the politically ambitious actor and comedian Volodymyr Zelensky. Born in a rough, mainly Russian-speaking industrial city in the south called Kryvyi Rih, he had cut his teeth as an entertainer and producer both in Kyiv and Moscow.

Here, the father of history makes another unexpected appearance in the story of Ukraine. In a dream scene in the satirical comedy *Servant of the People* – created by and starring Zelensky – Herodotus and fellow ancient historian Plutarch look down at the recently elected schoolteacher turned President, Vasyl Goloborodko, as he snores and talks in his sleep. They are discussing the situation in Ukraine, and the President gives a good summary of Ukraine's potential but how its rulers were failing its people: '[Presidents] come, they steal, then successors come and steal more.' He points out that Ukraine was number one in the world in sunflower oil production, number three in grain production and its thriving industrial sector made airplanes, combine harvesters and cars. Yet the country was one of the poorest in Europe, its economy facing default and the Maidan protesters' dreams of reform and joining the EU looked decades away. The fighting in Donbas doesn't feature in the show at all.

In an early episode, the newly inaugurated Goloborodko is introduced to his body double, who he is told 'will take a sniper bullet for you', but the team laughs that off as something that will never happen. The baby-faced, clean-shaven Zelensky looked faintly ridiculous in his expensive suit and surrounded by the pomp and opulence of the presidency. This was true both when he played the part of the President on TV and when he assumed the office for real.

When I finally met him many years later, his appearance had been scarred and deepened by the horrors. By then, he had long taken on the characteristics of the world's most famous war leader – the stubble, the olive-green military fleece, the piercing stare and gravelly voice.

He was elected President in 2019, riding a wave of popular anger against the establishment, in part on a platform to end the war in Donbas, which he apparently expected to be simple. 'Just stop the shooting' was his slogan. After negotiations with the Russians quickly broke down, he realised from bitter experience just how difficult it would be to do a deal with the Kremlin.

The Ukrainian military had not forgotten the threat from Russia, and they continued to rearm and prepare for what many saw as an inevitable larger war. During this period, Ukraine also developed a deep and complex relationship with the west. Ukrainian intelligence began co-operating seriously with the CIA against Russia, and western troops began training Ukrainian forces, who in turn provided their real-world experience fighting Russia and its proxies in Donbas. The war was an ideal training range – tough live fire and real combat, without being dangerous on the scale of a hot war. The tens of thousands of soldiers who cycled through here became the backbone of Ukraine's resistance in 2022.

Civil society also became more cohesive and patriotic. 'The Maidan was the moment of awakening, the activation of young people who had a totally different approach and vision,' Nayyem said. 'And during these next eight years, thousands of people grew up who started to believe the country belonged to them, not to government. And that was one of the reasons why, when invasion started, people [were] so well organised and proactive.'

Our research team met in Kyiv with Lieutenant General Serhiy Bessarab, then deputy head of the Ukrainian armed forces. We asked what Russia's plans were. He drew an oval on a piece of scrap paper to represent Ukraine. He started adding a series of arrows to represent various directions of attack. North-west, from the swamplands and forests of Belarus. North-east, from the plains of Kursk towards Sumy and Kharkiv. From the south, like a dagger into Ukraine's ribs, from occupied Crimea, and from the eastern Donbas territories that they were already fighting over.

Lord Ashcroft thanked the general for his insights and then said, with a wry smile, pointing at the rough squiggles, 'But one last piece of career advice. Please do not consider a career as an artist,' and the room burst into laughter. We were worried. Bessarab was not describing 'Russian hybrid warfare', the buzz-phrase of the day in European Defence Ministries, defined by deniable operations salami-slicing small pieces of territory, cyberattacks, propaganda and misinformation campaigns to destabilise democracies. This was a fully-fledged mechanised assault that hadn't been seen since the Second World War. It was politically unthinkable in the enlightened twenty-first century. Yet nearly four years later, those hastily drawn arrows would morph from being smudges of ink on a page to being tens of thousands of soldiers, tanks, armoured vehicles and artillery pieces barrelling towards every major Ukrainian city.

A TALE OF THREE CITIES

MARIUPOL, DONETSK OBLAST, FEBRUARY 2022

'Only God prepares in this country,' laughed Oleg Budnikov. A gregarious villager in his late sixties, his main concern was getting enough fodder for his animals and fertiliser for his crops. The Russian Army massing just over the border would have to wait. Occasionally, we heard a few shots of automatic rifle fire pinged back and forth between Ukrainian and Donetsk People's Republic forces.

THE DOGS OF WAR

It was the middle of February 2022, and I was with Canadian journalist Neil and Argentinian TV reporter Cecilia in the flyspeck village of Pavlopil, around ten kilometres from the port of Mariupol. At the town entrance, a rusting yellow 'Stop Mines!' sign with a skull and crossbones painted on it stood next to a dead tree in a sunflower field. It was a reminder that this was the front line of a European land war, and Ukraine's allies were desperately warning of the possibility of a larger invasion, but it didn't feel like it. Neither the locals nor the city authorities seemed to appreciate the situation. Budnikov said that people from the city administration had told them that there was training for evacuation plans scheduled for next month. But they had received no instructions to stockpile essentials or otherwise prepare for war. It was a similar story in Ukraine's capital.

I still have the ticket for the fateful flight I booked on a whim. PC1722, Pegasus Airlines flight Ankara to Boryspil, arriving at 1:15 a.m. on 24 January. It was supposed to be a short trip, to gauge the locals' feelings and write an article about living under the threat of war. The atmosphere in Kyiv was uneasy, and everyone seemed to switch from calm to panic at different points during the day.

Julia Tymoshenko, a consultant in her mid-twenties, explained to me: 'In Ukraine now, we live this surreal double life, where during the day we go about our work and lives as if everything is normal.' Tymoshenko (not to be confused with the former Ukrainian Prime Minister of the same name), told me:

> When we get home, we share strategies for survival – we discuss relatives we can stay with within western provinces, means of leaving the country or ways we could evacuate if Kyiv was attacked. Ukrainian people are living in a state of constant emotional terror,

trying to go day by day with routine tasks while starting to plan evacuation strategies and start packing emergency bags.

She referenced Kyiv's latest VIP international supporter, then Prime Minister Boris Johnson. 'We were even happy to have your Prime Minister here supporting us. We've been saying to ourselves, you know you are screwed when your best friend is Boris Johnson!' According to the polling data, Ukrainians in early 2022 were pessimistic about the future and apathetic about politics, and they did not trust politicians, political parties or most of Ukraine's domestic institutions. Zelensky was polling poorly, after his attempts to solve the Donbas conflict or widespread corruption had made little headway. When it came to a willingness to serve in the military or otherwise resist a foreign invasion, 40 per cent of respondents stated that they would not defend Ukraine. These responses suggested to the Russians that Ukraine would fold quickly and that its citizens owed no allegiance to the state.

Many people couldn't fathom the possibility of a war. 'The Russians are our brothers!' one young man in the streets of Kyiv told me. 'They wouldn't allow something like this to happen!' The war in Donbas and the annexation of Crimea had driven Ukrainians from wanting anything to do with Moscow's political ambitions. But at this stage, they still differentiated between Russia and its President. In one poll, 57 per cent of Ukrainians in government-controlled areas still held a positive view of Russia, even if only 8 per cent gave a favourable opinion of the Russian government or of Putin himself.

However, people in the army were more positive about Ukraine's chances. One wall of the central Kyiv branch of Leonid Ostaltsev's shop is covered in military patches and insignias, while on the wall is a map of Ukraine made out of spent shell casings. His desk was covered with a wide range of modern weaponry next to photos of his children. He said the Ukrainians were ready for anything. 'Now we are an absolutely different army,' Ostaltsev told me. 'We have something almost no other army in the world has: We have combat experience, and we know what war with a stronger enemy is, where you don't have anything, but you need to fight because it is your homeland.' The army, he promised, had improved greatly, adopting many western standards:

> The training was incredibly important. We learned to use new weapons like the Javelin [an American anti-tank weapon] and practised western tactical methods from NATO. Before 2014, our training was very basic – just shooting at targets. But after 2015, we started learning to fight like a modern army. The training made all the difference when the invasion began.

But no serious preparations were made over the months of January and February for an invasion until the very last minute. Yakut was on leave with his family in Dnipro in late February. He was immediately called back as his unit, the 25th Airborne Brigade, was stationed in Luhansk. He says no one suspected Russia would actually launch a full-scale invasion – everything seemed normal. Zelensky was worried that warning about an imminent attack would scare markets. The criticism he was focused on short-term political appearances over unpopular and difficult decisions that were necessary recurs repeatedly about Zelensky's actions during this war.

Back in Mariupol, the calm was almost complete. 'We've been at war here for eight years already!' one villager said, laughing off the threat. Mariupol had been briefly captured by forces belonging to the Donetsk People's Republic in 2014 before Ukrainians, mostly irregular militias including the Azov Battalion, had recaptured it. Azov set up a major base nearby, and the flourishing city became a symbol of Ukraine's independence.

While the Azov Battalion was originally far right, it was incorporated into the Ukrainian armed forces. An important part of conflict resolution is bringing armed militias under the state, so only the state has the monopoly on the use of force, but the association with Azov remained controversial among Ukraine's international partners for years to come.

In January 2015, a rocket attack from DPR-controlled territory hit a local market and killed thirty-one civilians, which resulted in many formerly pro-Russian residents thinking about the idea of seceding from Ukraine. Before I'd left Mariupol, I'd spoken again with Vitali Krasovsky, now the Ukrainian military attaché at the Ukrainian Embassy in London, who had identified Mariupol as a potential flashpoint of a Russian invasion. He said the Russians were behaving in ways that were confusing and contradictory. 'We are not seeing the signs that would accompany massive military operations,' he told me. The Russians were amassing thousands of troops, yes, but they were dispersing them across the entire border rather than concentrating them for an attack. 'They simply don't have the concentration of forces needed to break our lines.' Instead, he speculated that the Russians would try to capture Mariupol in a breakout operation from territory they already controlled in Donetsk. 'Mariupol is one of the sites in our chain of defences that are causing us real concern.' If the Ukrainian high command was concerned about the situation by the Azov Sea, that wasn't filtering through on the ground.

Before I arrived in Mariupol on the overnight train from Kyiv, I had expected to see a run-down rust belt town full of poverty and post-industrial distress. But Mariupol was beautiful. It was clean, flourishing, the people good-natured and helpful. The only sign of its past tragedy was the cinderblock that was the burned-out police station that had been the centre of fighting in 2014. In the words of Ponomarenko, who spent his university years here:

> The streets were miraculously smooth and clean ... New coffee shops, restaurant chains, and food courts that Mariupol never had before. New bike lanes and boutiques. What used to be just a long and dirty concrete breakwater prying into the sea was now a very good-looking, wood-decked pier with yachts and boats moored at its sides. New yellow-and-white buses rushed to and fro from glassed-in bus stops marked with little anchors ... Mariupol, once a depressed Soviet rust belt monster with a god-awful ecological legacy, was turning into a comfortable and quiet regional European city. With its cocktail bars, parks, and sushi places by the seaside, it was on the verge of becoming the finest recreational centre of East Ukraine.

I was checked into the Poseidon Hotel by the receptionist. She introduced herself as Helga Ihnatieva, and she asked if she could borrow my time before I retired. The hotel held a class for a local hairdressing studio and they needed a male model with long hair. By this time, I'd been growing it long enough that I looked like a Renaissance painting of Jesus, and I was due for a trim. So, I spent the first hour of my working day in front of a room of fifty people having various techniques and products demonstrated on me. My Russian being poor, I understood only a few words, but the audience were constantly laughing and thanking me. I still wonder how many of them are alive.

Helga didn't imagine a war coming. It was ridiculous, she thought, not something that could happen in the twenty-first century. Besides, there had been a smaller war going on next door for eight years. People had just learned to live with it! Meanwhile, we were being bombarded with requests to leave Ukraine. One highly placed American source dropped his diplomatic filter to say, 'You guys are retarded, staying there. I know, for a fact, there is going to be a war.' It was the raw, ugly certainty of someone who'd seen the intelligence. A British source was more delicate, but I could hear the trembling in his voice: 'It is entirely within the capacity of the Russian forces arrayed at the border to encircle Kyiv and envelop Ukrainian forces.'

Gung-ho, we ignored the warnings. Neil, Cecilia and I were soon met by our guide Eva, a bubbly young actress who was a stage director at the nearby Mariupol Drama Theatre. She'd caused a stir among the local drama community by being one of the first to insist on staging plays in Ukrainian. 'Mariupol is a Russian-speaking city,' they told her. Eva freely said that she still spoke Russian at home with her family and her boyfriend but insisted that public events should be in Ukrainian.

Eva's bright pink wool beanie made my colleagues and me look faintly ridiculous decked out in suits of body armour. In fact, there were no preparations of any kind going on in Mariupol. On a Sunday afternoon, we paid a visit to Central Hospital Number One. They were surprised to see us poking our heads in. 'There is nothing special happening here,' one of the nurses said, with evident irritation. 'What should we need? The situation is calm.' There were no additional beds, stockpiles of medicines, stretchers or any preparations for even a mild uptick in the fighting. The Russians, as anyone could see from satellite imagery the Americans released, were stockpiling blood and body bags and preparing mobile hospitals. Russian proxy officials in the DPR next door were warning of an imminent Ukrainian attack, ordering evacuations for women and children and beginning to mobilise the men for war. Only Oleg Gusack, a dour-looking dockworker, seemed concerned. 'There are no special preparations at all,' he said. 'Everyone is completely calm, the same for the whole city ... [The] city officials aren't doing enough. We should be preparing for war like they do in Israel!' It was as if the Ukrainian government wanted to stick its head in the sand and pretend nothing was happening.

In a local restaurant, I met with Tanya Azuaje, an American who worked as a monitor for the Organization for Security and Co-operation in Europe (OSCE) whose job it was to patrol the cease-fire. As her organisation worked on both sides of the front line, she had a unique opportunity to compare life in Ukraine with life under Russian occupation:

> Downtown Donetsk was a beautiful area. I was only there in the winter so didn't get to see their fabled roses. But it was really pretty; there was some nice architecture, a park area you could walk through in the centre of the city to some lovely views. There were decent restaurants.

But behind the pleasant facade, she said, was a constant sense of menace:

> We were warned that we were always being watched. One colleague took out his phone to take a photo of a nice building, and some men in plain clothes from the authorities came out of the shadows with guns and started questioning him. I was coming

back from a walk, and we saw a man who was clearly taking pictures of the licence plates of our vehicles.

Tanya, who is of Venezuelan heritage, said that she noticed one interesting contrast in Donetsk with other international postings she has had in her career:

> Being a woman of colour, I stood out; people would notice me. I actually found it surprising because I expected to be stared at or face racism or rejection because there were so few foreigners there, but I didn't experience it with people there. It was a closed space where people expect to be watched all the time, so everyone minds their own business. They are very focused on their own life and don't want to be seen as someone who would draw attention to themselves. It felt normal but also very dour. You didn't really see people smiling or laughing or playing around.

This was a huge contrast with Mariupol, where she arrived in early February 2022. As soon as she arrived, she said:

> When you crossed the border to Ukrainian-controlled areas, I felt a certain lightness, I felt like we could breathe easier. I felt like I had this heavy weight pressing down on my lungs and now I just felt better. Young couples holding hands and kissing, teenagers skateboarding, and I realised I hadn't seen that in Donetsk. There were cool trendy restaurants; it was very artsy and alternative, I could see it being the next Berlin!

I agreed with her impressions of the port city, but there was one thing that was unnerving me. I noticed the dogs in the city would not stop barking. It was a rhythmic and frantic barking, as if they were shouting a warning in unison. I walked onto the beach, and a local woman had lost control over her six dogs, and they began running around madly, scratching, clawing and biting at her and each other. Animals have a sixth sense for subtle changes in their environment, and they could have been detecting the growing fear and unease in the local people that they were unwilling to vocalise. Perhaps they had a premonition of things to come. I tweeted at the time: 'The dogs in Mariupol, Eastern Ukraine, have been barking non-stop.' Some half-remembered superstition from ghost stories I read in childhood came to mind that dogs will howl when death is near. A Slavic folklore tradition that says they are calling out to the approaching spectral hounds that come to collect the souls of the dead. I jotted in my notes: 'Do they know something we don't?' The next day, we took the train back to Kyiv, unnerved. A few days later, we sat around the television with a group of journalists and watched Putin's hour-long speech ranting against Ukrainian independence. 'Ukraine is not just a neighbouring country for us,' he said. 'It is an inalienable part of our own history, culture and spiritual space.' Now we knew all that we needed to about his plans.

On 23 February, the day before the invasion began, Eva went to a hill overlooking the port of Mariupol, a calm, chilly day with a light but bitterly cold breeze. There were two old women, looking gleefully out over the port, mumbling to each other like they were casting a curse on the people below. She said they looked ancient, their faces lined but smiling.

'What are you doing up here?' she asked them.

'Waiting for the boys!' one of them said, gesturing over towards Russian-controlled territory, where tanks and troops were massing to burst into the city streets the following day.

'What boys?'
One of the old crones cackled, like one of Macbeth's witches, then answered.
'Ours.'

CHAPTER TWO

CRY HAVOC: THE BATTLE FOR KYIV AND THE INVASION OF NORTHERN UKRAINE

> 'Bran thought about it. "Can a man still be brave if he's afraid?"
> "That is the only time a man can be brave," his father told him.'
> – GEORGE R. R. MARTIN, *A Game of Thrones*

> 'There was much in this that I did not understand, in some ways
> I did not even like it, but I recognized it immediately
> as a state of affairs worth fighting for.'
> – GEORGE ORWELL, *Homage to Catalonia*

A SPECIAL MILITARY OPERATION

BUCHA, KYIV OBLAST, FEBRUARY 2022

Three years on, Anastasia Alekseyuk can't look at sunrises, as they bring her straight back to Bucha. 'At the end of the first day, after constant explosions, everything went silent,' she told me. 'Non-stop. Boom, boom, boom. Then everything went totally quiet. I went outside, and I looked at the horizon because it had this very red, orange colour and it was super quiet. So now I have a problem with the sunrises!'

Anastasia, then twenty-nine, didn't know it at the time, but she was watching the most important battle of the entire war, raging just two kilometres from her home. She lived in the town of Bucha, a commuter city a half hour drive from Kyiv that would become a byword for Russian savagery. Just across from the town, over a leafy forest, was Hostomel Airport, the centrepiece of the Russian plan to swiftly take over Ukraine by decapitating its top leadership in Kyiv.

'My right ear was facing the window,' she continued.

All I [was aware of] was this insane pain and the noise from the fast plane, that goes 'shooe'. He maybe flew ten metres from our building complex. It has still been three years, but I don't hear properly on my right ear and my mum couldn't hear on her left ear for more than a year and a half. After night fell, I heard a ton of helicopters. When you look there… all that scenery was out of an apocalypse movie.

Many of the explosions Anastasia heard were, counterintuitively, shells fired by the Ukrainian Army. They were firing on their own airport runway to foil the Russians' plan for the war. Elite Russian paratroopers, known as the VDV, were flying in to capture Hostomel. They would seize control of the airport and then a larger group of forces would land and quickly enter and capture the capital. It would be a clean blow, like from an executioner's axe. Crucially, it would avoid a tough fight with the bulk of the Ukrainian Army in Donbas.

The pace of the operation took everyone by surprise. When one CNN reporter arrived at the scene, he asked waiting soldiers, 'Where are the Russians?' They looked at each other in confusion before replying, 'We are the Russians.'

After realising what Putin had planned, the Ukrainians diverted the one major artillery formation still based near Kyiv to making the airport inoperable. All night, Ukrainian shells rained down on the runway, leaving the facilities and airstrip in ruins. The Russians captured the airport, but it was a pyrrhic victory. They could not land their transport planes flying in from Belarus, so the first attack on Kyiv had been blunted.

This early battle reveals a lot, including the Ukrainians' quick-thinking and innovative use of their limited equipment, as well as their determination and desperation to resist the best Russian forces at all costs. But events here also show the crucial lack of planning that nearly cost Ukraine the war in its early days. US intelligence officials had previously alerted the leadership in Kyiv that the Russians may attack this exact location, but as in Mariupol, no special preparations to defend the capital were made until the final hours. General Valerii Zaluzhnyi, then the commander-in-chief of Ukraine's Armed Forces, made last-minute preparations, including moving air defence and aviation away from their normal positions, so they could avoid being hit by missile strikes, and ordering troops to move to defensive positions. Had he not done that, the war could have gone the other way.

'In all honesty... I think none of it happened,' Anastasia says, looking back on it three years later. 'It seems like I'm telling you a story that I've seen on TV. But everything is so blurry. I think my brain just forgot all of it because of the pain and to protect me.' She witnessed the opening salvo of a blitzkrieg designed to shock and overwhelm a sovereign democratic country in the largest challenge to the international order since the Second World War. No one who was in Kyiv will forget the scowl on the face of Vladimir Putin, hands clenching his desk as he declared a *'spetzialni voyenne operatsia*' (special military operation), pausing before each word before snarling it into the camera. Just before 5 a.m., air raid sirens were sounding throughout the country, missiles were slamming into buildings and barracks and huge columns of Russian troops were pouring over the border from nine different directions.

Putin has been ridiculed for his declaration in those frightening early hours of his 'special military operation'. Yet this phrase is critical to understand why early battles for northern Ukraine turned out like they did. It was not supposed to look like a traditional invasion. Michael Kofman, one of the top scholars of the Russian military, said, 'Military strategy starts at the political level. The Russian invasion was indeed structured as a "special military operation"; it was meant to be a coup de main. The core governing assumptions the Russian military had were driven by the political assumptions.'

The military assault was supposed to be a secondary component of a deeply flawed political fantasy. The Russians thought they had developed a large network of collaborators throughout Ukraine. The government in Kyiv, supposedly shocked and bewildered by the overwhelming Russian advance, would flee while traitors loyal to Moscow would turn the cities over to the control of the Kremlin's forces. Some were so confident they'd brought their parade uniforms in their tanks for a triumphal march through Khreshchatyk Boulevard. The Russian military would mop up any stragglers who refused to surrender. Then, they would enforce grim, brutal order on the people left under their rule. So confident were the Russians in their success that they advanced completely out of sequence and in ways that defied any sensible military logic. Large columns of armour, extremely vulnerable to artillery, airstrikes and drones, trundled forward without a care.

The biggest victims of Russian propaganda were the Russians themselves. A day-one prediction on Twitter by the pro-war channel 'Russians With Attitude' said: 'Man I don't even know what to tell you it looks like the entire Ukrainian military just disintegrated immediately on contact, from what I'm seeing Ukraine doesn't have an air force, air defence or fleet anymore.' Russians from Putin down believed that Ukraine had been captured by a fascist coup and masses of ordinary people would welcome them as liberators. When they came under heavy fire from Ukrainian defenders, most Russian forces were genuinely shocked. It is a factor that played into their horrific treatment of Ukrainian civilians.

It is only by looking at the Kremlin's strategy through this lens that some of the more baffling military decisions in the early days of the war become apparent. For instance, even though the Russian invasion would go on to produce an endless list of atrocities, in the first three days of the invasion, Russian forces were under instructions to minimise not just damage to civilians but even to the Ukrainian military itself. Kofman told me: 'They had very tight rules of engagement: they were told not to fire unless fired upon and to try to ensure Ukrainian soldiers had the opportunity to surrender.' The Russians also did not take out important aspects of Ukraine's critical infrastructure:

> They didn't hit a lot of the things we expected them to hit. Power plants, power grids, key bridges across the Dnipro, key transit nodes to stop assistance from the west, things that would paralyse key parts of Ukraine's electricity grids and key decision-making centres. They didn't start hitting communications until mid-March and didn't start seriously attacking the power grid until fall of 2022.

The Russians who invaded Ukraine were told they were on a peace-keeping mission that would be over with little fuss. All this gave Ukraine's startled military and political leadership crucial time to recover from the initial shock of the invasion and dig in for a fight.

They expected to capture Ukraine bloodlessly and intact, like they had done with Crimea in 2014. It was an old Russian strategy, based on 'Operation Danube' in 1968 when Soviet troops had crushed the Prague Spring in Czechoslovakia. This was a movement for national freedom where the country's Communist leadership wanted to part ways politically with the Soviet Union and open the country to free expression. No wonder Prague would become such a staunch supporter of Ukraine's war effort. They knew exactly what living under the thumb of Moscow was like – and would go on to save Ukraine's war effort.

Russia planned to capture Kyiv within seventy-two hours and wrap up operations around the country in a matter of weeks. Many governments and analysts in the west believed this. A report from the Center for Strategic and International Studies said of these analyses:

> Their judgements about Russian and Ukrainian military capacity were not merely off – they were wildly at variance with reality ... [This] was not a case of normal error or exaggeration. The expert community grossly overestimated Russian military capabilities, dismissed the chances of Ukraine resisting effectively and presented the likely outcome of the war as quick and decisive.

Kofman believes these arguments are fundamentally a misunderstanding of what the Russian invasion in the first few days really was – a political mission with a supporting military component, not a campaign against a well-armed peer military.

> If the intelligence operation failed [and] conditions weren't what they thought they were, then the military operation by itself from a strategy and force employment standpoint doesn't make any sense. That is why the correlation of forces made no sense. If you look at the leading formations going in, you will find the strangest configuration possible. Quite a few have Rosgvardia riot police in the lead, ahead of the airborne. If you ask me, as an analyst ... I'd say I've never seen anyone invade by this [method]!

It would be as if the United States had charged into Baghdad with campus police armed with tear gas and riot shields.

Most of the targets that analysts expected the Russians to strike weren't hit in the early days of the war, presumably as the Kremlin thought it would need to use them in an occupation. This included the power grid, the bridges of the Dnipro and key administrative buildings of major cities. The Russians hoped to simply intimidate Ukrainians into panic, then surrender. In some cases, the Ukrainians got very lucky. The country's military leadership, under instruction from General Zaluzhnyi, the head of the armed forces, only activated the plan to disperse its troops and air defence on the night of the invasion from their original staging points. Many of those were hit by Russian missiles in the opening salvos, and the troops missed annihilation by a matter of hours.

That first morning, I remember coming to my senses in a daze, my colleague shaking me awake and screaming, 'Tom, it's started, it's started!' It took a while to rouse me – we had been waiting for Putin's declaration until the early hours of the morning in various bars, and at first, I thought it was simply a bad dream and shoved him off. When I properly woke up, I walked to the window to see utterly empty streets. I checked my phone, which was full of messages of well-wishing and support. Anastasia had sent me a terrifying video from Bucha, full of men shouting and huge explosions sounding outside. But it wasn't until I saw a video on Twitter of dozens of helicopters flying over Kyiv Oblast, dropping flares and firing on their targets, that I began to realise the scale and scope of what was happening. Later that day, my colleagues and I went to a viewpoint over the city. We could see what to us was just a tiny wisp of smoke coming from a missile strike somewhere in the capital. 'Over that way, the Russians are landing. They want to take an airport and then they are going to land their special forces and swoop into the city,' an Australian photographer we'd been travelling around Kyiv with told me. This was no escalation in the simmering Donbas conflict, or a series of targeted military strikes meant to scare Ukraine into negotiations and intimidate NATO, as some had predicted. This was a full-scale invasion. I and most other foreigners there expected that Ukraine would fall in a few days.

Ukrainians had other ideas.

ROMEO AND JULIET

KYIV, FEBRUARY 2022

Nearly sixty metres underground, in the Leo Tolstoy Station of the Kyiv Metro, we took shelter with a few dozen shocked Ukrainian civilians, from what we expected to be a Russian aerial blitz on the capital that could reduce the centre to rubble. My nights here, now renamed Ukrainian Heroes Station, were the most terrifying of the war. Sure, I came closer to death on later occasions, such as in an artillery storm in the middle of a river. But by then, I was used to the rigours and dangers of war, the front lines were stable and we travelled with the Ukrainian Army who did their best to protect us.

In those first frantic, historic days, nobody knew what to expect. A few guards in the station, armed with assault rifles, swung shut the huge metre-thick steel doors at the entrance. It was built to survive a nuclear strike. We expected that we could go to the surface this morning to find Russian tanks patrolling the main streets of Kyiv in triumph. What would happen to us as journalists, no one knew; they could have easily lined us up against a wall and shot us. One of my first viral tweets was a quote from *Game of Thrones*, when a young Bran Stark asks his father, 'Can a man still be brave when he is afraid?' His father Ned replies, 'That is the only time he can be brave.'

I was comforted by the sight of a young couple next to me, the man pulling a tartan blanket over the woman cuddled up next to him. He was swigging from a bottle of Jack Daniel's, which he then offered up to me. We passed it around, doing our part to lift people's spirits. His name was Platon and he had a shock of thick black hair, slightly tanned skin and a cheeky smile. He was thumbing through a Russian-language copy of Dale Carnegie's *How to Win Friends and Influence People*.

We swapped phone numbers, and I noticed that his started with +7, the Russian dialling code, as opposed to Ukraine's +380. 'Yes, I've come from Russia, but I support Ukraine,' he told me. He began a lecture about the differences in philosophy between the two countries. 'I have been in Russia and Ukraine, and the difference is that Ukraine is a free country. I want to be rich, and here in Ukraine if you get rich, you are free. In Russia, if you get rich, you are still a servant of Putin.' Platon was clearly a little nervous, but he was putting on a confident face. I suspect this was to impress Barbara, who was cuddled up under his blanket. It was a moment I felt honoured to capture. I remembered one of the classic stories studied by budding foreign correspondents, from Reuters journalist Kurt Schork. While reporting on the Bosnian War, he had come across the story of a mixed Bosnian and Serb couple, Bosko Brkic and Admira Ismic, who had tried to escape the besieged city of Sarajevo but had been shot dead on a bridge – 'a wasteland of shell-blasted rubble, downed tree branches and dangling power lines'. Schork's dispatch, known as 'Romeo and Juliet in Sarajevo', was a simple human tragedy that brought a horror of war that was relatable anywhere. I thought of Platon and Barbara as my Bosko and Admira and wrote my own slightly sunnier dispatch for *New Lines Magazine*, titled 'Love Survives Russia's Onslaught in Kyiv's Underground'. The last time I spoke to Platon, several weeks later, he was fighting in the suburbs of Kyiv – 'killing orcs', he told me. Then, that number went dead – he could have changed it to a Ukrainian number, which would have been wise. To this day, I don't know the fate of the young couple.

This turned out to be one of the few examples of Russian and Ukrainian friendship during the war. The more common situation would be that these family links would be destroyed. I would often hear from Ukrainians their shock that their Russian family and former friends would just refuse to believe what was happening in Ukraine. 'I went to sleep in 2022 and woke up in 1941,' said Victoria Zavhorodnia. She was talking of the shocking week in June 1941 when Nazi Germany invaded the Soviet Union, a defining moment in the history of both Russia and Ukraine. 'I felt so depressed, weak and miserable,' she told me.

> We never could believe that Russia will invade us. It was absolute panic. I texted all my friends and family, and no one had any idea what to do. We were being bombed by our neighbour, where we

all have friends, relatives, even children. It is killing me from the inside – it broke my heart.

We still somehow had perfect internet reception this deep underground. Everyone was glued to their phones, searching for any scraps of material that would explain the military situation. Social media was the preferred means of sharing information. Military analysts like Rob Lee were already sharing Twitter threads featuring reports from soldiers that laid bare the extent of Russian advances, as well as the casualties Ukraine was inflicting on the invaders. Ukrainian soldiers were calling Putin's Chechen footmen 'TikTok soldiers' because they would post videos of them laughing and firing their guns madly, often well behind the front lines, Ukrainian soldiers told us.

The day before, Ukrainian Instagram had been full of concerts and plays and nightclubs. Now, it was video after video of explosions, lines of desperately fleeing civilians and masses huddling in Metro stations like we were. But the most popular clip was one of President Zelensky. In a grainy mobile phone video and flanked by his top officials, he addressed the Ukrainian people, saying that he was going nowhere. 'The President is here,' he said, before saying '*Slava Ukraini*', or 'Glory to Ukraine', with his men replying, '*Heroyam slava!*', or glory to the heroes. People were showing it around, and it was spreading smiles, enough to give people hope that this fight was not the foregone conclusion everyone outside Ukraine seemed to think. I was heartened by the camaraderie and determination but disturbed by what I saw lacking. There was nothing in the Metro that suggested any serious preparation on the part of the government. Everyone had brought their own sleeping bags and pillows; there were no signs of stockpiles of food, water or other essentials. If the city was surrounded, I worried deeply that Kyiv could end up cut off from the rest of Ukraine and we'd be unable to escape.

The signal was even good enough for me to do a live appearance on a New Zealand TV station where I predicted that the Russians would eventually capture Kyiv but be unable to hold it. I've never been happier to be wrong. At the end of my broadcast, I was interrupted by two of the armed guards, more bemused than concerned at what I was doing. They asked me a few questions – where I was from, what I was doing, who I had been talking to – before taking my passport and closely inspecting it. One of them mimicked handing me my passport, before yanking it away as I went to reach for it. He said, with a quizzical smile, '*Slava Ukraini!*' as if in expectation.

I knew how to stammer out the reply I would offer countless times.

'*Heroyam slava!*'

The guard smiled and handed it over.

KNOCK OUT

BROVARY, KYIV OBLAST, MARCH 2022

'Mayor, I need a weapon!' said the gruff, elderly guard at the hastily erected wooden checkpoint.

It was then that Vitali Klitschko knew he was going to win the toughest fight of his life. He had been a famous boxer, which turned out to be extraordinary preparation for his time as Kyiv's mayor during the city's darkest hour. Like most high-profile Ukrainian government officials, along with journalists and civil society activists, he was on a Russian 'kill list'. But no high-profile official in Kyiv turned traitor or fled their post. Like Zelensky, Klitschko would be a regular presence visiting troops on the front lines, and their presence in the danger zones was proof to most Ukrainians that their politicians were willing to suffer the same privations as the ordinary people.

The quiet commuter suburb of Brovary on Kyiv's eastern outskirts had transformed into a nightmare of steel and shellfire. The Russians had made a 'thunder run', a mad dash from their border with the Sumy region of Ukraine nearly 200 miles away. They'd expected little resistance, but a local spotted their approach with a drone he'd been using for hobby photography. He'd given the coordinates to Ukrainian artillery based in the area, who had blown the column to pieces. It was the first major use of a commercial unmanned aerial vehicle for military effect in the war that would go on to be dominated by such drones.

Klitschko, the former world champion, knew the importance of morale. 'As a former fighter, it is the biggest mistake to say that size and power are everything. In battle, much more important is spirit and the will to win,' he said. Imposing, square-jawed and muscular, he speaks slowly and deeply, each word landing like a blow from his fists. When he proposed evacuating the old man at the checkpoint who was wearing a jacket a size too big and holding a gun far too small to take on the tanks that were coming, he was rebutted: 'What, to leave my home town? I spent my life here, my friends and relatives live here, I don't want to leave. Listen, Mayor, can you give me a favour?' The elderly guard told the mayor what the motley crew of local men who had hastily gathered in the street really wanted: anti-tank weapons like the recently supplied US Javelin or British NLAWs that were toasting Russian armoured vehicles on front lines throughout the country.

Klitschko recalled:

I was very surprised. They don't ask me to help them save their lives; they don't care about that. They are asking about weapons, which means they are ready to fight! I tell these stories because these stories explain exactly the emotion, mood and spirit of the people. Civilians, peaceful people and professionals who would never have the idea to fight, but in this case, they were so motivated to fight and defend our home town.

Like so many who had joined the Territorial Defence, the branch of the army made up mostly of civilian soldiers, the men here had previously lived ordinary lives. I interviewed the mayor in his vast central Kyiv office, adorned with Ukrainian flags, trophies from boxing victories and mementoes of the war. It was almost a year to the day after these events, and he was gregarious, charming and full of confidence. But the circumstances were tinged with sadness. I had accompanied him to a memorial service in a small Kyiv church for two pilots who had been shot down performing a combat mission in Donbas. He had comforted the grieving family, bowing his head in front of them and gripping their wrists, his face tensed with rage and grief as he went on to press a bouquet of flowers onto the resting space below the coffins. He spoke briefly to the assembled mourners, saying, 'Ukraine will not forgive anyone. Ukraine will not forget anyone. Their memory will be eternal. If we remember them, as long as their memory lives on, they are alive in our hearts. Pilots don't die, they take off into the sky and don't come back.' By now, the war had deteriorated into a grinding stalemate that was killing tens of thousands of soldiers on each side. In February 2022, everyone was shocked that Ukraine was surviving day by day.

By the time the mayor was standing on the front lines, I was on a train winding my way back to Kyiv and I headed straight to

Brovary. It had taken a combination of courage and shame to get me to return here. When we went upstairs from the Metro station after those first nights, the streets had been empty except for a few military and police officers checking documents and flipping through camera rolls, looking for saboteurs. Then we jumped on a train, joining millions of Ukrainians on their way to the western border and the safety of countries like Poland, Romania and Moldova. I arrived in the western city of Lviv, heartland of Ukrainian nationalism. The hot water that flowed onto me as I disrobed and stepped into my first shower in ages felt miraculous, as it washed the muck and grime and dried sweat of three days of pure adrenalised terror and exhilaration off me. The four hours of sleep I got in a cramped hotel where we slept three to a room felt like a week in a luxury spa resort. The extreme stress of war plays tricks on your mind and body. I wrote in my diary at the time:

> It was only on this day that I really felt the stress of the war begin to weigh on me. For the first days, we were all living on adrenaline. But this day felt different, as our bodies finally processed what we were going through. I felt weird aches throughout my muscles, and I woke up in a hot sweat despite it being winter in a bitterly cold country. I would feel extremely energetic and then completely exhausted within the same hour.

The sound of the jets near the Polish border made me nearly jump out of my skin. The screech breaks the sound barrier, and it feels like a hole is being ripped in the air in front of you. They zipped over our heads, the last ones flying in formation. They were Ukrainian fighters, with their landing gear out, likely redeploying from destroyed bases further east towards western Ukraine, which was safer. It was around a week into the war, and Ukraine was still fighting. Every day, we had been expecting to hear the news that Kyiv had fallen or that the Ukrainian government had surrendered. It never came.

The queue at the Polish border stretched for up to thirty kilometres and I'd cut the line to deliver medical supplies and food to those who had been waiting for days. For the briefest of moments, I realised I'd be able to slip across myself to safety if I chose. My fate hung in the balance. Yet gnawing at me was the knowledge that I hadn't seen the war; I hadn't told the stories I'd come here to tell. I texted Rosa, a talented graphic designer I'd met, who I'd struck up a friendship with that was to grow close, that day. She was thirty-four, pale-faced, strikingly pretty with short blonde hair, from the southern city of Kherson. Her home town had been one of the first cities to fall to the Russians.

'Did you get out safely?' I asked, offering to help in any way I could.

'No. I'm still in Kyiv. Why should I leave, this is my home?'

I was hit with intense pangs of guilt. I'd forgotten to reach out in the chaos of the first two days. Here I was, playing a war reporter with all the bravado of someone who had just survived a combat deployment, a photo of me spread in my national newspaper with a camera slung over my shoulder, wearing a flak jacket and a helmet. In reality, I'd left brave Ukrainians, Rosa among them, to fend for themselves against overwhelming odds. If I left, I knew the shame would eat away at me – I know those who left who still feel guilt. So, I turned back and a few days later took the quiet train from Lviv to Kyiv. I'd expected it to be empty, but a fair few of the seats were full, mostly of men returning towards the front lines to volunteer to fight. Some had dropped loved ones off at the border, but tens of thousands of Ukrainian men had returned from abroad to join the armed forces.

The Ukrainian Army is known to have faced overwhelming odds throughout the war, battling a country with five times the population, ten times the money and a vast Soviet stockpile of tanks, artillery pieces and seemingly endless stocks of shells. Ukraine's defence is a real David and Goliath story for the ages. However, this can obscure some of the key facts about the military situation, especially early on. The Russians actually invaded with a peacetime strength army of around 120,000 that was missing many key logistics and support personnel and had seriously understrength battalions. Ukrainians realised straight away that they were fighting a war for their national existence. So they joined the army en masse. Within a few weeks, the Ukrainian armed forces had more men and women than they knew what to do with. They ended up with more soldiers in the country than the Russians did. The problem was that many of them had nothing to fight with. There was a mismatch between the two forces. The Ukrainians had the manpower but not the equipment to supply them with, and the Russians had a huge number of tanks and artillery, inherited from the Soviet Union's plans for a war against NATO, but not enough soldiers with which to properly use them.

I arrived back in Kyiv to the sight of the extraordinary city of 3 million people almost entirely empty. Its monumental granite and marble Stalinist-era buildings looked even more imposing and defiant. Only the occasional suspicious police officer on the street and the large queue outside a pet food store suggested that there was still a flicker of life in the area. 'Look who the cat dragged in!' said my colleague Oz Katerji, grinning after seeing me. 'You came back!' he said and slapped me on the back. There was still a small nest of journalists hanging out in Kyiv. There was a total shutdown on most activities and booze was officially banned, but one bar, a cramped underground Latin joint named Buena Vista, remained open. It became the place to be to trade war stories and share safety tips. They were more necessary than ever.

Two of Ukraine's new volunteers were Serhiy and Alexiy, a 52-year-old father and his twenty-year-old son, who were part of a garrison at a checkpoint at the entrance to Brovary when I arrived. They were comforted, Serhiy told me, by the fact that if the Russians broke through, they would die fighting side by side. 'Welcome to hell' was stencilled on a tank trap next to me. There were wrecks of civilian cars everywhere, coloured orange in the way that metal does when it oxidises quickly in the heat of shellfire. Some shells pounded in the distance, but nothing came too close. We got comparatively lucky. The following day, some of my colleagues drove in the other direction, towards the town of Irpin that the Russians were besieging. They took a back road and ran right into a Russian checkpoint.

No one in the car, nor the Russians, knew what to do. Oz, a British-Lebanese journalist who filmed a documentary, *The Battle for Kyiv*, about the early weeks of the war, told me, 'They were as surprised to see us as we were to see them! We were lucky to escape with our lives. We saw firsthand how close the Russians are to Kyiv and the devastation that they were inflicting on the people fleeing Irpin.'

Within the first two weeks, it was clear that the Russians had bungled their assault on the capital. First, the Ukrainians had resisted the attempt to land paratroopers in Hostomel Airport by blowing up the runway. Then, when the Russians attempted to reinforce their troops' advance with a huge column of supply trucks and armoured fighting vehicles overland, Ukrainian sabotage teams destroyed the vehicles at the top and the tail of the column, leaving a great headless snake curling its way, thrashing and useless, from the Belarusian border. The troops who had made it forward were pushing into Ukrainian defences in the towns of Irpin and Moschun and didn't have the firepower to break through to the capital. Elsewhere in the country, in Kharkiv, Donetsk and Mykolaiv Oblasts, the Ukrainians had stopped the Russian troops in their tracks. Only the Russians thrusting in the south-east, who had dashed from Crimea towards Mariupol, were on schedule.

The Battle of Kyiv is a story that has already gone down as one of the greatest underdog victories in military history. Zelensky's defiant selfie address to the nation is the 21st-century version of Winston Churchill's admonition to Britain that 'we will fight on the landing grounds'. The desperate fight to deny the Russians Hostomel Airport and the refugees flowing under the broken Irpin bridge are images that have become indelible in the world's collective memory of the Russian invasion of Ukraine. But it was only half the fight.

CHAS CHE

CHERNIHIV, FEBRUARY 2022

'My city has always been full of fountains,' Yuri Vietkin told me with a chuckle, 'so when the blood started spurting from my leg, I thought, it's just one more fountain!' He'd dreamed up a romantic scene of this moment before, he wrote in his memoir:

> I imagine myself dead, lying in a deserted meadow, and these

snowflakes falling on my face and not melting. What a great shot, but unfortunately it has already become a movie meme ... And all of this is accompanied by a song from, say, Quentin Tarantino's *Kill Bill*, when the Chinese woman, O-ren Ishii, who was wounded by the Red Mamba, falls on the snow, and the snow continues to fall slowly. Cinematic visuals also shape our consciousness. They give it pathos, an interesting, beautiful picture or an apt quote. That's why the death we see in movies is not as scary as in real life.

The grinning grey-haired man, aged fifty-seven, swung up his new leg, a prosthetic made of plastic and metal, and started twirling it around. The old flesh one had been blown up by an artillery shell. He had been trying to ferry supplies across a river, the only lifeline remaining for the 300,000 besieged inhabitants of the city. 'When I saw what the explosion had done, I knew I was dead. If the injury didn't kill me, I knew my wife would!' His smile and laughter were infectious, and he radiated warmth. It is often surprising how well survivors of trauma can thrive.

We were at a small drama theatre in the centre of Chernihiv, several years after his injury. Yuri beamed with pride as he handed me a hardcover of a slim book, the cover adorned with a photo of him in a field in front of a farmhouse, military gear on as a huge cloud of black smoke rises in the background. The title was *Chas Che*. It is a military slang term that means '[the battle] begins', while '*Che*' is also short for Chernihiv. He had written this memoir to tell the story of a battle that the world has forgotten.

Chernihiv is one of the oldest cities in eastern Europe, and its inhabitants like to claim it is the oldest city in Ukraine. It is a hidden gem, with its antique churches, winding parks full of oak trees and its cosy river beaches. It is barely a two-hour drive north from Kyiv, and with a population of 300,000, it offers a leisurely pace of life compared to the bustle of the capital. But for just over a month, the citizens here endured a collective nightmare, as the Russian 41st Guards Combined Arms Army drove south on their way to Kyiv. They expected to surround or occupy Chernihiv without fuss, then use the city as a logistics hub for a more concerted assault on the capital. The troops were so confident that the city would fall into their lap that the Russian Defence Ministry announced, 'The blockade of Chernihiv is complete and the AFU [Armed Forces of Ukraine] offer no resistance.'

When the first columns approached the city to claim their prize, they were met with a hail of artillery rockets fired from the highway. The junction the Ukrainians fired from, overlooked by a spectacular blue and white church, is where the city was first saved. 'No one knows this, but we were just as important to saving Kyiv,' said Andrii Titok, as he drove me through the countryside, its buildings still full of pockmarked walls and boarded-up windows, testament to the siege that occurred here. Titok is a Ukrainian journalist for *Suspilne Chernihiv* who reported on the battle every day that it was ongoing. 'We had about thirty-two tanks in Chernihiv region,' he said. 'The Russians had over a thousand.'

'A lot of old Soviet Army people retired here, so the Russians thought this would be an easy target,' Titok says. 'But we proved them completely wrong. Around 10,000 of our citizens signed up in the first days.' The Russians eventually came close to encircling the city, but they were stopped by a desperate Ukrainian defence near the town of Kolychivka just to the south. By this stage, the only way to resupply Chernihiv from Kyiv was a dangerous path through a forest or with small boats over a river, which were easy targets for Russian artillery. But the soldiers and local volunteers braved the freezing journeys regardless.

At one point, Russian tanks made it to the centre of Kolychivka, only to be lit up by a Ukrainian crew with an anti-tank launcher. Throughout the region, Russian columns would advance unsupported, easy prey for Ukrainian artillery and small infiltration units that could get up close and destroy them. They were also utterly unprepared for battle. 'Our morale was so high, we were fighting not just for our country but our home town,' Titok said. 'They were not prepared to fight. They didn't want to fight, and it showed.' Ukrainian General Nikoliuk, on the contrary, led his soldiers from the front, getting closer to the front line than any Russian general.

Yuri Vietkin survived to tell the tale, however. After his leg was amputated, he was evacuated to Munich, where his sense of humour remained intact, even if his body did not. 'Before I left Munich to go to Ukraine, I went to Octoberfest,' he told me. He would swing his leg up so his boot was facing skyward, where he would invite festivalgoers to put their pints of beer on his upturned prosthetic foot. They'd drink as he told war stories. He put many of them down in his book, including a section on the chaotic mix of emotions he called the 'cocktail of war':

> What does this cocktail of war consist of? What did that heavenly bartender mix in his shaker? Despite the physical sensation of a frosty hue, there is a smell of hope in the air that spring will inevitably come and 'quench' everything. It will quench everything and everyone with hope ... but hatred always fuels any war. Perhaps, so does fear. It was natural for war. First fear, and then hatred. Hate for what caused you this fear. The more fear you have, the

more hatred you have. But where does this fear come from? From the eyes of my wife, her sister, her godmother, the children hiding in the basement of my house?

With him, watching, was 26-year-old Alexiy Sokil, also a soldier from Chernihiv. He was a tall, muscular young man, with a masculine buzz cut. He was friendly. But his gait was unsteady, his handshake weak, his speech slightly slurred. When he sat down, he showed me photos of him on the operating table. There were huge, stitched scars in each leg. It seemed he'd caught the shrapnel from almost an entire artillery shell.

Sokil had also suffered a traumatic brain injury, and he was slowly healing both mentally and physically. 'It was so bad, that my first question when I woke up was not "Where am I?" It was "Who am I?!" They told my parents they had never seen somebody so badly injured survive. Somehow, I made it through.' He said, with a little trepidation, 'When my mother approached me, I gasped and asked, "Who the fuck are you?!"' I asked Yurii how he kept so cheerful despite what he'd suffered. 'I'm an old man, I've lived life. I want to set an example for the young guys like him, that life goes on even like this.'

THE GUT PUNCH

OKHTYRKA, SUMY OBLAST, FEBRUARY 2022

'Am I dying' was the first thought that went through both Stefan Weichert's and Emil Filtenborg's heads as the unknown gunman sprayed their car with bullets. They were in the small town of Okhtyrka, in Sumy Oblast on Ukraine's north-eastern border with Russia. There was no pain, Emil said, just a blinding shock. 'My friends call me a quarter now, because I was shot half as many times as 50 Cent,' he laughed. It took me a moment to get it. The fact that both his colleague and he survived despite being shot four times each was 'a complete miracle', he told me, although I thought of George Orwell's saying on being shot in the Spanish Civil War, that it was luckier not to have been shot at all. They were some of the first international journalists to be injured in a war that has gone on to claim many of our colleagues' lives.

The battle in Sumy comes the closest to the image of the desperate bedraggled civilian guerilla army fighting overwhelming odds. When the Russians marched in, even the Ukrainians expected to be overwhelmed here. Many of the city administration fled. The ordinary people of Sumy did not. A Ukrainian documentary, *The Gut Punch*, describes how the Russians attempted to encircle and then bypass Sumy with a massive armoured column, only to have small teams of defenders sally forth and knock out their logistics. These raids, on the exposed underbelly of a huge Russian force, were literal 'gut punches'. Videos show columns of Russian tanks driving on the roads, completely unsupported, sitting ducks for Ukrainian rockets and Javelins.

The Russians lost so many vehicles on this road that their repaired tanks were still being delivered to the Ukrainian stockpiles for four months after the Russians withdrew. They never thought that they would face resistance in Sumy. Most of the videos from here show Ukrainian civilians in normal clothes with assault rifles, with very few regular soldiers among them. In one case, a group of civilian soldiers bluffed a Russian armoured vehicle that had got lost into surrendering by yelling that they had a rocket launcher.

There were only around fifty professional soldiers in Sumy, with very little in the way of heavy weapons. So light were the forces that the Russians did not even bother to bring air defences to support their troops here, meaning that they became perfect targets for Ukraine's fleet of Bayraktar TB-2 drones.

Along the road from Sumy to Kyiv, the Russians left destruction in their wake, including one church in the village of Zavorychi. 'Those bloodthirsty bastards opened fire from their rusty tanks straight at my crib, my motherland,' Julia Tymoshenko said. 'This church was a symbol of that community and my childhood at Grandma's. I can only imagine the sorrow my grandma felt watching from her window how the church was turning into ashes. Everything that is left alive in me now burns.' The flaming church turned into another symbol of Russian brutality that galvanised resistance in the area.

As a report for West Point's Modern War Institute said:

> Ukraine's military had mounted a non-contiguous strongpoint defense of Sumy oblast ... While static defense forces held strongpoints that centered on urban and other key terrain, light infantry roamed the gaps between these strongpoints ... This effort, in both Sumy and the adjacent Chernihiv oblast, denied consolidation, resupply, and mass for Russia's main effort to encircle Kyiv.

In layman's terms, the Ukrainians fortified their cities to prevent an easy takeover while sending sabotage and diversion teams into the Russian columns. In Sumy, this effort was almost entirely led and self-directed by the citizens themselves, becoming a true people's defence force. One *Guardian* article described the odds as follows:

> Though there were only a few thousand civilians with rifles, a few dozen anti-tank weapons and no armed vehicles or heavy weaponry, by mid-March the Russians were scared to enter the

city. In an alleged recording of a phone call released by Ukrainian intelligence services on 16 March, a Russian soldier can be heard breaking down after telling his mother that they needed to take the road through Sumy city but 'not a single column of [theirs] had survived' ... Others joined in the days that followed as they overcame the shock, according to those involved. They said only about twenty out of 400 had previous military experience and coordination was carried out through messaging apps and phone calls, with groups riding around to locations in civilian cars and trucks to meet the incoming Russians.

That the locals were able to mount such a coherent defence of the city is a credit not only to their skill and the morale of average Ukrainians but to the extraordinarily poor preparation of the Russian Army that expected to steamroll through them.

'Formally, it was called the Territorial Defence Forces, but in reality, it was just people who had received arms from an army warehouse and formed reactive groups,' 29-year-old Ihor told *The Guardian*. 'It was so chaotic that it's even difficult to describe. There was no coordination or instructions from Kyiv or anything like that. We made [everything] up ourselves.'

When I visited Sumy, much later in the war, Alina, a local young woman, described to me how the city went into a frenzy of activity. 'My father and I made Molotov cocktails for the soldiers.' They were put to good use, as one video shows a civilian car driving up behind a Russian armoured personnel carrier on a highway, winding down the window and throwing the deadly concoction at the Russians. The Ukrainians watch the vehicle catch on fire as they drive away cheering.

THOUSAND-YARD STARE

IRPIN, KYIV OBLAST, MARCH 2022

Blood, booze, broken glass and human waste was spread everywhere – the floors, the couches, even the walls. Normally 'don't shit where you eat' is a just a metaphor. The Russians here hadn't even followed it literally. In one room, they had a cooking stove right next to a bucket in the corner, which they had used as a lavatory. 'Even animals wouldn't live like this,' Andriy, the owner, told me. It was the most disgusting thing I had ever seen in my life. The guesthouse, Stockholm Studios, had been taken over by the Russians and they had left it filthier than the most fly-ridden pigsty you could imagine.

Andriy told me about his bizarre escape from arbitrary death: 'They decided to execute me, but they didn't want to look me in the eyes while they did it. So, they closed the door to the kitchen and fired five shots into it. Thankfully, the door frame dispersed the shots and only one hit me in the foot.' He pointed to the four bullet holes in the door frame and pulled up his leg to show me the scar from the impact:

> Eventually, I climbed out the window that led back into the living room and my would-be executioner looked surprised. 'You are alive?!' he said. He decided not to shoot me again as it seemed to him that I wasn't meant to die. I escaped to another part of Irpin the next day and then walked to Kyiv on foot.

Andriy said this almost unemotionally, his eyes glazed over, as if the trauma had him disassociating from reality.

Outside the town as I drove in was a memorial to what to expect on the inside. Dozens of destroyed cars were piled in a huge heap at the entrance, all yellow and twisted. Inside, almost all the buildings seemed damaged, with blown-out windows and shrapnel holes on every wall.

I was later accused of Russophobia by the Russian Foreign Ministry because of my reporting in Ukraine. The first time I became physically sick by what I'd seen in Ukraine was in these houses, and I will admit that even now, my first association with the word 'Russia' is the filth and slaughter that I saw after the Russians pulled out of Kyiv Oblast. They had captured the towns of Bucha and Hostomel but had been stopped in Irpin, the gate to Kyiv itself. Through a series of quick-thinking manoeuvres, including blowing up a dam to flood the local river and destroying key bridges, the Ukrainians – at one point outnumbered nearly ten to one here – had slowed down the Russian advance. The desperate defence of the Ukrainian Army here provided the country with time to mobilise its troops, build up Territorial Defence Brigades and move in troops from bases around the country, particularly the west. The Russians, their logistics destroyed in Kyiv, Chernihiv and Sumy regions, with not enough infantry to support a mechanised advance, eventually retreated, but not before committing war crimes that live in infamy.

Many of the invading troops had been assured the Ukrainians were barely literate peasants, as Russian propaganda had long portrayed them. Yet many of the soldiers who invaded Irpin and Bucha had come from the poorest, most deprived regions of Russia to this affluent, green and pleasant city that was part of the Kyiv suburban commuter belt. People here lived comfortably, and for the Russians here who were from some of the most deprived regions in their country, it looked like luxury. They had been told by the Kremlin that they would be welcomed as heroes, but they met a population who hated them. One of my colleagues described how a family had returned to their flat with a bunch of empty bottles of booze next to some shot glasses. They also had a bottle of olive oil, with a shot's worth missing. The Russians, the inhabitants realised, had not even known what olive oil was, and thinking it was alcoholic, had tried to knock it back.

In their drunkenness and anger, the Russians became bloodthirsty. Ukrainians entered Bucha after the Russians pulled out to find bodies lying all over the streets. Mykhailo Podolyak, a close adviser to Zelensky, remembers how the scenes from Bucha changed how Ukrainians thought about Russia for ever. Speaking to me nearly three years after the town's liberation, he said:

> The Russian occupation regime is the vilest and brutal story, where we have the maximum number of victims among the civilian population. They are vengeful people, and they will be killing and killing again ... The UN [showed that] the Russian Federation [committed] systematic mass murders, torture and deportations in the Kyiv region. Everything was thoroughly planned, systematically agreed upon and a large number of Russians directly participated in this matter.

Putin gave a special award for 'mass heroism and valour' to the 64th Motorised Infantry Brigade, the unit responsible for much of the carnage. Even if he didn't directly order the massacres, he certainly approved of their actions.

In a field behind the Church of St Andrew the Apostle in Bucha, local workers were digging up a mass grave. Every so often, a crane would be lowered and pull out yet another body. I grimaced as I saw one laid on the ground, and a local woman was brought over, presumably a family member, to identify it. She slowly nodded and burst into tears. 'On the morning of 27 February, I was going to put on our service when a column of Kadyrovites came into the town and started shooting up the church,' said Father Andriy, dressed in simple priestly garments and carrying a cross.

> Every day it is burials and burials and burials. If I could ask Putin and others one simple question, it would be: if 'that happened after they had left', how is it that on Facebook, on my page, for example, there are videos of burials published on the 12 March? A miracle, it appears?

Ukrainian authorities say that at least 458 people were killed, including through summary execution, with many bodies showing signs of torture. Around a thousand more were killed in other towns in the Kyiv region.

The Russians claimed it was hoax or that it was committed by Azov troops or that the deaths were caused by Ukrainian artillery. Consistency didn't matter; all that mattered was that they flooded the zone with lies.

Andriy, a 69-year-old engineer who lived on Vokzalna Street, the site of one of the biggest battles in Bucha, looked at the wreckage, now being swept up, with grim resignation.

'War is war, but you need to carry on living … You see, the young ones here, they were afraid, and they hid in a cellar, then they moved to the kindergarten basement. Now they are in Poland. They didn't see these horrors, thank God.' Standing there in Bucha, I felt a slight sense of shame, as if we were intruding on private funerals.

There is an ugly side to the important job of bearing witness. Most disturbing of all was when a local woman began crying, and a group of photographers swarmed around her, trying to get the best and closest shot of grief. No wonder we were called the Vulture Club.

Bucha was not the only place the Russians committed crimes that locals say are unforgivable. In Yahidne, just south of Chernihiv, the Russians forced the entire 400-strong population at gunpoint into a school basement, where they were starved and not allowed to leave for more than a month. At least eleven people died from strokes or suffocation, their bodies left to rot next to their friends and families.

In the town of Borodyanka, just west of Bucha, a large teddy bear with glazed, vacant white eyes looked out into a destroyed building. Behind him was a huge crater, where twenty-seven civilians were buried in a Russian airstrike on 1 March. The locals had commemorated with a small memorial made from the possessions of the dead. 'I feel empty, like this photo,' Maria Litvin told me, as she pulled up a photo of the apartment block on her phone, showing me what the destroyed crater had once contained.

She was standing in what was left of her bedroom in an apartment in Borodyanka, a small town around 40 miles from Kyiv that the Russians had nearly razed. The floor was covered in broken glass and smashed furniture. Had Litvin been in the room when bombs rained down on 1 March, the glass could have ripped her apart. Instead, when they heard the jets flying overhead, she, her mother and her grandmother hid in their cramped shower and bathroom and were spared.

One resident said, 'This is what the *Ruskiy Mir* looks like. My neighbours here were a young couple with two children. All of them died in the basement.'

PARIAH STATE

The Russian invasion of northern Ukraine was one of the greatest political and military catastrophes in modern history, which set the stage for a bloody and bitter war. Almost nothing went right. Not only did the Russians fail to achieve their early objective of knocking out the Ukrainian leadership – they failed to conquer any territory that they could retain.

The Russians lost a huge quantity of armoured vehicles, many of which were repaired and reused by the Ukrainian Army. They also lost many of their best soldiers, such as the feared airborne, attempting risky manoeuvres like the landing at Hostomel. When they decided to refocus their energies on the Donbas region, their army had been badly mauled and they would never again gain a decisive advantage despite the huge differentials in resources and population between the countries. The Kremlin would later claim that the approach on Kyiv was simply a feint, designed to lure Ukrainian troops away from Russia's real objectives in the Donbas, and that their withdrawal was a 'goodwill gesture'. This is ludicrous, as no feint uses most of an army's fighting power and throws away their best soldiers. Furthermore, the Russians only started to make real progress in the Donbas after they had withdrawn from Kyiv.

The invasion was also a moral catastrophe. The photos that came out of Bucha in particular, where civilians had been slain and tortured, their bodies dumped in the streets, galvanised the west into providing unprecedented quantities of military and financial aid to Ukraine. The fierce resistance also forced the United States to consider sending more advanced weapons systems, whereas they had previously considered it a foregone conclusion that they would fall into the hands of the Russians. Atrocities in Bucha and elsewhere galvanised the Ukrainian population into hatred of the Russians. These discoveries also blew up cautious negotiations that were taking place between Ukrainian and Russian delegations in Istanbul on ending the war. After it was clear that Russia's initial shock and awe attempt had failed, negotiators from both countries met to try to reach a diplomatic solution. Negotiating teams came close to reaching a settlement. They decided to put the issue of territorial control of Crimea and Donbas off, potentially for decades. Ukraine was apparently willing to give up on its ambitions to join NATO, if it received some security guarantees protecting its future sovereignty.

The breakdown in the talks is still not fully understood. But it seems three factors played a role. The first was the last-minute Russian attempt to insert clauses that would have given them a veto over Ukraine's security guarantees, as well as put serious limits on Ukraine's armed forces. The second was a visit by UK Prime Minister Boris Johnson to Kyiv, where he apparently warned Zelensky against trusting Putin to abide by a deal and promising that the west would increase its military support. Johnson has denied he had anything to do with sabotaging peace arrangements but has never been entirely clear on what he discussed in Kyiv. His walkabout in the centre of the city became legendary, however, and he remains a folk hero in Ukraine with murals, mugs, T-shirts and even cupcakes featuring his likeness and messy blond mop of hair.

The final one, and the killer blow to an early peace, was the discovery of the Russian atrocities. With the Russians occupying 20 per cent of the country, it became unthinkable that Ukraine could allow more people to suffer fates like those in Bucha. It was also a major contributor to the hatred that Ukrainians developed not just for the Russian Army but for ordinary Russians who seemed to either be supportive or be sticking their heads in the sand. The breakdown in the Istanbul talks, and Russia's crimes in Bucha, convinced many Ukrainians that further negotiations were futile. Podolyak, who participated in the Istanbul talks, later told me that after meeting the Russians, he realised:

> Russia does not negotiate for peace; negotiations are a tool of pressure. Russia does not want a partnership, she wants dominance through the tools of aggression, escalation, blackmail, pressure and provocation. If you are not psychologically ready for this, if you believe they are ready to concede something or use logic, you have already lost.

In a museum in central Kyiv, you can see the face of Vladimir Ovcharov, a Russian soldier, who was just nineteen years old when he died invading Ukraine. As I wrote then:

> His passport photo, on display at the museum, has the look of a boy barely out of high school: baby-faced, with a slight gap in his teeth and wispy hair combed across his head. 'He's so young ... you'd almost feel sorry for him,' says Yana Troianska, a 28-year-old woman from Mykolaiv, while visiting the museum ... The personal documents of other Russian soldiers, as well as captured battle plans and journals, are displayed on tables in the center of the main room. It was an interesting curatorial decision, I thought, in that it actually humanized the invading Russian soldiers who killed tens of thousands of Ukrainians.

Thousands of young Russian men like Ovcharov would die senselessly.

Ukrainian morale skyrocketed after their victories throughout northern Ukraine, and the battles here with their citizen soldiers are part of the great lore of their history. As Yuri Vietkin wrote of the citizen soldiers who saved Ukraine: 'Heroes live among us. They do something, go to work, drink with friends, fall in love, break up, live real lives. Nowhere in the world can we boast of so many heroes per square kilometre.'

Yet it was obvious that the crimes in Bucha were not isolated. The whole world was watching with horror the atrocities being committed in that once glistening seaport, Mariupol.

AFTERWORD: PUPS OF PEACE

CHERNIHIV, APRIL 2025

'Woof, woof!'

Patron ran towards me, narrowing his eyes and letting out a few loud barks before sitting down in front of me. 'Who is this strange-smelling man coming onto my territory?' he must have thought, as I walked to the local branch of Ukraine's demining service, DSNS, in Chernihiv. Only by dangling a puppy treat in my fingers was I to get him to open his little mouth, and he jumped up and down until he snatched it from me. He smiled, tongue out and wagged his tail. 'Good boy!' I said, and he barked softly back. We were friends now, but the look in his eyes was warning me not to get too comfortable. He ruled the roost here! The war here had finished in a month – the clean-up would take years.

'Warning: as soon as we put his jacket on, he gets even more confident,' said Mykhailo, Patron's human 'father', as he plopped a jacket with the logo of the DSNS onto the wiry energetic five-year-old Jack Russell terrier. With his pointy brown ears and distinctive red line running up his snout, Patron is a superstar in Ukraine. Mykhailo had bought him for his son, picked specially from a litter born to prize-winning parents. Trained from a young age to smell explosive residue and gunpowder, Patron and other sniffer dogs search for unexploded ordnance – a term referring to shells, grenades, mines or other ammunition that haven't detonated but can remain deadly for decades to come. When they find something, they call to their humans, who come and safely disarm the device.

'When the full-scale invasion broke out, Patron reported for duty right away. He had grown up and been trained around explosions. So, he wasn't scared on the first day, unlike almost everyone else!' Mykhailo says. 'I found him right next to our truck, ready to work.' Around halfway into the siege of Chernihiv, Ukrainian air defence shot down a Russian jet over the city. When a team of soldiers came, Patron started barking loudly as they approached – he'd smelled something he didn't like, and it wasn't just the Russian flying the plane. When the team moved closer to investigate, they noticed that the jet still had a 500kg bomb attached to it, which could detonate at any moment. Thanks to the pup's expert nose, they were able to carefully remove and defuse it. When the Russians retreated, Patron and his friends were some of the first to enter liberated areas to make them safe for human habitation again.

His 'mother', Irina, said he had a unique role to play in the education of Ukrainian children. 'It is our job to go around schools and teach children about the dangers of mines and explosives. We noticed that many of them would zone out and not listen. This is very dangerous.' So, she came up with the idea to use Patron as the mascot for the service. They took him around schools and introduced him to the children. Irina reported that the younger kids would say, 'Patron told me not to pick up these things. Patron told me to tell an adult.' He didn't just appeal to children. Everywhere

I went in Ukraine, I saw plush-toy Patrons, Patron fridge magnets and little ceramic models of him. He featured in a cartoon show and a comic book series.

Some audiences required a good cop/bad cop act. Patron would also work with a DSNS employee called Kraken, who would pull up his trouser leg to show his shiny metal foot. The original one had been blown off when he'd stepped on a mine during a job in the liberated Kharkiv region. 'This is what will happen if you don't pay attention,' he says.

For Patron's efforts, President Zelensky had awarded him a medal for courage, and he was the first dog to be named a UNICEF Goodwill Ambassador. 'They also like him in Canada,' Mykhailo told me, as he'd barked and bit at Prime Minister Justin Trudeau when he'd tried to pick him up when Zelensky had presented him. Patron is a hardened veteran, having completed tours of duty around former front lines in Mykolaiv, Kharkiv and Donetsk Oblasts.

The real-life Patron was a bit more cocksure and haughtier than his on-screen character, but he is one of the bravest and most adorable creatures it is possible to meet.

Anthony Connell, a New Zealander who worked for a Swiss demining NGO in Chernihiv, allowed me to join his crew as they worked. It was tough and tedious work. 'It looks nothing like *The Hurt Locker*!' one of the deminers told me. The six men with me would advance slowly and cautiously, one step at a time, waving their metal detectors over the ground. When they found paydirt, a pouch of grenades that had been buried, they attached cables and painstakingly winched them out of the ground from as far away as the spool would stretch. One wrong move could mean the loss of a limb or even a life.

Irina remained haunted by what Patron and his dog colleagues had found in some of the homes that the Ukrainian Army had liberated in the Chernihiv region. The Russians left explosive booby traps all over civilian dwellings. They would be in fridges and cupboards, under bodies, even dug into people's gardens.

'In some cases, the Russians would take pets, like a house cat, and put him in a closet next to an explosive. When the owner returned home, they would hear the cat screeching, and the first thing you think to do is go and let him out!' Then the mine would be activated.

It had taken two years to demine 20,000 hectares of Chernihiv region, where fighting had only gone on for a month. To demine Kharkiv region, or the Donbas, would be an extraordinary feat. 'It will take decades, and billions of dollars', Anthony says frankly.

In the meantime, I was glad to see that dogs in Ukraine were far more than portents of doom. For Irina, Patron is crucial for keeping up morale. 'In the midst of all of these terrible things, it is great to give people some joy, something to be hopeful for.'

CHAPTER THREE

THE EMPIRE STRIKES BACK: THE CONQUEST OF THE SOUTH AND THE FIRST BATTLE OF DONBAS

'No, you do not know a night in Ukraine! ... The moon shines in the midst of the sky; the immeasurable vault of heaven seems to have expanded to infinity; the earth is bathed in silver light; the air is warm, voluptuous, and redolent of innumerable sweet scents.'
– Nikolai Gogol, *Evenings on a Farm Near Dikanka*

'I was delighted with most of what the war had offered me: chicks, kicks, cash and chaos; teenage punk dreams turned real and wreathed in gunsmoke.'
– Anthony Loyd, *My War Gone By, I Miss It So*

FIRE CONTROL

LYSYCHANSK, LUHANSK OBLAST, MAY 2022

Everything was in flames.

When we'd driven this road the other way two hours ago, a group of Ukrainian soldiers had already set up camp by a bend in the road. Beside them was a large self-propelled howitzer they were using to shell advancing Russian attack teams. Now, their vehicles were on fire and the men's bodies scattered across the remains of their gun emplacement. 'Judging by the smoke, we missed this strike by about five minutes,' said Anton, the Ukrainian soldier driving us back and forth from the battlefield. Depending on the day, this highway to the besieged city of Lysychansk was known by two names. When it was quiet, it was the 'road of life' that brought desperately needed supplies, ammunition and reinforcements to the troops holding Ukraine's crumbling defences. If it was a loud day, it was the 'road of death' because the Russians had brought their artillery to within range and could pour hellfire down on it at will and any trip could mean death. It was like an exposed artery that spurts blood with each hit from a mortar or artillery shell. This situation is euphemistically known in military lingo as being under 'fire control' and that was a very literal description today. Anton slammed the accelerator and pushed it up near to 150 kilometres per hour. Three Ukrainian tanks rumbled past us on their way to the battle, towards the very inferno we were escaping.

As we drove, we passed the sign that said 'Luhansk Oblast' in white lettering against a blue background. It was an ominous name that had become the byword for a terrifying secret about Ukraine's military position. For most of the first two months, Ukraine had notched up victory after victory, pushing the Russians from Kyiv, then from the outskirts of Kharkiv and halting their advance on Odesa in the south. So, the Russians had refocused their assault to the provinces of Donetsk and Luhansk, collectively known as the Donbas.

After pushing all around the front line, the Russians had finally found a weak point. Slowly but surely, their military machine was bringing to bear its overwhelming firepower to lay waste to Ukrainian towns and cities. They would destroy every building in sight until they left the Ukrainian Army with nowhere to hide and they were forced to retreat. This had happened in one nearby Ukrainian stronghold over the last few days. 'They didn't capture Popasna – they destroyed the city and moved into its ruins,' a deputy mayor in the nearby city of Bakhmut told me. I wonder if he knew by then what fate had in store for his own home.

The lynchpin of Ukrainian defences here were the twin cities of Lysychansk and Severodonetsk, separated by a small river. Inside Lysychansk, there were scenes of panic and devastation, the horizon itself obscured by the thick black smoke rising from Russian shelling at a nearby oil refinery. 'What's the news?' said Tatiana Malorezka, one of the few remaining civilians in the city, as she ambled up to us. 'We have no electricity, no mobile signal, no idea what's going on. The Russians say they have captured Severodonetsk?!' We reassured her that the Ukrainians held the neighbouring city, and she nearly cried with relief.

We'd got here through a lucky break. We'd tried to hire a local from Luhansk region as a fixer but, in all bluntness, he'd had a breakdown on us. One moment over the phone he said, 'Ah, I see you guys want to get into the shit!' and was promising us a bevy of military contacts to take us to positions near the front line. The next, he was calling us drunk at 11 p.m., swearing at us and saying, 'Going there is suicide man. We are all going to die.' As luck would have it, we'd picked up the number of a local volunteer, a man named Oleksiy Ovchynnykov, and we decided to call it. His smooth voice and calm manner instantly put us at ease. He was from Slovyansk, a former dancer who owned a series of studios across the Donbas. Now he was working as a volunteer bringing aid into besieged towns. He was due, he said, to help the military bring some supplies to Lysychansk and invited us for the ride.

'My nerves just can't take it anymore, you know?' Tatiana said, her hands shaking. 'I don't want the Russians to be here!' Tatiana said she could live under almost any circumstances without power or running water if it was under the Ukrainian flag. 'I can never live under Russian occupation,' she told us. 'It is the only thing that would make me leave.' She handed us three numbers of family members who have fled to western Ukraine. 'Please call them and tell them that I and the rest of the family are OK,' she pleaded. One of the numbers was for her son, who is in the army and is fighting on the front line. She hadn't been able to contact him and has no way to know if he is dead or alive. We had a Ukrainian colleague call, but I don't know what happened to either of them, and the fate of Tatiana is one of those I still reflect on.

Severodonetsk was the regional capital of the Ukrainian-controlled part of Luhansk Oblast, after the Russian-backed separatists had occupied the main city of Luhansk and some surrounding regions back in 2014. Now the Russians wanted the lot. When Russian forces refocused from Kyiv, the war became much more recognisable to one from our history books, seeing mass bombing campaigns, intense urban warfare and endless gallons of blood spilled on both sides. However, the Russians had lost many of their best troops in the initial invasion, so they would struggle to maintain enough soldiers in the field, despite possessing much more firepower when measured by tanks or artillery.

Ukraine, meanwhile, had an enormous number of troops mobilised, but much fewer artillery pieces, shells or armoured vehicles. The Russians fired an average of 20,000 shells per day during this period and likely averaged 15,000 over the course of 2022. For comparison's sake, at this time the United States, once a colossus of military manufacturing, produced just under 15,000 artillery shells per month. To outside observers, the Ukrainians seemed like they had the situation under control. 'The Russian advance in the Donbas has stalled,' said one daily British Defence Ministry intelligence update. Some Ukrainian politicians had gone even further. Oleksii Arestovych, an adviser to the President's office who would later fall out spectacularly with the administration, said that the Russian assault was failing so badly that Ukraine would be soon taking back Crimea and that Putin's regime was on the brink of collapse. This was wishful thinking at best and hinted at greater problems to come. 'You should make it clear that we believed him,' said one friend when I showed her this passage. 'They gave us hope – false hope it turned out – that the war would all be over soon and that we would have victory. Now "victory" is kind of a dirty word.'

It was an interesting insight into what would soon become clear: that sources of information in this war would be diverse and varied, and many supposedly reliable institutions would fail in their analyses. Instead, a cottage industry of amateur experts cropped up to track the war through open-source intelligence (OSINT). Most well known in the west was Oryx, which tracked the numbers of destroyed tanks and other vehicles based on publicly available photos and videos. On the Russian side, there were war bloggers with Telegram channels such as Rybar, War Gonzo or Strelkov, belonging to former FSB Colonel Igor Girkin. While their political views were always tainted with Russian propaganda, they often provided reliable information about battles on the ground or exact lines of territorial control. They were some of the few outlets that would openly criticise Russian strategy or command. The Ukrainians were usually cleverer at keeping tight operational security to prevent their troops' locations being spotted, so correspondents embedded with the Russians often had a closer view of the battlefield than others on the Ukrainian side. This often had terrible results for the Russians. In one infamous incident, a pro-Russian blogger left an identifiable marking on a building where their troops were based; the Ukrainians promptly destroyed it with long-range artillery, killing around twenty soldiers.

Instead, the Ukrainians often promoted stories about local heroics to raise morale – like the story of the soldiers on Snake Island, who had told Moscow's Black Sea flagship the immortal line: 'Russian warship, go fuck yourself'; or the Ghost of Kyiv, the (almost certainly invented) pilot who shot down dozens of Russian planes. These usually blended an element of truth and myth; there is no record of Zelensky saying the punchy line: 'I need ammunition, not a ride,' but it certainly captured the sentiment he conveyed. As the war became fought in the information space alongside the battlefield, the only way to part the fog of war was to go to the front line yourself.

The recent fighting in Luhansk had centred on a suburb to the north-east called Rubizhne over a small river tributary. Russians hadn't occupied Rubizhne, that was true. But the soldiers we were visiting in Lysychansk told us that things were not going nearly as well as they were being portrayed to the wider world. Roman, one of the soldiers, revealed that the precise lack of movement on the maps was misleading. He himself had participated in the battle for Rubizhne, which ended with his unit and the rest of the Ukrainian troops being forced out of the town the previous night by overwhelming Russian artillery fire. 'We were forced to retreat last night,' he said. 'We didn't have the forces to hold the town, so we blew up the bridge and pulled back to Severodonetsk. We hold it now, but the battles will be hard. The Russians are coming.' The main problem, the soldiers said, was artillery. The Ukrainians had exhausted almost all their Soviet stockpiles in the defence of Kyiv and other cities. Now, they were waiting desperately for promised western supplies. The Russians, on the other hand, had seemingly endless stockpiles.

The Soviet Union had been keeping these shells for what it saw as an inevitable land war against NATO forces in western Europe. Instead, the two biggest successor states were using these to inflict bloody carnage on each other. In some places, the Ukrainian soldiers said, the Russians were shooting ten shells for every one they could fire back. The west had promised military aid, but it wasn't arriving in time and in sufficient quantity to offset the Russians' enormous advantages. 'They just destroy the city block by block with artillery,' said the commanding officer here, a tall, fair-haired Ukrainian major with the callsign 'Spartak'. 'They do here just what they did in Mariupol.'

WAR DIARY

MARIUPOL, DONETSK OBLAST, MARCH 2022

'Day 9. A strong glow is visible over Vostochny, probably from a fire ... We are worried because Mom is there.' Helga Ihnatieva had no idea if her parents or any of her loved ones were still alive. "'Have you seen a Ukrainian night...?" Gogol wrote. "Yes. Ukraine is on fire," Dovzhenko would answer.' Less than a month ago, she'd been checking me into her hotel. Now, as she expressed in a captivating diary that she gave me, she and her family were experiencing a hellish trial of faith.

Nikolai Gogol is one of the most famous Ukrainian writers who had written paeons to the bucolic Poltava region of his childhood. 'No, you do not know a night in Ukraine,' his wistful story continued with the quote that opens this chapter. Gogol had written entirely in Russian, however, and had once represented the happy coexistence between Russia and Ukraine. Russians claimed him as one of their greats – Dostoevsky saying, 'We all came out from Gogol's overcoat.' Gogol had never been able to choose his allegiance and said, 'I don't know whether my soul is Ukrainian or Russian.' Well, now it was the time for everyone on the land of Ukraine to make that choice.

Oleksandr Dovzhenko, on the other hand, was a Ukrainian director who had made a 1943 film called *Ukraine in Flames* about the Battle of Kharkiv between the Soviets and the Nazis. Gogol's vision of Ukraine was being destroyed, replaced by Dovzhenko's vision of endless war. I was astounded by the fact that Helga had the presence of mind to incorporate literary criticism into the war diary she was writing by candlelight in a desolate basement while bombs smashed into the street around her.

The same day, Helga said, she had been called by her neighbour in a shrieking fit of terror. 'A piece of shrapnel hit her one-year-old son in the head, and he started bleeding. They drove to the hospital under the bombing, where the doctors tried to save the child, but he died after ten minutes.' The city was crucial to Russian plans for the south, where they wanted to build a land bridge between the occupied Donbas regions and the Crimean Peninsula. It didn't matter how many innocents died on the way. The annexation of Crimea remained the biggest feather in Putin's cap, the great achievement of his 22-year reign. But after he annexed it, the Ukrainians had blocked the water supply from the Kakhovka Dam that it had relied on. It was isolated from the Russian mainland, and the only way to supply it was through a huge bridge that the Russians were building from Kerch. If that bridge was taken out, the Ukrainians could isolate and potentially destroy the Russian position in Crimea over time. The city was to suffer the cruellest bombardment of any in Europe since the Second World War.

Helga's diary continued:

> Day 10. Only a couple of hours have passed since I described the 9th day. An air raid. Hands are shaking. The face began to distort as if from a stroke, the smile turned out crooked and unnatural and, of course, involuntary. They dropped a bomb not far away from our house. It is unclear how far the plane flew and whether it is possible to go to bed. It's scary. It's unclear where a shell or bomb will come from: from above, from below, from the left or right. Bang. Bang a lot. It's impossible to open a window to the street: everything around stinks of burned rubber. We are sitting and cursing one person. A well-known person. Putin.

As we've seen, the original Russian concept of operations completely fell apart around Kyiv. But it was different in Ukraine's south. Michael Kofman says this was a successful example of Russia's model of the 'special military operation', which failed miserably elsewhere.

'The Russian intelligence operation against Ukraine was not hallucinated!' he told me.

> In the south and in the east, from Luhansk through Donetsk, Kherson and Zaporizhzhia, Russian forces advanced very rapidly in the early days of the war and were almost unopposed. Nothing that was done in Ukraine's north to stymie the Russian advance took place in the south or the east, until about the Kharkiv region. Nobody tried to resist them from exiting Crimea to the borders of Mykolaiv Oblast in the opening of the war, and we should ask why that is!

There were many signs that here, the appointed Ukrainian collaborators had come through for them. The Ukrainians had planted landmines by the narrow isthmus of Perekop that separates Crimea from the mainland. But they didn't explode when the Russians drove over them. Someone had supplied the Russians with maps of the minefields so they could avoid or disable them. Major bridges that were supposed to be destroyed to stop the Russian advance, like the large one over the Dnipro near Kherson, were left intact. One after another, small cities surrendered to the Russians without a fight. Nova Kakhovka, Melitopol and Berdiansk fell like dominoes. By 28 February, the Russians had linked up with their proxy forces controlling the Donbas and scored a major victory. The Ukrainian defenders in Mariupol were encircled. Of the Ukrainian territory occupied and still held by the Russians during the full-scale invasion as of 2025, around two-thirds of it was captured during this lightning assault in the south.

The Ukrainians have conducted investigations into events here, and the head of Ukraine's Security Service was fired over the failings. Some Ukrainian troops woke up with the Russians outside their base and surrendered right away. The Russians were so confident they'd won, that they allowed the troops to retreat to Ukrainian-controlled territory without taking them prisoner.

Helga wrote:

Day 15: Our morning began at 3:30. I slept for a total of three hours and then we were woken up by shells. That day there was a lot of thunder, everything around was exploding. At about 10:45 they dropped a bomb from an airplane into the neighbouring yard. We saw a blast wave, things fell from tables and nightstands.

AGAINST ALL ODDS

The Ukrainian Marines realised early on that their fight was probably hopeless. Among other things, the Russians had wiped out Ukraine's air defences in this area, so their jets could fly freely. They'd destroyed the Ukrainian Navy almost entirely in 2014, so they could bring missile-bearing ships and submarines right up to the blockaded port. Against this level of firepower, the Ukrainian defenders never stood a chance. Shaun Pinner, a former British Army soldier who lived in Ukraine with his wife, recalled that they knew the battle was lost almost before it began: 'We had good defences to the east, towards the Donetsk People's Republic, and they held up pretty well. But the real attack came from the west, from Crimea, and it just punched right through us.' Yet they kept fighting on orders from their high command. The Russians were expending huge quantities of troops and ammunition here, meaning that they could not use them to assault other parts of the country. It was vital that Mariupol's defenders hold on for as long as possible.

Helga documented:

Day 19: I don't want to put medals on myself, beat my chest and shout: yes I do, yes I do, do you know what I've been through? Every resident of Mariupol ... has experienced it. But I want to tell you how it was. This text is being written right now on the 9th day of the war that a small bald dwarf decided to start against my Fatherland. I am Ukrainian and yes, I speak Russian. Why are we at war? Because the man who is now sitting in a bunker in the Urals decided to expand his territory. And all of Russia is afraid of this man, even more so the whole world. One fucking dwarf,

People are afraid that they are being put in paddy wagons, and what's more, children are being put in them. It seems that Russia has forgotten what a revolution is and that there are 140,000,000 of them. Just think about it! Only a few of them are trying to fight it.

One of Helga's friends had told her that a green corridor to evacuate civilians had been organised. As they packed what few belongings they had and prepared to leave, they got word that the deal had fallen apart. Anyone who did try to leave via that route was shelled and many were killed.

On 16 March came one of the worst Russian crimes of the entire war. Just before 10 a.m., a Russian airstrike smashed into the Mariupol Drama Theatre that had been a shelter for thousands of civilians. A sign painted outside that read '*deti*', or 'children', became infamous as a sign of the Kremlin's willingness to kill anyone in their way. Around 600 people died in the worst mass casualty event of the war to date. By this time, Eva, the guide from my February trip, had managed to leave and was in Germany. She told me:

> When I saw that, it was still a part of me. Something inside me had died. It sounds so silly, but the theatre itself was a sign of the city's life. It's a terrible feeling when you can do nothing for the place and people you love. I want to know who is there and who stayed alive. When you search pictures for Mariupol it is the first that comes up. It was the place people would always meet and walk around, the hub of the city. It was the symbol of Mariupol. It felt to me like if there is no more theatre, there is no more Mariupol.

These terrible weeks saw tragedy after tragedy. Some became famous like that of Iryna Kalinina, a pregnant woman who was carried on a red polka-dot stretcher as she bled to death from a strike on a maternity hospital, immortalised by *Associated Press* photographer Evgeniy Maloletka's World Press Photo award-winning picture. Others are less known. 'I saw a great number of dead bodies of civilians,' Helga told me. 'Two of them were our former neighbours, lying in the courtyard. We wanted to bury them there because no one could come to collect the bodies, but the ground was frozen, and we couldn't dig. We had to leave the bodies in a plastic bag.'

She wrote:

Day 20: Our area is being shelled very heavily.

Dropping bombs and rockets became the order of the day. The vibrations from the explosions were very strong, plaster was falling, concrete slabs were blown out, doors and windows were blown out. The shelling became so frequent that it was simply unsafe to go outside even for a short time. The most everyone did was boil a kettle for boiling water, no one cooked food. Shells were already falling and exploding near us, we all survived, Denis [then Helga's fiancé, now husband] was briefly stunned. Around 12 midnight on the 17th day, city buses were parked right next to our house. It became obvious that there was now a line of defence, that is, the front line, under our house. There was no longer any talk of sleep.

Three weeks into the war, the seemingly impossible had happened. An agreement for a short ceasefire, merely a few hours, was reached to allow a convoy of vehicles to move out of Mariupol and into Ukrainian or Russian-held territory. Helga managed to find a place in the vehicle for the family that remained around her. On the way, they passed through the notorious Russian filtration system. These were camps set up by the Russians to check whether anyone leaving Mariupol was civilian or military. The Russians checked phones, documents, wallets and especially bodies for the slightest sign of combat. Any cuts or scratches, calluses that could have come from holding a rifle, a tattoo with symbols of Ukraine – just one of these could be enough for you to be whisked away to a grisly fate. If you were deemed a threat, you could well be 'disappeared' into the hellish Russian prison system, with its constant physical and psychological torture.

Helga recorded:

There were probably around twelve Russian checkpoints. It was the 21st day of the blockade of Mariupol. They made the boys undress three times. They would check their backs, they were very exacting. They told one of our guys the scratch on his back was from body armour. They almost took him captive. My fiancé had a ketchup stain on his pants, they said it was blood and he definitely had been somewhere in a field killing Russians. This was even though we had been shelled for three weeks and blood wouldn't have been a surprise. But we got out in the end.

The Ukrainians had a mighty fortress from which to make a last stand. With its back to the sea, and surrounded by a river, the Azovstal metalworks became the site of a defence verging on mythic. Mariupol witnessed some of the most daring Ukrainian heroics of the war. Two thousand people, both soldiers and civilians, were held up in a vast labyrinth of steel. There was no way to supply the fortress by ground or sea. The Russian ground forces surrounded three sides, and their navy controlled the fourth, with powerful radar systems to monitor any aerial activity. The solution lay in the ingenuity of Ukraine's air force, who found a way to reach the plant unseen. Early in the mornings, fog often covered the sea and visibility from land to the sea was nearly non-existent, so they could swoop in undetected. Ihor and Andriy, who were twenty at the time, flew their helicopters deep into enemy territory, carrying food, weapons and supplies, as well as a few suicidally brave soldiers who had offered to be dropped in to fight alongside the bedraggled defenders.

'We were flying into Mariupol at the height of the siege. We came from the sea to avoid being spotted by Russian defences, flying at altitudes of less than ten metres … It is extremely dangerous because you can run into power lines or trees,' Andriy said, dragging on a cigarette in a training ground near the city of Lviv. Despite being only twenty-two when I met him two years after his descent into Mariupol's hell, Andriy had already flown more than thirty missions. But he told this to me without a hint of excitement or emotion, describing his extraordinary work as if it was as dull as washing dishes or filling in spreadsheets. The exhausted defenders were bewildered to see them, expecting that they had been abandoned to their fate. The supplies and reinforcements were dropped off and the worst of the wounded were evacuated back to the safety of Ukrainian-controlled territory. Throughout the war, however difficult the situation, they tried to leave no one behind.

Eventually, the Russians got wind of the plan and the helicopters that flew in afterwards were shot down. The survivors endured miserable conditions there for another month while Russian forces bombarded the plant with bombs of all sizes and types. Fortunately for those taking shelter, the area had been designed by Soviet engineers with the intent that the tunnels could withstand a nuclear attack. Completely surrounded and under relentless attack, the Ukrainians heroically held their ground and launched counterattacks against the Russians. Small units snuck outside the industrial area, carrying anti-tank weapons on their shoulders, ambushing armoured vehicles amid the ruins and destroying one tank after another.

The fight for Mariupol would eventually end. After two months of bloody fighting, the soldiers and civilians who sought shelter in tunnels beneath the Azovstal steel plant surrendered. They had run out of food and ammunition, and Ukrainian forces did not have the ammunition or armoured vehicles necessary to launch an assault on the city that could relieve them. On 16 May, the last defenders of Azovstal were ordered to surrender. Mariupol had fallen at last. Shaun Pinner didn't make it to Azovstal. During the fighting, he had become separated from his Marine unit. He was nearly killed trying to link up with other Ukrainian forces. Eventually, he ran solo into a Russian patrol and was forced to surrender. The defence was not in vain, however. It bought crucial time for Ukraine to raise its forces and receive western supplies. No other city in Ukraine would be surrounded like Mariupol.

'All that Russia has brought to my life and my city is death,' Helga wrote in her final diary entry after leaving the city. 'I don't have a home anymore, the same as 500,000 Mariupol citizens, I don't have my city, some people don't have relatives, friends, memories,' she said. 'We will never come back there. We're on our own now and our life starts anew.'

SCAR TISSUE

The wound of Mariupol may never heal. In the nearby city of

Zaporizhzhia, where most of those who could leave Mariupol fled, there is a refugee hub, 'IMariupol', to help the displaced. A young English teacher was giving a lesson to a group of children while medical specialists in a doctor's clinic and dentist's office were examining patients. Ludmila Shevchenko works at this clinic. She was a doctor who fled Mariupol last March but not before witnessing some of the war's worst horrors. For four devastating weeks, Shevchenko worked in one of the city's hospitals, treating a never-ending stream of civilian and military patients.

These refugees all carry a great deal of trauma. 'I noticed how children seemed to suffer much more,' Shevchenko told me. 'I remember seeing a group of kids playing a game, where they would role-play as amputees, saying "Let's cut off the hand" or "Let's cut off the head."' She says, 'We have a specialist mental health clinic that can prescribe anti-depressants or therapy,' but she admits it is difficult to heal those who have suffered such deep psychological wounds. 'Some of the symptoms don't show at first,' she says. 'It will only be after the victory when the symptoms of post-traumatic stress in the country will bloom everywhere like flowers.' Shevchenko had two elderly colleagues, who managed to leave Mariupol for Kyiv, only to die of heart attacks caused by their stress in the following months.

Shevchenko keeps in contact with relatives and friends still living in the now destroyed and occupied city who describe a horrific humanitarian situation that the Russian authorities are totally unequipped to handle. 'There are so many amputees in the city, people without arms or legs,' she says. 'Now that it is summer, and people wear lighter clothing, this is far more visible. There is no power in most of the city, so elevators don't work, and some disabled people are trapped on the upper floors of their buildings.'

The Russians have never allowed independent investigators into the city, so no one knows the true death toll, and we may never know. Mariupol's mayor says it could be up to 25,000.

In the autumn of 2024, I visited Eva in Berlin, where she was living with her partner. She had left very early, just before the battle started. I asked what her defining memory of Mariupol was, and she mused and returned to the old women she'd seen looking over the port waiting expectantly for the *Ruskiy Mir*. 'I often wonder where those women are now. Did they get what they were waiting for? Or are their bodies, like those of so many other Mariupol residents, buried beneath the rubble of apartment blocks destroyed by Russian rockets and bombs?'

THE VULTURE CLUB

'The Russians have hardly bombed us today at all,' said Alexandra, a bright-faced seventeen-year-old. 'We've been able to be outside almost the entire day,' she beams. We were in the courtyard of a school in Lysychansk, where some of the city's few remaining civilians were taking refuge in the basement. Alexandra beckoned us inside, and her bright red hair was lit up by dim candles, which became most residents' main source of light. There was no power or running water here, so families collect water from a well. Worst of all, they say, is the lack of phone signal or internet access, so they have no idea of the military situation or any way to contact friends and family who have left.

'We didn't leave the basement for almost one entire month,' says her brother Daniil, a sixteen-year-old student at the school. 'The shelling was too heavy. Today, for some reason, it's light,' he shrugs. Beds were crammed closely together, forming two thick rows lining each wall of the main underground chamber. Preserves and other non-perishables lay on tables: jam, pickles, cans of stewed meat. An unpleasant odour, a mix of sweat, bleach and dried urine, was always present in these shelters.

The Russians were trying to create what is known as a 'cauldron' of Ukraine's troops in the Donbas, where they could surround the Ukrainian armed forces and gradually shell them into submission. It would mean they would not have to storm headfirst into Ukraine's trench networks and minefields, many of which Ukraine had been building since 2014. To plug gaps in its lines and prevent the Russians from encircling them, Ukraine threw a lot of its hastily trained Territorial Defence units, made from local volunteers with no previous military experience, into the bloodiest battles. Many died, but their sacrifice bought Ukraine valuable time to build up its military resources and receive supplies from the west. Many of these units were originally set up to defend their own regions as far away as the Romanian border. Yet none protested when they were sent to the hottest parts of the Donbas front; Ukrainians were determined to defend every inch of their soil from Lviv to Donetsk.

This has been a dark chapter, full of hopelessness and despair. You might be wondering why anyone would willingly come to a place like this. Ukrainians had no choice; it was their homes being destroyed and their people being killed. But war zones have many draws for young, ambitious people with a low sense of self-preservation. There were four of us on that trip. Along with me there was Neil, a tall, gruff and sweaty Canadian, whose fluent Russian saved us from more than a few scrapes; Caleb, a soft-spoken blond-haired American with a boyishly handsome face who seemed to have no inbuilt fear and never flinched no matter how close a shelling came to us; and Hugo, a darkly funny Frenchman with curly black hair who chain-smoked so much it seemed cigarettes grew from his hands. Hugo's girlfriend, an elegant and witty French photojournalist named Ines, dropped in and out of our trips.

Ukraine was different from other wars. It sounds strange for those who have never experienced it, but reporting the war in Ukraine was in many ways an easy job. Readers had tired of conflicts in Iraq and Syria, which seemed to be endless bloodbaths between different jihadi cults and various murderous dictators. The morality here was also simple: Russia was clearly the aggressor and Ukraine, for all its flaws, was the heroic underdog. Everyone who was anyone in respectable society in the west was on the same side. Even the US military, who were supplying Ukraine with weapons, and the CIA, who had predicted the invasion and were giving Ukraine detailed intelligence on Russian troop movements, were the good guys here, no matter their sins elsewhere in the world. Along the road you could stop at various gas stations for some of the best fast food you could find in Europe; a hot dog or burger from the chains WOG or OKKO, washed down with an apple and kiwi flavoured Burn energy drink became the basis for any nutritious meal in the Donbas. One particular station – people familiar with the region will know what I refer to – operates so close to the front lines that I have no idea how it has not caught a Grad rocket barrage or an Iskander missile by now.

Above all, Ukrainians were simply glad we were there. Having foreign journalists covering the war was not just a morale boost. It was a crucial part of Ukraine's messaging strategy, and they saw a direct link between international media coverage and the flow of desperately needed weapons and humanitarian aid. One soldier from Mariupol later told me, 'After Bucha, it was you guys covering Russian atrocities that meant that we got as much support as we did.' This confluence of interests had great practical advantages as well. In Syria, journalists who picked the wrong fixer or rebel group to embed with could get just as easily sold to Islamic State, as nearly happened to Anthony Loyd, whose quote opens this chapter.

In Ukraine, you worked with a highly professional, competent military who was on your side and had a personal stake in both your survival and your ability to tell the story. So much in the country worked that you wouldn't expect. Cell service was perfect almost anywhere except the very front line, and even there you had Starlink. Despite the Russians' best efforts later in the war, the electricity grid never collapsed. As I discuss in a later chapter, you could have a very good life behind the front lines in Kyiv or other major cities. It wasn't perfect, far from it, and the combination of dozens of young, hot-headed, brash and confident young people, foreigners and locals alike, often made for combustion. War zone drama was absurdly common. There were endless affairs, rows and disputes over money, credit for photos and stories between journalists, fighters and volunteers (I'm afraid I was not exempt). Of course, the most common drama was over romance. These were so common that Ukrainians working here called the latest scandal a 'Santa Barbara', after an old American soap opera of the same name that was popular on late Soviet television (I'm afraid I was not exempt).

It comes across as callous and uncaring to those suffering in other conflicts to say that people cared about Ukraine because they saw more of themselves in Ukrainians, but I'm afraid it is true. Every newspaper wanted the latest battle dispatch. Every magazine wanted a Ukraine angle on their particular niche. *Vogue* put Zelensky and his glamorous and courageous wife Olena on their cover. *Rolling Stone* profiled Sviatoslav Vakarchuk, the Ukrainian rock star who interspersed his sellout world tours with concerts for soldiers in underground command centres close to the front line. I wrote about the latest developments in drone warfare for *Popular Mechanics* and the commemoration of the war in Ukrainian museums for the New York culture magazine *Atlas Obscura*.

Our tiny guesthouse, Hotel Gut in the city of Kramatorsk, became the hub for the small group of journalists covering Donbas from the ground. It was a stodgy affair, with rather hard beds and a cramped kitchen with a kettle that occasionally worked, some bitter instant coffee and a sugar jar that had been there for so long all the crystals had stuck together in one lump. Yet it was also a homely place, with the sense of community and camaraderie of a backpacking hostel. At night, as the sun set, people would gather to smoke by the backdoor and you could hear dogs barking, birds singing and the ever-present and now familiar sounds of war.

Every day, we'd set off in our various directions towards a town that was under fire, and then evenings would be sitting around a table drinking vodka and sharing stories of the road. There was a startling feeling of equality here, as journalists from the most storied outlets like the *New York Times* would share digs with YouTube bloggers and scrappy freelance journalists. Out in Donbas, the wild west of conflict journalism, your only value was in the bravery of your reporting or the standout nature of your scoops. Ukrainian society here had a similar equality. One day, in a pizza parlour in Slovyansk, the city where the Russian separatists had started their war against Ukraine, we ran into Sviatoslav Vakarchuk himself. The headliner of Okean Elzy usually draws sold-out crowds in major stadiums, yet here he was sitting and discussing the military situation with his security escort, a young Ukrainian soldier. He had taken the idea of the 'cultural front line' very literally. He would swing from major shows in Kyiv, Warsaw and London straight to intimate personal shows in bunkers and trenches for Ukrainian soldiers, where his crooning, romantic lyrics would coexist with the whistling of shells and the crack of gunfire. He had just come from Dolyna, just north of us, where he'd sung a new song, 'Misto Mariyi', for the soldiers of Ukraine's 95th Brigade. He was affable and unassuming and thanked us for being there.

'It's all about making people comfortable, not putting too much pressure on them,' said a videographer who had just arrived from Agence France-Presse. He got his iPhone out and showed us a video of a farmer, whose house had just been destroyed. 'People get scared when you shove a camera in their face, but if you just take your phone out, say, "Oh, I'm just going to make a small record of this," they open right up.' He had rimmed circular glasses, an infectious smile and a light French accent that seemed to coat every word with honey even when describing the most terrible events. I took a liking to Arman Soldin immediately. He was an obsessive football fan who had once been selected for an academy before an injury had ended his chances of playing professionally. He'd switched to covering news and sports in London, but those stories were too light for his liking. He'd signed up to cover Ukraine eagerly and was soon known for his grace and good humour under pressure.

One of these late-night reveries turned into one of the most combative experiences of my career. I was sat around a table with Donatella Rovera, Amnesty International's senior crisis researcher, telling her that their upcoming report would be received very badly. We were in the kitchen of Hotel Gut, the constant crack of artillery in the distance being drowned out by our stern, raised voices. Rather than expressing shock at the relentless Russian bombardment, the Amnesty staff seemed much more concerned with the fact that a Ukrainian Army unit had taken refuge in the basement of a college building. They were preparing a report on what Rovera told us were *Ukrainian* crimes – specifically, having its armed forces in cities. 'All governments lie to you. Your job as a reporter or researcher is to be strictly impartial and report only the facts,' Rovera said. We'd all been to the building: an abandoned language school in the city of Bakhmut which had been turned into a temporary barracks for a Ukrainian unit. This is not a war crime. A military is perfectly entitled to set up in an evacuated educational institution, although of course that building can no longer claim civilian protection and there was a mainly civilian apartment block over the road, where some residents were still living. The government and military had been urging residents to leave these towns from the start, but as in any war, some civilians refused to leave.

These circumstances are far more common than people unfamiliar with war may realise. Schools are a series of large buildings capable of housing hundreds of people, with connected water and sewage systems, often with basements. Unlike civilian apartment blocks, they can be evacuated easily, with the military not having to worry about people who refuse to leave. In a pinch, they are an ideal military base. When the Ukrainians killed around 400 Russians who had set up base in a school in Makiivka, occupied Donetsk, this was a totally legitimate target. But Rovera was insistent that this military presence in a populated area was a 'violation of international humanitarian law'. When I pressed her on how the Ukrainian Army was supposed to defend a populated area, she said that it was irrelevant.

By that logic, I continued, Ukraine would have to abandon the major locations such as the city of Kharkiv. 'Well, they must avoid as far as possible taking positions in a populated area,' she replied. 'International humanitarian law is very clear on this.' This is false. I suggested that her coming Amnesty International report would be criticised if it failed to differentiate between defensive and offensive operations in urban areas. But it appeared the authors' minds had been made up: Ukraine was endangering its own civilians by the mere act of attempting to defend its cities. The discussion got heated and went on for about half an hour. I jotted some notes of the conversation down and honestly wondered if I'd misheard her. When the report was released a few months later, she stated exactly what I remembered.

When the report came out, it said that 'such tactics violate international humanitarian law and endanger civilians, as they turn civilian objects into military targets'. Almost every sentence of the report was either a falsehood, an exaggeration or a misunderstanding of the laws and customs of armed conflict. The overall impression created was that Ukraine was using its civilians as human shields. Amnesty's secretary general invited even more scorn when she refused to address any criticism of the report, labelling those contesting her findings 'Ukrainian and Russian trolls'.

'Most residential areas where soldiers located themselves were kilometres away from front lines. Viable alternatives were available that would not endanger civilians – such as military bases or densely wooded areas nearby,' the report said. Yet it would have been impossible for Rovera to know.

When I called Jack Watling, a land warfare expert at the Royal United Services Institute, he was scathing of Amnesty's work:

> The report demonstrates a weak understanding of the laws of armed conflict. You need to balance military necessity with proportionality, so you need to take reasonable measures to protect civilians, but that must be balanced with your orders to defend an

area. If the enemy is attacking a certain urban area, then you are going to need to occupy it. There is no war in history where civilians have completely removed themselves from the combat zone.

He summarised the report's concerns as pointless, frivolous and trivial.

Another thing that was galling about Amnesty's response to these criticisms was the shocking way in which it handled them. Initially, Amnesty's secretary general dismissed her critics – whether journalists, conflict experts and even the head of Amnesty's Ukrainian branch, who resigned in protest – as 'Ukrainian and Russian trolls'. A later internal report by Amnesty International (which I did not participate in) came to similar conclusions as I did. According to the panel, Amnesty International failed to do this vital work, seemingly because it 'failed to meaningfully engage with Ukrainian authorities' and made little, if any, effort to understand or fairly assess the rationales behind Ukrainian military practices. The panellists concluded:

> The only evidence that Ukrainian forces could have located in other, equally beneficial places more removed from civilians is the opinion of the researchers themselves. Amnesty did not have information from the Ukrainian military concerning why its forces located in the positions that they did. Nor did (the report) itself consider any potential justifications for the positioning of Ukrainian forces.

Rather than admitting fault, Amnesty first put pressure on the reviews to remove or tone down their criticisms. Then it refused to release the report, which was leaked to the *New York Times*. For an organisation that prides itself on holding governments and militaries to account, whose entire purpose is to scrutinise powerful institutions, it was unwilling to focus that on itself.

Amnesty's failing would not be the only example I'd see of respected international organisations failing their core missions in Ukraine. I would not always strike the right balance in my own criticisms of them. And not everyone at that table would stay alive.

THE IRON GENERATION

IVANIVKA, DONETSK OBLAST, JUNE 2022

'The national flag is good for peacetime,' said Oksana Krasnova, twenty-six, with a rifle slung over her shoulder. 'Our flag, with the colours of blood and death, is for war.' Like many Ukrainian nationalist groups, the modern iteration of the Organisation of Ukrainian Nationalists uses a black and red flag, several of which were hanging around this outpost near the city of Slovyansk. The colour contrast with the Ukrainian flag, which is bright blue and yellow, is intentional and symbolic, says Oksana. In the field adjacent to us, we saw a patchwork of Russian shells smash into the ground. The smoke rising from the impacts began to blanket the area, and with the light of the sun at dusk filtering through it, it had an eerie, almost beautiful appearance. The sound of shelling was mixed with the warbling of the birds, which were thoroughly undisturbed by the war of men, women and machines around them.

Oksana and her husband Stanislav had gone through heaven and hell together, and they were now fighting side by side. They met in the 2014 Maidan Revolution, the uprising that toppled Ukraine's pro-Russian government. They each sustained injuries, Oksana from rubber bullets and Stanislav from a stun grenade. Soon after, they married. Stanislav, thirty-five, comes from Crimea and has even greater reason to fight Moscow's attempt to seize more of Ukraine. 'I lost my home town that year,' he said of his native Simferopol, a major city in Crimea. 'Now, they want the rest.'

'Mainly, it is an artillery battle here now,' says Oksana. 'We sometimes fire back, but we don't have massive artillery guns. We just dig and stay and hold our lines so the Russians can't destroy us. Our only job is to never let the Russians pass our lines.' Just a few months ago, they were both working at a law firm in Kyiv. Now, they were together other in the Donbas trenches. 'I'm not frightened; I'm bored… I've heard this a million times now,' says Oksana, as she nods to the artillery thundering over the barracks where she and several others from their unit of seventy soldiers are enjoying a few days of relaxation, if you could call it that. It was hard to believe the degree of intellectual talent packed into this farmhouse. Both Oksana and Stanislav had been studying for their doctorates in law, which they had put on hold to join the armed forces.

Alongside them was Nikolai, a young soldier from the city of Cherkasy who says he planned to celebrate his twenty-second birthday the following day with his first day of fighting Putin's army on the zero line a few kilometres ahead of us. Then there was Ricochet, slim and brooding, who fought near the airport in Donetsk in 2015. He was one of the men responsible for defending Zelensky from would-be Russian assassins in the first days of the invasion. Oksen Lisovyi, with a tall, muscular frame, thick ginger beard and slow, melodic voice, was introduced as an academic superstar, a warrior poet. He had a thick sniper rifle, and he was loading and unloading it while showing us the various parts. He was a pacifist philosophically and got no pleasure from 'working on the enemy', as he gently put it, but it was his job, and he performed it without remorse. 'They are like red dots on a screen,' he said. 'You just have to hit them.' Soon after we left, Zelensky would personally recall him from the battlefield.

Some of the Russian artillery is hitting just a kilometre away. Oksana points to a farmhouse right next to the barracks, which is burned-out from a recent artillery strike. 'Luckily, they got the wrong building,' she says, insisting she wasn't worried about her own safety – just her five cats, who are back in Kyiv being looked after by her parents. Stanislav showed me drone footage of our frontline positions: soldiers' dugouts on a green, vibrant field being covered with black shell craters like gangrene moving up a once healthy limb. It looks like something from the Second World War. We were on the northernmost front line of Donetsk Oblast, staying the night in a farmhouse that was a converted military barracks. An artillery emplacement was in the field next to us, making us an uncomfortably close target. Yet they enjoyed the chance to talk about something other than the war. Oksen wanted to swap stories with my American colleague about roadtripping; 'I don't want to talk about guns, I want to talk about mountain bikes!' he laughed.

I was fascinated by the people here, whose learning could have put the faculty of many universities to shame. I realised a horrifying truth about this war that night. If you take a moment to read obituaries and headstones from the First World War, you see so many of the young men killed were graduates from the top universities like Oxford and Cambridge; they were the ones with the advanced degrees and best careers in law, academics and finance in London. They had signed up in huge numbers, as it was the patriotic thing to do. This had decimated the young men of Britain, leading to a lost generation. The same thing was happening in Ukraine, where the best and brightest were the ones who were volunteering in their tens of thousands to fight the Russian invasion. It was the smartest and most talented who were catching the shells and shrapnel and being brought home in body bags.

The Donbas was also the site of one of the worst, little-known Russian crimes of the war. The occupation forcibly rounded up thousands of the young men in occupied Donetsk and Luhansk and threw them against entrenched Ukrainian defensive positions, sometimes with decades-old rifles and a single clip of ammunition, forcing Ukrainians to kill their own countrymen or be killed by them. Independent Russian media outlet *Meduza* reported deeply on this.

One of their sources described how

> this mass of untrained, unequipped and unmotivated people were thrown into the assault on Volnovakha, Mariupol and Maryinka. There, where the Ukrainian armed forces had been preparing for war for eight years, digging in and pouring concrete into positions, people were trained by specialists from NATO countries and armed with the latest weapons! What is this if not a crime?

This caused a rare protest against Russian conduct during the war in these territories, by some of the female relatives of the soldiers, who were quickly repressed by the People's Republic's secret police.

After a night in the trenches, and being shaken awake by an artillery barrage, we bade Oksana and her team farewell, and I headed west. I left Ukraine in the first week of June, after nearly five months of non-stop reporting, and entered Romania. I'd expected to feel some relief. Instead, I felt the worst depression and disassociation of my life. I spent three weeks in a haze and funk, struggling to process the contrast of the vibrant city lights and relaxing and partying crowds of Bucharest, London and Warsaw with the scenes from the Second World War that raged on nearby. I had trouble relating to friends, finding their concerns about making rent or putting in long hours at their jobs or fights and break-ups with their partners trivial. I felt myself numb to most emotions – except anger, and for a while, I developed a combustible temper. After more times coming in and out of Ukraine, I came to manage this better, but this unease of shifting between two worlds never entirely subsided.

A few weeks after I left, the Russians finally made a breakthrough around Lysychansk, and the Ukrainians were forced to withdraw in a hurry or else be surrounded, shelled or starved into surrender. They withdrew from Lysychansk under heavy fire, with the Russians in hot pursuit, but they managed to save most of their force. The Russians declared the total 'liberation' of Luhansk Oblast. They'd notched up one of their major victories of the war.

Around this time, papers reported the death of Roman Ratushnyi, an environmental activist and an anti-corruption firebrand who'd become famous on the Maidan. He had been killed on the very same section of the front line that I had been on, and his unit had been ambushed just a few kilometres from where I had spent that night. He had been one of the first people on Maidan Square in 2014, and his death caused an outpouring of grief among friends in Kyiv. In July, at a conference on Ukrainian reconstruction, European Commission President Ursula von der Leyen said:

> He fought for a sovereign Ukraine and paid the highest price for it. Roman's life was taken too early, but his dreams live on. The dream of a new Ukraine is not only free, democratic and European but also green and flourishing. A place where the Ukrainian golden generation can finally feel its own.

I had looked into the eyes of those members of this generation who were fighting and dying, and they no longer glittered like gold, but they were hard and unshakable. These men and women had been forged into swords, spears and shields by the infernos that erupted on the road of death – or over the roof of Azovstal. An iron generation.

AFTERWORD: BACK FROM THE GULAG

DNIPRO, AUGUST 2024

'The first thing they did was stab me in the leg,' Shaun Pinner told us, as he sipped tea from his favourite mug emblazoned with a Union Jack. We were sitting in his house in Dnipro, where he now lives with his Ukrainian wife. 'They knew I was trained and that the best time to escape was going from point A to point B. It was three inches deep; I'm lucky they didn't nick an artery!'

Most captured Ukrainian soldiers, a total of 211, were transferred to a prison camp in Olenivka in the Donetsk region. Prisoner accounts show that systematic torture and executions remain routine in the camps. Satellite images show new mass graves, as well as open, empty graves, suggesting that the Russians were preparing for mass executions of prisoners of war. In the middle of the night on 29 July 2022, an explosion occurred in the camp, killing fifty-three prisoners and seriously injuring seventy-three others. The Russians blamed the Ukrainians, but an analysis of footage taken shortly after the attack, which was posted online, suggests that the explosion was caused by a bomb placed on the ground. As with any atrocity that occurred in Russian-controlled territory, independent international investigators were not granted access to the site.

Now, twenty-one months after Russia's full-scale invasion, many of those who survived the siege of the plant and the prison camps have been freed in a series of prisoner exchanges with Russia. Most recount stories of horrific torture and abuse during their time in Russian captivity. Pinner experienced extreme torture and deprivation, yet he recounts the ordeal in his cockney English accent with a bit of a grin on his face. He is animated and expressive, and he has used his horrific experiences as fuel for his current project to raise awareness of the war in Ukraine. He says he still sleeps very soundly and that he suffers from little long-term trauma, which he says is a result of his extensive training. The fifty-year-old moved to the Ukrainian port city of Mariupol in 2017 and joined the Ukrainian Marines. When the Russians invaded, he was already at the front lines and fought for seven weeks until being captured while trying to break out of the city.

He described a range of torture methods: 'Their favourite is electrocution ... They ask you if you want to "phone home", and they connect a phone wire to you and run a current through it. Everything in your body tenses, it feels like your muscles are going to burst out of your skin.' After six months of gruelling captivity, including being tried in a sham court and sentenced to death, Pinner was exchanged in a swap facilitated with the help of Russian oligarch and Chelsea FC owner Roman Abramovich and Saudi Prince Mohammed bin Salman.

Despite his captivity, Pinner does not express hatred towards the Russian people. 'There are even some humanitarians there. Some people who would try to get you a bit of decent food or stop people torturing you. They might have believed all the rubbish Putin told them, but they just didn't like seeing us being treated like that.'

Ukrainian officials say that at least 3,500 Ukrainians are being held in Russian captivity at the time of writing in 2025, many of them captured in Mariupol. Every few months, many of the family members stage protests in Kyiv. Here I met Anya, whose brother was taken prisoner in Mariupol. She said her job was to remind the government of its obligation to bring their loved ones home. They were involved in lobbying government representatives, as well as the Red Cross, to make sure their family members' names were included on the list of those prisoners to be swapped.

Sometimes, they also trade crucial information about their loved ones trapped inside. At one point, we saw a woman speak with a young man, Andriy, who had been released in a recent prisoner exchange. He said that before he had been released, he had seen her son, who was alive but sick. The woman started crying – it was the first news she had heard of her son in months. Andriy, who we spoke with briefly, had suffered grievously. He had been in a psychological ward since release and requested that I didn't photograph his face. He stuttered when he spoke and couldn't look us in the eye. He had few physical scars – he explained that his torturers preferred not to leave marks. So, they would force inmates to drink boiling water, searing their internal organs but leaving them outwardly unharmed.

For Pinner, thoughts of those of his unit remaining in captivity are always present. 'Most of my unit is still inside. I went through captivity as a middle-aged man with a lot of combat experience. Some guys still inside are eighteen/nineteen-year-olds and it was their first combat experience. I can't imagine how it is for them.'

CHAPTER FOUR

HERO CITY: THE FIRST UKRAINE COUNTEROFFENSIVE AND THE UNBREAKABLE DEFIANCE OF KHARKIV

GIVE PEACE A CHANCE

IZIUM, KHARKIV OBLAST, SEPTEMBER 2022

'If you want to visit the torture chamber, please follow Svetlana,' the middle-aged blonde-haired khaki-wearing press officer said dryly. 'But don't be late! We need to be back at the bus by 1:30 p.m. to go to the mass grave!' With her strict, schoolmarmish tone, she sounded like she was herding a class of rambunctious primary-age children around the world's most macabre school field trip. Izium, a drab town of around 50,000 people about ninety minutes' drive from Kharkiv, had been unexpectedly liberated in one of the Ukrainians' most daring and stunningly successful military operations of the entire war. Just days earlier, a surprise Ukrainian assault had broken through poorly manned Russian lines to the west, using clever diversion and subterfuge to hide a large build-up of troops near the city. It had shattered our preconceptions about an inevitable creeping Russian advance. But just as in Bucha, everyone's enthusiasm was tempered by a grim anticipation of what would have been left behind. As was routine in areas that the occupiers had fled, they had left abundant evidence of war crimes. I was jammed, along with two dozen or so other colleagues, into a creaky, rusted old school bus and driven in, during a break in the fighting, to tell the world what we saw. We'd been promised one of the grimmest spectacles of the war, and our guides wanted to make sure we had all the grisly details.

Along the path to the police station that had been turned into the centrepiece of the Russian terror regime, we walked through the courtyards of three high-rise blocks, all chewed up by artillery fire, rubble sprawled all over the grounds, then past an apartment complex with a wall-sized mural of John Lennon, skilfully spray-painted. The Beatles' frontman's scruffy hair, jet-black eyeglasses and sleek denim jacket, with the words 'give peace a chance' written in Ukrainian next to him, contrasted curiously with the scenes of destruction all around him. Something had exploded in the street next to him, pockmarking the monument with shrapnel, just enough to give John a rugged edge but not to disfigure his famous features. Frankly, he looked cooler and fit better into his surroundings with a few scars.

The walls and floors of the station were bloodstained, the rooms littered with gas masks, ropes and electrical cables. The Russians hadn't innovated in their methods. It was all about inflicting as much pain as possible to get Ukrainians to comply with their rule and to try to flush out 'subversives' who were still dedicated to helping their country. The reasons could be suspicion of spotting for enemy artillery or as arbitrary as speaking Ukrainian. People didn't want to leave their houses as the Russians would often check people's phones on the street. If they found a message or photo they didn't like, it could be straight to the torture chamber.

When Russian soldiers burst into Artyom's house just after capturing his town in March 2022, they dragged him in for questioning, and the first thing they asked him was: 'Why did you have a Ukrainian flag on the wall?' He replied, puzzled, 'Because this is Ukraine! Should I have had the Japanese flag instead?' The Russian soldiers didn't see the funny side and beat him senseless to teach him a lesson. He considered himself one of the lucky ones. He would frequently hear the familiar crack and sizzle of electricity being prepared, then the grunts and screams as cables were shoved into the skin or orifices of the prisoners in adjacent cells. We got to see the remains of all these, with a friendly Ukrainian local police officer who showed how a suspect would be worked over. As he demonstrated the ways the Russians would beat, shock and waterboard you, his tone was as plain and jolly as if he was giving an instructional scuba diving lecture. 'We never met a single member of law enforcement or the military who was arrested who wasn't tortured,' he said dryly. These prisons were found all throughout the liberated territories. A pattern of seemingly random scratches on the wall of one of them turned out to read: 'Our father who art in heaven.' The beginning of the Lord's Prayer in Russian. I wondered how the tortured scribe had felt as he carved the line 'as we forgive those who trespass against us'. Had he managed to keep his faith in a just God?

'Hop on the magic school bus,' another reporter joked, as we piled onto our vehicle. This dark humour is typical of those who've spent too much time around death and his companions. The bus would clank and sputter whenever the key was turned. It seemed ready to fall apart around us any moment. A few minutes' drive from Izium, in a field just outside the city, was a small patch of fenced-off forest, with dozens of holes dug into the ground. The luckier people had a personal grave, their name carved on a simple wooden cross, perhaps even a wreath of flowers adorning it. Others were buried unmarked and, too decomposed to be identified, were given a number tagged onto a piece of string tied around any limb that was still solid enough. I remember #412 being attached to one corpse, probably a rotund middle-aged man, who was so far gone I wouldn't have been able to tell him from the corpse of an animal. 'A man hath no pre-eminence above a beast,' Ecclesiastes says. 'All are of the dust, and all turn to dust again.'

'DE-NAZIFIED'

KHARKIV, MARCH 2022

'Russian terrorists did this,' Galina said, gesturing to the wreckage of the Soviet-era housing block behind her. Her face was twisted into a scowl as she continued, 'And my father is Russian, from Belgorod!' She was a 63-year-old woman, a native Russian speaker and had been a cashier at a local supermarket. A few days earlier, a Russian airstrike had smashed her apartment to pieces. Galina and her husband were picking through the pile of debris that had been their lifetime home, loading what possessions had survived the fire into a handful of shopping bags. The walls, windows and floorboards that the people had lived in for decades had been scattered over the grass of their front lawns in an instant.

It was late March, and my first day in Kharkiv, Ukraine's second-largest city. The Russians had launched an attack here on the first day of the war, at the same time as they'd launched their assault on Kyiv. They'd quickly blazed their way down from the Russian border, and a Spetsnaz division had walked right into the centre of the city. Apparently, they expected to meet little resistance and to be greeted by local collaborators who would hand them the keys to the city. Defending Ukrainian troops could barely believe their luck that the enemy's crack troops had advanced in small numbers and entirely unsupported by artillery or air power. 'They came up to the gates expecting people to just run around in despair as soon as they entered the city,' said one Ukrainian soldier who participated in the defence of Kharkiv. It was here that a column even advanced from the border with riot police in the lead, armed with batons and shields, showing how easy they thought the fight would be. The Ukrainians instead drove a tank unit into the path of the Spetsnaz and forced them to retreat into a local school, where they had a shootout lasting nearly eighteen hours. By the end of it, most of them lay dead and the Ukrainians had held the city.

Like Kyiv, the Russians expected Kharkiv to fall into their lap with a little prodding. Their plan was even less well formed than it was for the invasion of Kyiv Oblast, and they likewise had no follow-up plan for if their initial thunder run failed. They ended up trying to storm a city of a million people with a few hundred men. There were Russian mechanised columns advancing close behind them, but they were repelled at the northern edges to Saltivka, the northernmost district of Kharkiv, by heavy artillery fire from Ukrainian guns hastily moved in and around the streets. So, the Russians took positions concentrated in the town of Tsukuryne, just a few kilometres to the north. From there, they expected to shell the city into submission over the course of a few weeks. Instead, Kharkiv would become the site of some of Ukraine's most extraordinary victories. On the surface, the Russians had reason to expect Kharkiv to fall easily.

Geographically, it lies barely thirty kilometres from Russia and like other eastern cities, the population was overwhelmingly made up of native Russian speakers. It had traditionally voted for pro-Russian parties, although not by the margins of the neighbouring Donbas oblasts. In 2014, a group of pro-Russian rebels had briefly managed to capture key city locations and declare a 'Kharkiv People's Republic', but this was quickly snuffed out by a series of Ukrainian police raids before it gained serious momentum.

In Donetsk and Luhansk, much of the population stayed passive in response to the pro-Russian takeover in 2014, and the Russians expected the same to happen in Kharkiv. But the citizens here were determined to resist fiercely. To understand how Kharkiv avoided falling in 2014 and 2022, I met with Ihor Terekhov, Kharkiv's mayor, in the reinforced bunker that was his office – decorated with Ukrainian flags, the city emblems and small models of different weapons systems, including Patriots and HIMARS.

> I remember everything that was happening in 2014. According to the considerations of the Russian Federation, they needed to start from Kharkiv, that was their plan. People were divided about the position of RF [Russian Federation]. There were a lot of supporters of the RF, and I remember 1 March when pro-Russian activists wanted to seize the Kharkiv regional administration. There was also a peaceful rally on the square, but after the Russian provocateurs arrived – there was a fight. I remember there was a shooting and a lot of blood, but luckily, we managed. There was a kid who died because of the bomb, if you remember. Now the school is named after him. It was in 2014.
>
> Society back in that time was ambiguous. The mentality of the civil population, well, we didn't know what they wanted. The

Russian provocateurs understood and used the situation in their advance. But with all the administration, we've managed to resist this situation and went through this. They wanted to get into the administration and the mayor building. On 13 April 2014, they wanted to do this, but we resisted. We raised a Ukrainian flag. The battle was inside the building and in the backyard. Since then, the Russians did not try to repeat this.

They think if people here speak Russian, it means they support Russia. Many militaries who protect us speak Russian, but they are protecting Ukraine, and they are defending Ukrainian values.

He said that, like the other mayors in the region, he'd received a text from a Russian number asking him to collaborate with their attempt to take over the city and had ignored it.

Kharkiv's air was thick with the sounds of war. The sounds of artillery duels were almost constant; there was broken glass over many of the streets. Windows and doors were boarded up everywhere. In the centre, next to its long and majestic main boulevard, the central administration building lay in ruins. It had been hit directly by two Russian Kalibr missiles, killing twenty-nine people. Strikes on residential buildings were killing civilians almost every day. As Galina said to me: 'Kharkiv is – or at least was – a pro-Russian city! Everyone here speaks Russian and has family over the border… They've come to *liberate* us from our apartment blocks!' This incredulity, the sense of shock and betrayal, could be heard all over the city. Near the destroyed apartment blocks was the Church of the Holy Myrrh-Bearing Women. The church's head priest, Father Vasili, was tending to a group of civilians taking shelter in the church's basement. I still remember his ornate silver crucifix, a symbol of his dedication not just to God but to the Russian Orthodox Church, whose patriarch had come out in favour of Putin's war. For Vasili, Kharkiv's shared history with Russia made the assault even more senseless:

> One-hundred and fifty metres from this church, there is the Russian Pushkin Drama Theatre. About 600 metres from here, there is the Kharkiv National University, which has a department of Russian language and literature. There are three to four streets close by named after the prominent Russian poets and writers: Pushkinskaya, Lermontovskaya, Dostoevskovo ... They've come to 'de-nazify' what? Their people and their language!

In Kharkiv, much of the population was passionately pro-Ukrainian, because the city had a proud history deeply intertwined with that of the wider nation. The city existed near Russia, and absorbed Russian culture, but never became truly Russified. The experience of war in Kharkiv was different from that of people in safer regions. First, there was the fact that the war was on their doorsteps. Once a city comes within about twenty-five to thirty kilometres of the front line, it is now within artillery range. This meant that the Russians could pound a city with their huge and intensive stockpiles of artillery ammunition. Air defence can't help you here. The only way to protect yourself from artillery is to either be underground or destroy the guns that are launching the shells.

For the first three months or so of the war, Russian forces were around two kilometres from the northern entrance of Kharkiv, so they could shell any part of the city at will. Anyone who stayed in Kharkiv long enough experienced the full fury of the war. The city's proximity to Russia, and residents' longstanding family ties, meant that the invasion felt like a deep betrayal, as if their own brothers, fathers, cousins were the ones pulling the triggers.

This could be literally true: I spoke to several Kharkivites whose family over the border had joined the Russian Armed Forces. Most traumatically of all, most people's friends and family in Russia had swallowed the Kremlin's propaganda line enthusiastically.

THE PASSENGERS

'When we were evacuated, I looked out the windows of the bus. I saw parts of destroyed vehicles and parts of dead human bodies' a 61-year old woman, also called Galina, told me. But this was not the most traumatic part. 'When I called my daughter, who lives in Russia, to tell her what happened to her home town, she told me I was lying.' She'd seen on Russian TV, she said, that 'Ukrainian Nazis' had been the ones responsible for all the destruction. When confronted with the choice over whether to believe Kremlin talking heads or her own mother, she chose the former in a heartbeat. The agony of betrayal was etched into Galina's eyes and the thick lines on her face. She was living in one of Kharkiv's Metro stations and was a teacher in regular life. She had curly auburn hair. Wearing a green puffer jacket, her face still had the faint shadow of her former kindly smile, but her eyes were flickering, bloodshot and downcast. For three weeks, she and her remaining family had not left their basement except to get snow to melt for drinking water. Eventually, an evacuation bus managed to get in and get them to Kharkiv. 'I can't process how my daughter won't believe her own mother.' Galina broke down sobbing and put her hand over her heart.

Because of the constant danger of shelling, life in the city moved almost entirely underground. Metro stations – Heroiv Pratsi (Heroes of Labour), Peremoha (Victory), Studentska – became the names of their own little towns and communities. The twitchy policemen guarding the entrances would scrutinise your documents and then usher you down into an underground settlement crammed with hundreds of people. The smell was the first thing that hit you, a pungent mix of sweat and cleaning fluid. The floors were covered with mattresses, sleeping bags and suitcases. In the Peremoha station, we were immediately escorted to the 'mayor', 29-year-old Olya Filipskaya, who scanned us once over with her eyes, then asked a few piercing questions. Officially, she was just a 'volunteer', but she oversaw everything in the station. She directed medical care, organised the distribution of meals and coordinated the deliveries of humanitarian aid. She introduced the community in the station as 'The Passengers', named not just because of where they were living but to emphasise it was a temporary stop on their journey, which they hoped would end with a Ukrainian victory and a return to their life on the surface. I empathised with them, having spent the first days in terror curled up in a sleeping bag on the cold, hard floor of a Kyiv Metro. They had been there for nearly three months.

Olya's English was flawless, a rarity in Ukraine, and she quickly dropped her initially sceptical demeanour and became chatty. She was remarkably calm given the circumstances. Why, I asked her, was everyone putting their trust in her? She sighed, and her face took on a shadow for a moment. 'Because I've been through this before.' She went on:

> I am from Stakhanov in what is now the 'Luhansk People's Republic'. I was there when the conflict in Donbas started eight years ago. I had been through the start of a war before, so I didn't feel

as shocked, and I knew what to do... I knew what all the different sounds were, whether something was outgoing or incoming and exactly what amount of danger we were in when we heard something... This is what we've gone through for eight years.'

She didn't even seem tired despite the dazzling pace of her activity but confessed 'every day or so, I need to take five minutes to have a breakdown. Then I'll shake myself off and get back to work.'

The Passengers had managed to convert back offices into showers, and a regular cleaning schedule stopped the place from becoming too dirty. Some of the residents had not left the Metro in months. 'Why would we want to go outside when every step is a lottery with our lives? Nowhere in the city is safe,' said Nastya, a 23-year-old woman living inside.

A quick trip to the northernmost suburbs of Kharkiv would show us why they stayed underground. 'Look, this is *Ruskiy Mir*,' a volunteer called Serhiy said, gesturing angrily at one of the houses we drove past in the northern suburb of Danylivka. It was cleft almost neatly in two, the right half burned to pieces, the left almost untouched in a neat continuum. Most big aid organisations were afraid to send their foreign staff to Kharkiv, so aid delivery was almost entirely done by local volunteers. The streets were green and full of trees. We stepped into one backyard and saw that flowers were blooming everywhere. But poking through them was a simple wooden cross. 'One of the ladies who lived here died from the shelling,' Serhiy said, as we walked through the backyard. There were a few elderly people still here, many who had built their houses with their own hands and would rather die at home than risk leaving. Somewhat remarkably, we could still order an Uber to this area, but the driver would be driving about three times the speed limit in and out. I was profoundly moved by the resilience of the citizens in Kharkiv. The city authorities made a less heroic first impression.

The policeman's face was close enough to me that I could smell the pungency of vodka on his breath, his twitchy, undisciplined finger on the trigger of the gun he was pointing at my heart. I wasn't confident my flak jacket would stop a bullet at the range of a few centimetres. 'Why the fuck do you have a camera,' he was screaming at me in Russian. We'd been interviewing a woman who had been teaching at a school that had been bombed, before driving her back to her apartment, where three police officers had been hovering outside. 'Well, we are journalists, we have been interviewing this lady, we are taking her photo.' He was unconvinced. 'Well, why do journalists take interviews? Why do they take pictures?' he snarled at me before grabbing the camera I'd had slung over my shoulder. I'd barely begun stammering out a lecture on the first principles of journalism when his two equally nervous but visibly embarrassed colleagues caught up to us.

For the first couple of weeks of the war, everyone was obsessed with the possibility of spies giving information to the Russians. It was a real threat, and Ukrainian intelligence spent months breaking up spy rings after the invasion began. In this febrile atmosphere, several people, particularly in Kyiv, ended up getting killed by friendly fire. Later that evening, I arrived back in the city of Dnipro with Neil to an apartment a local friend had lent us. We began debriefing about the day's events, then he went into the next room to get a drink. I heard the front door open, a thud, and more shouting in Russian. God's sake, I thought, this again already? Two men in balaclavas swung around the corner, one with a pistol, the other an automatic rifle, and in a flash, I was on the ground being frisked, hands pinned behind my back, gun at my head. Yet of my would-be killers that day, this guy was by far the most pleasant.

They quickly realised we were reporters rather than spies and dragged Neil back in the room. They were officers from the SBU, Ukraine's feared internal security agency, responsible for rooting out spies. 'Guys, the neighbours saw young men with body armour they didn't know going into an apartment and making noise,' the masked man said in surprisingly competent English. They left with a warning to be more careful – and watch out for spies ourselves.

Kharkiv had shut down almost completely, but there were a few businesses that kept quietly pumping along. One was Protagonist, a small cafe near the centre of town. Every frontline city had one of these, a single restaurant or bar that stayed open to serve foreign journalists and the local military garrison. It was brave and dangerous work. Places frequented by foreigners, along with the few hotels open, were regular targets for Russian strikes. The food at Protagonist was consistently exceptional, and I would fill up at every chance with a dish of chicken thighs, spicy meatballs and a massive side dish of locally grown vegetables. I didn't care much for their coffee, but keeping such a high quality of cuisine under a siege was a small miracle. The only other place we saw open was Oleksiy and Anna Subotina's tattoo studio. Uniquely, they said, business was the best it had been in years thanks to the influx of soldiers. 'Nothing is open, and they have nothing to spend their money on, so they spend it here instead.' I became one of their customers, getting my forearm inked with a design of the Mirror Stream fountain, a famous city monument that was on fire, with the phrase *XAPKIB* 22, the city's name in Cyrillic, below it. The tattoo is a popular attraction. Whenever I meet someone from the city and show it to them, without exception they pull out their phones and ask for a photo of it.

RIDERS OF ROHAN

ROHAN, KHARKIV OBLAST, MAY 2022

A bang filled the sky, then another, then another, and we looked up to see dozens of rockets fly over our heads. '*Nashi*,' said one of the Ukrainian officers, meaning 'ours', a simple way to tell us not to worry. In the field behind us was a Grad launcher, named after the Russian word for 'hail', and it is one of the most terrifying and ferocious weapons on the battlefield. A series of metal tubes hoisted together on the back of a truck, it fires up to thirty unguided rockets within seconds of each other, blanketing an area with explosive power. We watched these fly in a parabola towards Russian positions a few kilometres away.

'I wonder what Miss Wade would think if she could see this,' my companion turned to me and said in a dry New Zealand accent. Nick Fisher had been my classmate at intermediate school back home, when we were between ten and twelve years old. Nick was taller and squarer-jawed than I remember but still had the flash of blond hair and mischievous grin from his childhood that you can see in a school photo of us taken in 2004. It had been nearly twenty years since we'd seen each other, and his mention of our old teacher perked up our spirits. Next to us was a busted-up Russian tank, with a white Z scrawled on the side of it. As a young man growing up in New Zealand, I had longed to see the world in all its rough and tumble. The first piece of serious reporting I ever did was for a student newspaper about an earthquake in our home town of Christchurch. I remember how my old classmate and trainee police officer Leon started digging under the rubble to rescue those trapped underneath when a building collapsed near him. There were countless parallels, of ordinary people made extraordinary by circumstances outside their control, happening in Ukraine.

Soon after, I left New Zealand to study at Oxford, then worked as a reporter and a parliamentary researcher around Westminster, but I had grown tired of interviews in the same hotels and swanky bars in central London. So, when the war between Armenia and Azerbaijan broke out over Nagorno-Karabakh, I flew to Armenia on a whim. That's where my career as a war reporter started. Nick had gone on to do something very similar, albeit taking a very different route. After working as a tour guide and horticulturalist in the South Island of New Zealand, he'd taken a gap year to go travelling which had never ended. He began filming his trips and by the time I met him again, he was one of the world's most well-known adventure travel bloggers with over 2 million YouTube subscribers on his channel Indigo Traveller.

His output had gone from the cringy and shakily filmed handheld phone videos of early gems like '10 Vietnam Motorbiking Tips You Need to Know' to serious conflict reporting from every continent, including in hotspots like Afghanistan and Somalia. News editors used to complain that no one was interested in foreign coverage, and they didn't have the patience to watch anything longer than a few minutes. Nick was proving this wrong. His videos from North Korea and Nigeria had over 8 million views each, despite being nearly half an hour long. I'd convinced him to come and do his next series in Ukraine during the war.

Now here we were, after twenty years of adventure, having converged at the same point, standing near the tiny village of Rohan embedded with the Ukrainian Army in its fight to take back

Kharkiv Oblast. In a strange twist of fate, we grew up near another Rohan. The Kingdom of Rohan in Peter Jackson's second *Lord of the Rings* epic was shot in our home province. These films were all anybody I met in Ukraine usually knew about New Zealand. They'd taken metaphors from them to describe their own war. The Russian soldiers were known as 'orcs', and Russia itself was 'Mordor', while the Ukrainians and their western partners were the alliance of elves, dwarves and men. Stylised descriptions of such creatures sometimes appeared on Ukrainian recruiting posters. Most of all, Ukrainians loved the moral simplicity, the good vs evil nature of Tolkien's mythos that they passionately believed mirrored their own existential struggle.

I was speaking into Nick's camera, describing the situation, when another volley of rockets started flying next to us. The viral clip was viewed millions of times, and I've been recognised in the street and in hostels from it. When I contacted Miss Wade, now Jude Garrett, she replied, 'I always said there were amazing kids in that class who would go far in the world – not sure I was anticipating a war zone!'

The soldiers here were upbeat about their prospects. They'd just finished a small-scale counteroffensive and pushed the Russians back from the ring of towns closest to Kharkiv. One man I'll call Andriy, because his position was sensitive enough that he wore a green balaclava the entire trip, said that the Russians were having significant difficulty with their artillery, as many of their guns in this area were rusted, poorly maintained or missing crucial components. The Ukrainian soldiers had been incensed by how Russians had shelled Kharkiv, where they had killed hundreds of civilians. 'It's like a slow-motion Mariupol,' one said. But unlike Mariupol, the Russian operation to capture this city was falling apart. Despite the indiscriminate damage they were doing, the Russians were performing especially poorly in this area.

While the Russians had taken significant territory in the south and were slowly advancing in the Donbas, in Kharkiv, they were steadily retreating. Ukrainian guns were visible in the fields we passed and helicopters flew over our heads. When an army is visible on the battlefield, it usually means that they feel they've suppressed enemy fire enough to move freely. Putin, despite being notorious for rewarding loyal but incompetent servants, fired the commander of Russian Army Group West for his failure to capture the city. Before we left Rohan to go back to Kharkiv, Andriy said that a swift Ukrainian victory here was inevitable and that the invaders would be pushed out of the entire region within weeks. I thought at the time that this was just bravado, putting on a brave face for his visitors. I was to be proved dazzlingly wrong.

A few months after I left Kharkiv, on a cloudy day in early September, 'Yakut', the Ukrainian soldier who had told me about his fight for Slovyansk in 2014, was summoned with the rest of his unit from Donbas to a small farmhouse near Rohan. The lines here had moved little for the past four months, but the Ukrainians were simply biding their time, slowly building up their forces. There, Yakut found that thousands of other soldiers had gathered as part of a secret plan. Just one night before the mission, they were told their objective was Balaklia, a nearby Ukrainian town that had served as a Russian logistics point. Their ultimate prize in the operation was to be Izium, the central command city in the region. The soldiers had serious doubts at first. Ukraine was already engaged in a separate offensive in Kherson, which, by all accounts, was tough going. General Zaluzhnyi, still the head of Ukraine's armed forces, thought that the priority of any offensive should be the Russian land bridge to Crimea, but he was overruled. The Russians had moved many of their troops from Izium to Kherson to fend off the Ukrainian assault in the south, so their positions in Kharkiv were especially vulnerable.

According to a *Washington Post* report of the battle, the US also assisted deeply with the planning, providing M777 howitzers, tens of thousands of shells and detailed intelligence about potential Russian logistics and command targets. The night before Yakut and his team moved, a huge storm of artillery pounded Russian positions all throughout Kharkiv Oblast. Then, like the Riders of Rohan at Helm's Deep, they charged and, as in Jackson's film, the 'orc' positions simply melted away. 'As soon as they saw the wave of our forces coming towards them, they fled almost immediately,' Yakut told me. The Ukrainians successfully exploited their numerical advantage and the poor quality of the Russian troops here, who left behind a treasure trove of tanks, artillery and ammunition, enough to re-equip many of Ukraine's depleted brigades. They captured so many vehicles that Ben Wallace, then UK Defence Secretary, told me in an interview in November 2022 that the biggest donor to the Ukrainian Army was now the Russian Army itself!

By the time my colleagues and I arrived in Izium, most of us had been inured to the sight of death. What really shocked us was the smell. I've been told many times that I must have 'not been able to believe what I've seen' or some variant. Actually, I can convey what I've seen to you quite easily through photos or videos. It's not particularly more impactful to see death in person. What is impossible to convey is the experience of war to your other senses. The deafening shriek of a shell as it flies past you; the way an explosion's shockwave radiates through your whole body, shaking every muscle, nerve and bone; the way the particles carrying the stench of death seem to jam their way into your nostrils, suffocating them to any other smell.

After poking around Izium's mass grave, I needed to wash my clothes three times before they smelled wearable again. Later in the week, I went to a barber shop. Picking and scratching through the knots in my hair thick with the dust of the dead, the hairdresser screwed up his face and exclaimed, 'Where have you been?'

When we clambered back into the 'magic school bus', it was the only thing we could talk about. It had been terrifying enough to see the bodies in Bucha, but many of those had been dead for a few weeks at most and were at least recognisable as human beings. But Izium had suffered six months of occupation. Bodies had decayed and putrefied beyond recognition. Men clad in white overalls, with thick facemasks and bright blue gloves and shoe coverings would dig the body from the ground, load it into a jet-black body bag and take it for forensic examination.

The graves in Izium told a similar story to what we saw in occupied territories in Ukraine. Russian 'liberation' always looked the same: pits full of bodies, basements of police stations and schools full of dried blood and torture instruments, broken houses, broken bodies, the land salted with mines and shells. The premature lines and grey hairs on the faces of survivors.

We did find one strange moment of levity. When we walked around a small nearby village to find accounts of survivors, we stumbled upon a family who had been collecting the spent shells of rockets. Eight-year-old Nikolai and his mother posed for us in front of one of them – he flashed the peace sign while holding up a jagged piece of metal taller than he was.

Ukraine's Kharkiv victory was a huge success, what became known as the 'Miracle on the Oskil'. It was one of the most impressive military victories of modern manoeuvre warfare, and it upended traditional expectations that said that Ukraine was destined to slowly lose more territory as the war dragged on. The armed forces had showed that they could conduct serious offensives and work closely with NATO advisers and officials. They reversed months of hard-fought Russian gains in a matter of days.

Inside Russia, the failure of the invasion and the extraordinary crumbling of the Russian lines in Kharkiv meant that even the Kremlin could no longer disguise the failure of its invasion. Pro-Russian bloggers, even those who had accepted the Kremlin line about the invasion of Kyiv being a diversion, could not disguise the reality that this was a devastating blow. The Twitter account 'Russians With Attitude' tweeted: 'Huge fuck-up by Army Group West', and called it the first major Ukrainian victory of the war.

Like all other offensives in this war, however, it eventually ran out of steam. Yakut's unit was ordered to encircle and capture the town of Lyman, in the Donetsk Oblast, which had been captured by Russia in April. Here, the Russian garrison made a stand. For weeks, Ukrainian units battled through the forest around the town, before the exhausted Russians pulled out. It was near here that Yakut's war would come to an end. His unit tried to push on to the Russian-controlled town of Kreminna. But the Ukrainians had exhausted all their resources and lacked the strength to move further. They held the line here for six months.

One day, Yakut was in a trench at the zero line for the last time:

> I heard the whistle of the shell coming in and managed to push myself into cover between two other guys who were with me. After the explosion went off above us, I let go of my head and fell down. I had a massive concussion and couldn't see out of my right

eye. At first, I thought my face was badly damaged. I tried to stand up but could only stand on my left foot.

When I met him, over a year later, it was at a rehabilitation centre in Kyiv. He was in a wheelchair, his right leg intact but full of scars. He had suffered extensive nerve damage and his leg wasn't functioning, he told me, and the doctors couldn't figure out why. It would eventually be amputated.

The Kremlin realised that its initial plan of invading Ukraine with a peacetime strength army had failed and Russia's positions in Ukraine were in danger of total collapse. Putin could either try to find a face-saving way out or double down. The internal deliberations in the Kremlin are murky. Some reports say that the Russians put out peace feelers to the Americans, who they always believed controlled Ukraine's government, transmitting an offer to freeze the line of contact and make concessions. Bob Woodward, in his book *War*, says that the Russian strategy was much more aggressive. The Americans picked up signals that suggested the Russians were planning to use nuclear weapons in Ukraine if the Ukrainian Army advanced further, especially in the southern region of Kherson. But what is for sure is that the Kremlin did decide to massively increase its investment in the conquest of Ukraine. Russia moved civilian factories to a war economy and began building relationships with Iran and North Korea to buy huge supplies of drones and artillery ammunition. Most crucially, Putin ordered a partial mobilisation of young men registered in the military draft. That quickly doubled the number of men that the Kremlin could send to the front.

There are a number of reasons why Ukraine's Kharkiv offensive was so incredibly, unexpectedly successful. The main one is that Russian units here were running out of ammunition and manpower, with the best troops having been diverted to other battlefields. Some units were so understrength that they were deploying soldiers from random parts of their armed forces, such as military band members and sailors. Russian bloggers and units on the ground apparently warned about a Ukrainian build-up in the area at the time, but their high command failed to properly prepare for it.

Michael Kofman says:

In Kharkiv, the Russians were completely depleted. They hadn't conducted mobilisation. They had anywhere from 25–40 per cent manning rates. War hadn't been declared; the Russian military wasn't operating under wartime conditions. It wasn't just eaten away through losses but also from people who left their formations! As contract servicemen, they could tear up their contracts, only putting in a negative stamp in their military passport [a dishonourable discharge] and that was it. And they'd say between dying in Ukraine and getting a bad stamp, I'll take the stamps. The Western Military District had been largely destroyed as a fighting force ... The advancing Ukrainians saw the Russians had no real established line of defence and were completely undermanned. It was wildly more successful than the Ukrainians expected.

It also potentially gave a false impression of how easy it would be for Ukraine to liberate territory elsewhere. 'It was a very well-executed operation, but it wasn't going to be easy to replicate elsewhere,' Kofman concludes.

REQUIEM FOR A DREAM

Two and a half years later, with Ukraine's position looking bleak, many Ukrainians remember the period of the Kharkiv offensive as the halcyon days of the war. Some observers say that if Ukraine had been properly supplied with all the necessary weapons – western tanks, F16s, long-range ATACMS missiles – from the start, this could have led to a final victory while Russian lines were buckling during this period. Yaroslav Trofimov, the chief foreign correspondent for the *Wall Street Journal*, who was with Nick and me on our excursion to Rohan, described it as 'how the best chance to win the Ukraine war was lost'. In his book on the first year of the war, *Our Enemies Will Vanish*, he writes:

> Kyiv's pleas for Western tanks and fighting vehicles kept getting turned down. Meanwhile, Russia's new commander for the war, Gen. Sergei Surovikin, had hundreds of thousands of fresh troops at his disposal. Ukraine's advantage in manpower was over. Surovikin ordered these men to spend the winter digging, creating nearly impregnable fortifications along the entire front line.
>
> All the hardware that Ukraine was begging for in 2022 – Leopard and Abrams tanks, Bradleys and Strykers, and Patriot batteries – was eventually provided the following year. 'A mountain of steel,' is how US officials termed it.
>
> But, by then, it was a different war. The Ukrainian offensives of 2023 gained little ground against an entrenched, prepared and more numerous enemy. Putin's nuclear brinkmanship had gained him time – not just to prevent a military collapse, but also for indispensable military aid to Ukraine to get caught up in the United States' own domestic politics.

Kofman, as usual, has a more complicated, pessimistic view of the situation, saying, 'It is a poorly thought through counterfactual that is not supported by the evidence or the logic.' He explains further:

If you've never worked in government, you don't understand the physics of it. Magic was not an option! The challenge with that argument is that in order to do these things, it took 2022 to build the organisational capacity, establish the physical presence to transfer to the equipment to Ukraine and train Ukrainian troops. SACEUR [the organisation that coordinated Ukrainian military assistance] was only set up in 2022. All that took considerable time. As far as equipment and all these things go, it was a huge learning process. If we'd done it two months earlier, it wouldn't have made a difference for the war in 2022.

In terms of training, Ukraine did not have the brigades to send us because they were under high pressure and taking heavy casualties. They weren't able to take men off the line and often haven't been filling their training spots in the west. Ukraine wouldn't have had nine brigades of men! They didn't have excess force capacity they could send out of the war. Did Ukraine have a second army that none of us know about it could have teleported out of Ukraine and brought back in three months?

Best case scenario, they would have got to key supply hubs in Luhansk and maybe wrapped around Severodonetsk. The war would have continued with the lines closer to the Russian border and Russians would have declared mobilisation like they did. Ukraine's military leadership doesn't believe that it would have made that big a difference.

Pondering the deaths of friends and colleagues, along with the thousands of houses destroyed since then, I often wonder about exactly that. Kofman is right, I believe, that a more successful Kharkiv offensive would not have ended the war and may not have progressed further if Ukraine had been better equipped. But two months could have been made up here. As Jack Watling notes in his Royal United Services Institute report on the 2023 counteroffensive: 'Ukraine's international partners wasted four months in deciding to act so that only a part of the pledged equipment arrived in Ukraine prior to the offensive.' So, there were several decision points where a quicker understanding of the situation could have built Ukraine's military resources up faster. Individual decisions to move faster from the beginning may not have changed the outcome of specific battles. But I believe a real effort from the west to back Ukraine to the hilt from the beginning would have had the most effect.

For all three years it oversaw western aid to Ukraine, the Biden administration obsessed over whether a particular delivery, say of tanks or long-range missiles, would tip Putin over the edge and encourage him to use nuclear weapons. Putin played the 'madman theory' perfectly.

In reality, he had escalation options before the nuclear – the most obvious of which would be to order a full mobilisation and call as many young men as possible in Russia to the front. War hawks like Strelkov were already demanding this. In the end, none of the west's deliveries of aid even pushed him to do that.

If they had not been as cowed by these threats, western allies could have begun training F16 pilots and tank crews from the first month, bolstering artillery deliveries before Ukraine ran out of its own stocks and immediately approving Challengers and Leopards and long-range strike missiles (which were eventually approved long after they would have changed the situation on the ground), and I think there is a realistic prospect that the war could have been over by now. It could have meant more equivalent offensives, better protection and lethality for Ukrainian troops, and it would have meant fewer lives lost. Ukraine would not have won the war in 2022.

But the sum total of these efforts would have meant Ukraine had a better chance to win it later, or at least settle it on favourable terms, rather than be dragged into the gruelling attritional stalemate that would soak thousands of miles of Ukrainian land with blood.

UNBREAKABLE

KUPYANSK, KHARKIV OBLAST, MARCH 2024

'Same shit, different day,' Serhiy said. He was drinking a beer, smoking a cigarette and about to drive me to the front line. It was 9 a.m., but somehow it seemed totally normal at the time. He'd become my usual driver after taking Nick and I to Rohan those two years ago. Events here had become terrifyingly routine.

'You are very lucky to be here today!' the commander, codenamed 'Leshy', told me as we approached his M1230 howitzer, a Soviet-era piece donated to Ukraine by Slovakia. 'We got a big delivery of shells.' Leshy, a 48-year-old man with a bushy white beard and a faint and raspy voice, was a veteran of the first war in Donbas and had been fighting since 2014. He said that this was a particularly good day and they had not had a shipment of ammunition like this in weeks. In the tarpaulin-covered dugout where they stored their ammunition, their stockpile of spare rounds looked to be fewer than a dozen. Leshy said that they constantly requested fresh supplies of ammunition but had little control over when it would arrive. Ukraine's Kharkiv offensive had stopped just over the Oskil River, near the city of Kupyansk. The men there had been holding their positions against constant Russian counterattacks for nearly two years, and the exhaustion showed on their faces and in their movements.

It had been a frightening drive to Leshy's position. The Russians had conducted airstrikes throughout the region, and we could see black smoke rising from the fields all around us. In the distant sky, we could see the vapour trails of a Russian jet, as it fired a glide bomb towards Ukrainian positions. The heady days of Ukrainian victories felt like a lifetime ago for the soldiers who had manned the trenches here ever since.

As we sat inside a dugout less than ten kilometres away from the Russians, one officer joined us, his eyes red and his head in his hands, looking like he could fall asleep at any moment. These men, and one woman, would have had two weeks' leave to go home if they were lucky. In their trench command post were a few mattresses and laptops and other electronic equipment, including drone detectors, perched on a small table in the corner. They had fashioned a small shelf packed with coffee, cigarettes and snacks.

Our interview was interrupted when Leshy received a radio call. A Russian assault group was attacking a trench about six kilometres ahead of us, trying to take advantage of Ukraine's ammunition shortage. Time to 'work on the enemy'. We rushed out, and several men ran forward to clear the camouflage netting off the front of the artillery piece to allow it to fire. Another ran forward with a shell over his shoulder to load the gun. They fired around ten rounds towards the Russian assault group, before declaring the job completed. Leshy told us that they'd struck two important targets and that the Russians in the area would be licking their wounds. The mood of the soldiers improved. Leshy called us over to speak again. His message was simple: he wanted to show us that if he still had the shells, Ukraine could still do the job and the Russians would be stopped in their tracks.

I visited Kharkiv possibly a dozen times over the three years I've been in Ukraine, and I visited several of the front lines again.

Whether the Kharkiv counteroffensives gave Ukraine false hope of further victories or not, there was one unquestionable benefit. From June onwards, the 'Passengers' in the Kharkiv Metro Station began to slowly to emerge to the surface. After the second offensive in September, the city was finally out of range of Russian artillery. Olya Filipskaya remembered that the first time she returned to the surface felt like being able to breathe again after suffocating for months.

But the return to the surface was difficult for many, she told me:

> In the Metro, everyone was together, there was a sense of community. Everyone had company. We got the best food, cooked and delivered from the local restaurants. Some of the old ladies were delighted to get tuna sandwiches. It is very expensive [in Ukraine], so many of them couldn't afford it on their pensions.

When they returned to the surface, many of them were again isolated, scared. The consequences in some cases were tragic, as Filipskaya recalled:

> I remember one elderly man died of a heart attack shortly after he returned. He'd had one in the subway, but we were able to get him medical attention because he collapsed in front of us. But at home he was alone, and no one was there to see him.

The fighting had settled into a stalemate. The Russians opened a second front to the north of the city in May 2024, trying to regain the territory they had been so embarrassingly pushed out of. They got stopped by stiff resistance in the middle of the cities of Vovchansk and Lyptsi and never progressed further towards Kharkiv itself.

I spent my time here digging into the history of the city, which had a rich legacy of art and culture that Ukrainians were rediscovering after decades of Soviet suppression. Tetyana Pylypchuk, the director of Kharkiv's Literary Museum, was determined not to let cultural life here die. She and her staff kept open one of the few museums still operating during this period, devoted to Kharkiv's cultural history. In the 1920s, Slovo House (*slovo* meaning 'word' in Ukrainian) had once been the meeting point for the country's most esteemed poets and authors. What Oxford's Eagle and Child was for Tolkien and Lewis, Slovo House was for Ukraine. Their slogans were unabashedly nationalist: 'Death to Dostoyevskyism! Up with the Cultural Renaissance!' and 'Away from Moscow! Go to Europe!' This movement would eventually be crushed by Stalin, who had more than 200 participants killed after sham trials. They are known today as the Executed Renaissance.

Having survived so much already, the museum's curators were not about to let Putin close it down again. Pylypchuk told me when I visited:

> In real life, Ukrainians are the freedom lovers, the fighters. Russians thought that we count them as a 'big brother' or an 'old brother', but in the reality it was never like that. We want to build our own country, not invade others. From the cultural point of view, because it was throughout the centuries as they were killing poets, musicians, repressing them and sending to concentration camps – this time they had expected something the same.

People here still struggle with what to do about Kharkiv's complicated history with its neighbour. 'But I saved my books in Russian,'

Pylypchuk told me, 'my whole library. If your mother read you Pushkin's [a Russian poet's] tales, it is about your childhood, your memories maybe, but it is not about Pushkin.'

There are elements of the shared past that are harder than others to let go.

'Now, for example, they want to dismantle the monument to the Kharkiv division, which fought in Kharkiv [during the Second World War],' Pylypchuk said. 'And I still feel such a dissonance. It cannot be dismantled, it must be reinterpreted, rethought.' She wanted Ukraine to reclaim these elements of its history as part of its own national story, not simply wipe them away because of their association with Russia.

From this point on, there would be active front lines and packed nightclubs within a twenty-minute drive of each other. Kharkiv managed to be simultaneously deserted and full of life. You'd walk through an empty main street, only to see a bridal party posing to take photos on the next corner. They were only allowed fifteen minutes for the ceremony, the maid of honour told me, best friends and family only. You'd see a closed shop, then a barricaded building and then a raucous street party. On the same day, you could take photos of soldiers manning their artillery near Vovchansk and dolled-up models enjoying bottle service at Che1654, a posh cocktail lounge. 'If there was an explosion in the next street, people might stop to take photographs, but then they'd get on with their night,' one partygoer said.

The city was still dangerous. One morning I was walking from the train station to my hotel when I heard what I thought was the screeching of a jet, until the sound became deafening, and it was clear it was the crash of an explosion. It was about two blocks from me. Then another screech, another crash, another explosion. These were glide bombs, the Russians' latest devastating weapon. I rushed to the scene.

As I watched, a crew of firefighters in red overalls and hard helmets smashed through a broken door to make space for a family to leave a burning building after a Russian missile strike. A young boy, Timofiy, barely ten years old, was later pulled dead from the rubble still wearing his red and black Spiderman pyjamas. The city's shops and restaurants carried on as normal, absorbing this one tragedy as it had so many others.

Here everyone lived each day as if it were their last. 'You get used to war so quickly,' Olya mused. She recounted a phone call with a friend in Kyiv. 'What are you doing after this?' the friend had asked. Olya replied that she was going to the gym and then teaching an English class at a local cafe. 'A gym? A class? You are in Kharkiv! Are you crazy?' When I arrived on my last trip, I arrived in the station and was picked up by my affable fixer Boris. Immediately, my phone started beeping and a message popped up that said 'TAKE SHELTER IMMEDIATELY'. It was more impactful than a regular air raid siren, given when the Ukrainians had knowledge of a serious inbound threat. I asked Boris what we should do. 'Give me your phone, I'll turn the alert off for you. We get it every day,' he said, and we drove off. Kharkiv was not for the weak.

Because of Kharkiv citizens' ability to live their normal lives in the middle of one of the hottest parts of the war, people from around Ukraine, amazed at their defiance and resilience, began to call the city 'unbreakable'. Olya, who I imagined as one of the key representatives of this iron generation, disagreed. 'I hate it when people call us unbreakable,' she told me, and she shared a journal entry with me:

Honestly, I get what they are implying, I get that this is sort of motivation not to give up, to stay strong, to keep living. But this is also a huge emotional forbiddance to feel sad, to be scared of death, to grieve and to say goodbye to a lot of things we lost in this war. The human mind and body are not made to endure such kind of stress, resist the 500kgs bombs or its blast wave. So, we break.

Ihor Terekhov, the mayor, still believes that Kharkiv has a bright future after all this pain, and its children are the future:

We will keep seeing the city as the student capital, for me it is so important for the city to become full of its youth again. We will return to peace and rebuild everything we have lost during the war. Run our universities offline, not online, bring back IT professionals, build the scientific park we have planned.

Already, prestigious French architects were preparing plans to rebuild a vibrant and modern city, preserving the grand constructivist facades of Kharkiv's National University and imposing City Hall, both already bombed and quickly rebuilt. There were red and blue painted cranes already dotting the skyline in Saltivka, hard at work rebuilding Kharkiv's most destroyed district. All that remained was for the shooting to stop.

If you want to see the real heroism of Ukraine, start in the nearby town of Chuhuiv, where you can see a huge mural on the side of an apartment block recreating Ilya Repin's iconic painting *Reply of the Zaporozhian Cossacks*, where the bald-headed, moustache-spouting, scimitar-wielding warriors compete to come up with more profane and offensive insults to send to the Ottoman Sultan after he demanded they submit to his rule. It's the 'Russian warship, go fuck yourself' of the nineteenth century.

As you drive north on the highway from Donbas, surrounded by bright yellow sunflower fields and the empty ruins of once loved and now abandoned towns, you see billboard after billboard that memorialise the fallen. 'He died so you could live,' is the caption under the smiling headshot of one young soldier, his dates of birth and death giving his age as twenty-five. 'She gave everything, so you'd suffer nothing,' reads another.

Finally, the road crests and you see the gleaming city skyline, the grey smoke rising from a bomb strike, and read 'Welcome to the Hero City of Kharkiv', emblazoned on the final sign at the entrance to the city. Kharkiv has become the place where the bounds between war and peace dissolve, where the sounds of artillery and electric guitars, shellfire and birdsong mix together in an orchestra that plays the music of heaven and hell together in one great symphony.

It wasn't the worst fate that awaited a city in Ukraine.

CHAPTER FIVE

THE WRATH OF THE RIVER: OCCUPATION, LIBERATION AND AGONY IN KHERSON

'I want the Kiev authorities and their true handlers in the west to hear me now, and I want everyone to remember this: the people living ... in Kherson ... have become our citizens, for ever.'

— Vladimir Putin

THE TEMPEST

KHERSON, JUNE 2023

Even the dead had not seen the end of the war. Corpses floated downstream, the tempest having washed these poor souls from their resting places in the village graveyards that had once dotted the banks of the Dnipro. The great river's levees had burst, and thousands of metric tonnes of water were flowing downstream, washing away anyone or anything not firmly moored to the ground. A Ukrainian soldier aptly described the flooded city of Kherson at this time as 'Venice from Hell'. Instead of intricately carved wooden gondolas carrying honeymooning couples down the antique Italian canals, Ukrainian soldiers on small rubber speedboats were ferrying desperate civilians to safety under deadly fire.

The violently exhumed bodies of long-dead Ukrainians were not the only form of foulness the water was carrying: oil and industrial chemicals mixed with landmines and unexploded ammunition swept from hastily abandoned frontline positions on both sides of the river. More than 600 square kilometres of dry land, much of it being Ukraine's most fertile, was submerged by the torrents. Several times an hour, a boat would pull up to the street and civilians would pile out. Sometimes desperate relatives would be on hand to embrace them, other times they would be taken straight to a humanitarian shelter for aid, food and water. Others carried terrified and soaking pets in cages – Ukrainian people's care for the most vulnerable members of their communities, including animals, never ceased to touch my heart.

It was on the river that I heard the faint whistle, which turned into the screech of a banshee as I saw the rocket streak down in front of us, smashing into the water perhaps fifty metres ahead of our boat. It wasn't the sight, which was over in less than a second, but the sound and the shockwave that were overwhelming. The cacophony of shells heading towards you is utter terror that no video can convey. It is otherworldly and the second it takes to close in on you feels stretched into an hour. The first shell in front of us landed, then I closed my eyes and heard another, then another. Each of us on the boat knew we may die, and there wasn't a thing we could do about it.

Once this volley had passed, the laid-back Dutch journalist next to me on our tiny craft, Chris, said that shortly before the ride, he'd bought an engagement ring that he was carrying with him like a lucky charm. 'I'm going to ask my girlfriend to marry me next week, so we have to make it out of this!' On the way back to shore, we saw a speedboat piloted by a Ukrainian special forces soldier with two civilians in tow zip past a partially submerged sign. It had a photo of a Ukrainian soldier saluting with a slogan in bold lettering running across. 'Kherson is Ukraine', it said. But what an awful price the city had to pay for its freedom.

The people here had spurned the idea of the 'Russian World', and now the Russians would punish them by raining an endless hell on the thousands of civilians left behind.

How different the scenes had been just over six months ago, when Volodymyr Zelensky strode through a jubilant crowd waving Ukrainian flags, singing the national anthem and ripping down the Russian propaganda posters that adorned the streets. Kherson had just been liberated from eight months of violent occupation, and the President had told a waiting pool of reporters – me among them – that this was the 'beginning of the end' of the Russian war on Ukraine. Here was just the latest in a string of Ukrainian victories, the national mood was buoyant and the Russians were retreating throughout the country. The city itself had survived the recent fighting almost completely intact. Who could blame him for his optimism?

Yet two hours later, we could have all been dead after a Russian artillery shell hit the clearing across from our press bus. I wrote at the time that it was a sign that 'the city is not out of danger yet'. No one could have known the agony that awaited Kherson. 'Hell is empty, and all the devils are here,' as Shakespeare wrote in *The Tempest*.

LAST STAND

In a quiet park in the south of the city, lying next to the riverbank, a crooked wooden cross pokes out of the top of a blasted tree trunk.

It is ringed by some sparse wreaths of flowers, and the Ukrainian flag flaps in the wind beside it. Perched at the top is a photo of an unknown soldier. Aside from a sprinkling of these mementos sticking out of the ground, this is the only sign that men died here. Erected after the pleading of relatives in May 2022, it is a monument to Ukraine's forgotten heroes. On 1 March, the forty-three men of Kherson's Territorial Defence knew that the odds were hopeless. The city was encircled and most of the local authorities had fled. The regular army had been ordered to retreat to defences that were being hastily erected around the city of Mykolaiv, around sixty kilometres west.

Still, Mykola Zozulia and his comrades loaded their Soviet-era rifles, prepared Molotov cocktails, shared a few grenades that they'd gathered from an abandoned police armoury and took up positions in Lilac Park to fight the huge Russian forces arrayed against them. The battle was over in less than half an hour, and eighteen of them lay dead. The standard narrative says that Kherson surrendered without a fight, handing the keys of the city to the Russians. But don't tell that to Zozulia, who helped stage the desperate last-ditch defence: 'Until about midday, the Russians were afraid to advance into the city. They thought the Territorial Defence would really lay into them.'

Despite their bravery, the capture of Kherson was an early triumph for the Kremlin after its initial blitzkrieg on Kyiv had failed. While the airborne landing at Hostomel outside the capital had to be aborted after a Ukrainian fightback, the Russians managed a successful landing by the Antonivsky Bridge linking Kherson to the left bank of the Dnipro. It was never intended to be the main goal of the Russian advance. Their troops were supposed to use the city as a bridgehead over the river to launch a larger assault along the Black Sea coast to make Ukraine landlocked and gain control of a glimmering prize.

Kherson was founded by Russian Empress Catherine the Great, and the settlement was named after the famed colony of Chersonesus that the Greeks had set up in nearby Crimea. The Russians called it part of Novorossiya, 'New Russia'. The most famous son of the region was Leon Trotsky, a son of Jewish farmers raised in the small village of Yanovka, one of many Ukrainians who would rise to the heights of power in the Soviet Empire. He described his homeland as follows: 'On the boundless steppes of Kherson ... was a kingdom of wheat and sheep, living by laws all its own ... Only the numerous barrows on the steppes remained as landmarks of the great migration of nations.' He would spend months imprisoned in the city for his early revolutionary activity, the same dungeons in which the Russians would imprison Ukrainian dissidents more than a century later. He ironically would also do more than almost anyone to break Ukrainian nationalism in the region, when he led the Red Army to crush their troops throughout Ukraine in the Russian Civil War.

If Russian forces captured Odesa, they would slice the country in half, cut off Ukraine's access to the sea and cripple the export-based Ukrainian economy, even if the rest of the country managed to hold out. Russian soldiers were to be issued medals for the 'liberation of Odessa', intended to be swiftly annexed into the Russian Federation, as opposed to the 'capture of Kiev', where they were merely to impose a puppet state.

Many were shocked by the speed of the collapse of Ukraine's defences in this region. 'There was not a single headquarters to organise defence. Not one. They ran away,' a Ukrainian Territorial Defence soldier told *Ukrainska Pravda*, a Ukrainian website that wrote a gripping account of the battle to resurrect the reputation of the city and its defenders. 'The police and the SSU [Security Services of Ukraine] left the city on day one,' said another. In addition, the Antonivsky Bridge was never blown up, allowing the Russians to quickly move troops and equipment outside Kherson. The unprepared Ukrainian regular troops in the area were outnumbered by nearly three to one and decided to retreat. The Ukrainian authorities later pursued treason charges against some of the senior city officials, but the exact reasons for the quick fall of the city remain unknown.

With Kherson secured and a solid bridgehead established, the Russians pursued their next objective. The city of Mykolaiv was the main target standing between the Russians and Odesa, and they expected to quickly take it. But it was here that their plans for Ukraine's south quickly became unstuck.

There are no memorials for the dozens of Russian soldiers incinerated by artillery on a cold winter's day in early March 2022. Instead, in an open field just a few kilometres east of Mykolaiv, the ground is dotted with twisted metal and scorched earth. Anatoliy, a Ukrainian Army officer, said that a Ukrainian farmer had seen Russian armour massing for an assault on the city. He quickly alerted the Ukrainian authorities and sent them coordinates, allowing the hastily assembled defenders to pound the force with artillery. There are dozens of Russian vehicle carcasses scattered through the fields thanks to the farmer's quick-thinking. The Russians attempted to encircle the city by sending a rapid assault force north, but a stiff Ukrainian defence in the town of Voznesensk quickly stopped them.

THE WRATH OF THE RIVER

MYKOLAIV, MARCH 2022

The explosive charges that the Ukrainians had placed so that they could blow up the bridge over the Southern Bug River to Mykolaiv showed that the Ukrainians were determined not to repeat the mistakes that led the Russians to capture Kherson. When I arrived in early March 2022, I saw sandbags, tank traps and other fortifications everywhere. Overnight, the calm city of just under half a million people had been turned into a fortress. It was the last major city on the road from Kherson to Odesa, and Ukraine needed to hold it whatever the cost.

While the whumping of artillery could be heard throughout the city limits, the defenders had mostly repulsed the Russian advance. The Ukrainians were bullish about their chances. 'They have no will to fight ... We captured a lot of their military equipment,' Andriy, a local Ukrainian soldier helping organise the city's defence, said. 'They just abandoned it. It says a lot about their complete demoralisation!'

It also says a great deal about the Russians' shambolic preparation for the war effort. After their initial success in Kherson, they failed to realise that the rest of the country was now banding together and preparing to fight the invaders. Locals were saying it felt like a rerun of the Second World War. The sandbagged fortifications in front of the Odesa Opera House that I saw looked almost identical to those used in the same location in 1941, when the city was preparing for a Nazi assault. The famed beaches that are usually packed with international tourists at the height of summer were now covered with explosive mines in expectation of a Russian amphibious landing.

The photogenic Ukrainian Governor of Mykolaiv, Vitaliy Kim, had become a Ukrainian internet icon due to his taunting of the retreating Russians. The governor, who is of Korean heritage, was in high spirits as he walked into a courtyard outside the Mykolaiv city administration building.

'We have offered the Russian forces near the city to surrender to us,' he said to me and the small group of reporters who had braved the freezing cold and Russian bombardment to meet him. 'They thought that we would greet them with flowers! Plenty of Russians are already lying dead outside the city.' He told us to come back in a couple of days to hear their answer. A few weeks later, the building would be destroyed in a Russian rocket strike. Thirty-seven workers, mostly civilians, died in the blast. Kim would survive, despite being the Russians' primary target. He later thanked the gods he had overslept and been late for work.

The Russian plan, premised on meeting little resistance and steamrolling disorganised and demoralised Ukrainian units, failed in a similar fashion to how their assaults in Kyiv and Kharkiv had burned out. But unlike in those regions, the Russians had captured a regional capital of significant importance. For now, they were determined to hold on to their one prize of the early invasion.

Kherson was in a unique situation, as it was captured without significant fighting and with a majority of the 250,000 or so population remaining. If the Russians expected their new subjects to be quiet and obedient, they were soon disabused of that notion. In the first days of the occupation, Ukrainians protested every day in their hundreds. On 13 March, the anniversary of the joyous day in 1944 when the city was liberated from the Nazis by the Red Army, more than 5,000 people took to the streets, waving the Ukrainian flag and calling for the Russian forces to leave. They shouted 'Kherson is Ukraine! Go home!' They ignored warning shots fired by Russian troops attempting to get the protesters to disperse.

The city had been mostly Russian-speaking, and its residents had tended to vote for pro-Russian parties in the years leading up to the full-scale invasion. But as in Kharkiv, this was a totally different matter from the residents desiring a violent occupation. Protests were held almost every day until the end of March. Serhii Vodotyka, a writer living in Kherson through this period, wrote 'The people of Kherson had more or less calmed down emotionally; they were convinced of the victory of Ukraine. At least, it had become clear that they did not accept the "*Ruskiy Mir*" and were unanimous in their hatred towards the occupiers.' By the third week, the Russians started to clamp down more and more on civil resistance. After the failure of their assault on Mykolaiv, they were turning to consolidate power over the city they did control. They began to break up rallies using tear gas, live ammunition and arresting the organisers.

Many expected a swift Ukrainian counteroffensive here. The doom of the opening days had been replaced by determination throughout the country, and Ukraine's successful repelling of Russian forces from Kyiv, Chernihiv and Sumy made residents think that their own liberation was imminent. But Ukrainian forces were also bruised and recuperating. They counterattacked and pushed the occupiers almost completely out of Mykolaiv Oblast, but soon a front line formed that mapped quite neatly onto the outline of Kherson Oblast. Instead of waiting to be rescued, many civilians decided to leave of their own accord.

My friend Serhiy said that he and his wife tried several times to leave Kherson with their family only to be rebuffed at Russian checkpoints. Eventually, a bribe of cigarettes and vodka was enough to get him and them over the checkpoint and into free Ukrainian territory. By September, more than half of the city had left – most to other areas within Ukraine but others to Russia via Crimea.

Some decided to take matters into their own hands. They would not let the Russians stay in their homes without putting up some kind of fight. Denis Tsurkunov was first captured by Russians four days into the war, when his Territorial Defence unit just outside the city was overwhelmed. 'They cut our hands with their bayonets, broke our ribs with their boots and shot next to our heads as we lay face down on a cold floor,' he said in an interview by encrypted messenger. His captor told him, as he smashed Tsurkunov's head into the floor, that Russian soldiers were being killed because of 'scum like you'. He was one of the lucky ones, released from captivity early.

In response, the Russians put together a network of detention centres and torture chambers for civilians they considered to be helping Ukrainians. Those under most scrutiny were former soldiers and law enforcement, as well as anyone known to authorities as a pro-Ukrainian activist. Speaking Ukrainian was seen as particularly suspicious.

Olga Balan, a woman living in the town of Velyka Olexandrivka, told me:

> They took [my husband] Serhiy captive and tortured him with electrocution very badly for five days. These are incredibly horrible people. When they found people with Ukrainian tattoos, they would cut them out of their skin. They went from house to house, shooting people's dogs! Every morning you wake up, look out the window and see that the Russians are still there, and we ask ourselves, 'When will they leave?'

She was cradling her five-month-old daughter Eva in her arms. She'd given birth to her in the family shed, she told me, because the Russians had placed her under house arrest as her husband

Ira Hadetska, twenty-eight, from the southern city of Mykolaiv, stands outside the university that was her alma mater, which was badly damaged by a Russian missile in August 2022. 'All we want is for Russia, and Russians, to get the fuck out of our country,' Ira told me just after I snapped this.
© Tom Mutch

Ukrainian soldiers rest on the fast train from Kramatorsk to Kyiv after coming off the front line in the Donetsk region. The railways have been one of Ukraine's minor miracles during the war. They continue to function smoothly, ferrying desperate refugees to safety one way and taking ammunition and supplies the other.
© Tom Mutch

Kateryna Petrenko and Serhiy Pixel were due to be married until their engagement was tragically cut short when Serhiy was killed fighting in the Kursk region, where Ukraine launched an offensive in 2024. He was a drone pilot, and now she is training to take his place.   Courtesy of Kateryna Petrenko

ABOVE A drone pilot in the basement of a farmhouse near Kupyansk, March 2024. When the US Congress cut off aid to Ukraine in late 2023, the armed forces had to adapt, and a home-grown defence industry based around drones sprang up. Now, the battlefield is dominated by them, and they are responsible for the majority of casualties.
© Tom Mutch

LEFT MIDDLE Rescue workers search for remains at the site of a missile strike in Vinnytsia in June 2022. Twenty-three people were killed by five ballistic missiles fired from Black Sea submarines. There seemed no military logic to this strike – Vinnytsia was far from the front lines.
© Tom Mutch

LEFT BELOW A father returning from a year of fighting in the Donetsk region in eastern Ukraine reunites with his daughter at a train station in the city of Lviv in March 2023. Many Ukrainian soldiers have served in the trenches for years with perhaps two weeks off.
© Tom Mutch

Ukrainian soldiers ferry civilians to safety on speedboats in the city of Kherson amid the floods caused by the destruction of the Nova Kakhovka Dam. The sign behind them reads: 'Kherson is Ukraine. We thank the AFU [Armed Forces of Ukraine].'
© Tom Mutch

Two students celebrate their graduation from Taras Shevchenko University in Kyiv, the country's most prestigious higher education establishment, in June 2023. Despite the war, life continued nearly as normal in Kyiv, and schools and universities remained open.
© Tom Mutch

A rescue worker with an axe slung over his shoulder walks through the site of a missile strike in Kharkiv in October 2023. Sitting less than fifty kilometres from the Russian border, Ukraine's second-largest city was bombarded with all manner of shells and bombs, but the people remained defiant, and the city never fell.
© Tom Mutch

A boy and his mother display the shell of a missile that they collected in a small town in the Kharkiv region shortly after its liberation from Russian occupation in September 2022. The Kharkiv counteroffensive was one of the most extraordinary turnarounds in the history of modern warfare. But it also raised expectations that Ukraine would never quite be able to live up to. © Tom Mutch

A soldier of Ukraine's 57th Motorized Brigade runs to reload a Gvozdika 2S1 self-propelled howitzer on the front lines near the city of Kupyansk in the Kharkiv region in March 2024. The Ukrainians had liberated the city a year and a half previously, but both sides had been stuck in a gruelling attritional battle nearby ever since.
© Tom Mutch

Four soldiers from Ukraine's 121st Naval Infantry Brigade pose for a photo following an interview about their cross-river operations in the Kherson region in August 2024. Ukraine held a bridgehead over the Dnipro River for nearly eight months but could not make serious headway towards occupied Crimea.
© Tom Mutch

A young girl looks into the barrel of a Russian tank, which is displayed as a trophy on Kyiv's Khreshchatyk Boulevard, in August 2022.
© Tom Mutch

Body bags holding the remains of civilians are buried in a mass grave near the city of Izium in the Kharkiv region, shortly after its liberation in September 2022. Everywhere the Russians retreated from, evidence of murder and torture was rife.
© Tom Mutch

Ukrainian President Volodymyr Zelensky walks through the main square of the recently liberated city of Kherson, flanked by his guards and chief of staff Andriy Yermak, in November 2022. This was the high-water mark of Ukrainian success in the war, but the situation gradually deteriorated after the Russians started taking the war more seriously.
© Tom Mutch

LEFT Vadim, a Ukrainian officer, looks at a destroyed statue of the founder of the Soviet Union, Vladimir Lenin, in the town of Sudzha in the Kursk region of the Russian Federation. Vadim was part of the daring Ukrainian offensive that captured around 1,000 square kilometres of Russian territory, but they were gradually pushed out of it by a combined Russian–North Korean offensive. © Tom Mutch

ABOVE Oksen Lisovyi, then a soldier with a Ukrainian National Guard unit, prepares his sniper rifle in Donbas in May 2022. Shortly after, he was recalled by Zelensky to become Ukraine's Minister of Education and Science and was responsible for opening the first in-person schools since the beginning of the full-scale invasion. He represents how the highest ranks of Ukrainian society fought in the war.
© Tom Mutch

LEFT Rosa's depiction of life in Kyiv. The snake in the tree represents the ever-present nature of death in Ukraine, which always lurks around the corner, no matter how peaceful the city may seem on the surface.
© Mella Rosa

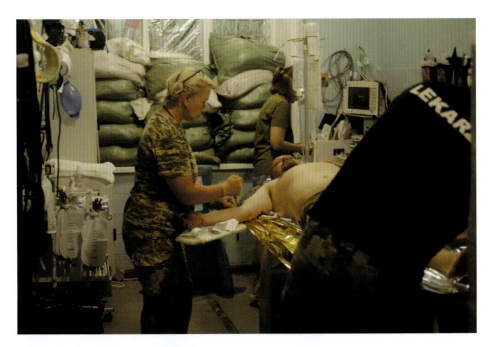

ABOVE Ukrainian medics work at a stabilisation point near the occupied town of Soledar during Ukraine's 2023 counteroffensive. This military operation was a brutal failure and marked the end of Ukraine's hopes of regaining the territory it had lost to Russia since 2014. © Tom Mutch

LEFT MIDDLE A mannequin lies against a tree near the village of Novopetrivka in the Kherson region shortly after Russian occupying forces withdrew in November 2022. The Russians left decoys to fool Ukrainian scouts and drone pilots into thinking they were still there so they could withdraw safely.
© Tom Mutch

LEFT BELOW Wife and husband Oksana Krasnova and Stanislav Krasnov near their base on the front line of the Donetsk region in May 2022. Stanislav was badly injured in the Kharkiv region six months later but recovered and returned to combat duty. Both of them are still working on or near the front lines.
© Tom Mutch

Soldiers from Ukraine's 80th Air Assault Brigade fire a D-30 howitzer towards Russian positions on the front line near the city of Bakhmut in May 2023. The Ukrainian leadership's decision to hold the Donetsk city to the bitter end after the military situation had deteriorated remains highly controversial. © Tom Mutch

The turret of a Russian tank destroyed by fighting in the Mykolaiv Oblast in August 2022. Some Russian tanks had a structural weakness where a well-aimed explosive could set off the ammunition belt and blow the turret clean into the air. Ukrainian soldiers made a game of it, calling it 'turret toss'.
© Tom Mutch

'Pes Patron' is one of Ukraine's most recognisable celebrities. He works as a member of the canine unit in Ukraine's demining service, the DSNS, sniffing for mines and unexploded ordnance. Ukraine is the most heavily contaminated country in the world, and it will take decades and billions of dollars to make it safe.
© Maria Syrotiuk

was a person of interest. They wouldn't even allow her to go to the hospital.

The Russians made a show of giving out humanitarian aid in Kherson, but it was almost all items they had looted from the city's closed shops and forcibly requisitioned from local farmers.

The Russians were right about the population's 'disloyalty'. Because most of the Ukrainian population loathed them, they regularly assisted the nearby Ukrainian Army. Kherson residents would regularly take photos and note coordinates of Russian military equipment, logistics points and ammunition storage. One civilian would later tell me that the reason that the city was so undamaged was that the Ukrainian Army had extremely good intelligence on every Russian military asset in and around the area. 'The occupiers never slept soundly,' he said. Local partisans also carried out a campaign of retribution against those in the city who had dared to join the Russian collaboration scheme.

Still, even under these circumstances, life always finds a way to resume a certain normality. Vodotyka wrote:

> Kherson lived in a dual reality: the Russian military was in the city, but the blue and yellow flag flew over the city council. Mayor Ihor Kolykhayev was present in the media space, reporting on the work of city services, and disseminating information on his social media pages that was important for survival ... The streets were cleaned better than in peacetime, and garbage was regularly collected. Water, gas, and electricity continued to function. About a week after the occupation began, trolleybuses started running again, and small private shops opened ... It was surreal.

When driving, I saw the six signature white streaks, one after the other, as the payload of six rockets was sent into the skies, then turned down on their target with minute precision. This was the real game changer of weapons sent by the west – High Mobility Artillery Rocket System (HIMARS). The rockets these systems used could fly up to 90 kilometres before hitting a target with extraordinary precision, making them ideal for hitting logistics nodes and command posts.

The Russians had nearly 30,000 of their crack troops in the region, more than enough to mount an effective defence of the city if they wanted to fight street by street. But their logistics were the Achilles heel of the Russian operation in Kherson. It took far more than a single arrow from Paris to cut the tendon of the Russian occupation in Kherson. US estimates say that nearly 400 HIMARS rockets slammed into the Antonivsky Bridge before they put it out of commission.

RECLAMATION

By the end of August 2022, Ukraine finally looked to be able to counterattack against Russian forces. The regular Russian Army was still smarting from the Kremlin's decision to launch a major European land war without actually declaring war and building up its forces. Their original invasion army was bedraggled and exhausted. The 'people's militias' of the so-called Donetsk and Luhansk People's Republics had been eaten up, thrown callously against Ukrainian defensive positions in Luhansk Oblast. The grinding campaign against the fortress of Bakhmut was ongoing, but the Wagner Private Military Company, of whom we will hear more, was leading this assault. Ukraine had also received a large influx of western weapons and ammunition to replace its nearly depleted Soviet-era stockpiles.

On 29 August, Ukraine began a full offensive. Ukrainian strategists said they hoped to be in Kherson quickly. On the ground, soldiers gave more sober assessments. The Ukrainian push at first seemed a failure, making very few gains at high cost. I was in Mykolaiv again at the time, and the sunflowers were already wilting when I spoke with Dmitro Pletenchuk, a spokesperson for the military administration. He pointed out that the Russians had extraordinarily deep minefields, thousands of their crack airborne troops and the flat, open ground made advancing Ukrainian troops vulnerable to Russian aircraft stationed in Crimea. He also provided a shopping list of supplies and weaponry the Ukrainians would need. Ukrainian officials often acted as if all journalists they met had a direct line to US State Department decision-makers.

This slow progress convinced Kofman, who visited at the same time, that any Ukrainian assault on even better prepared Russian positions in Zaporizhzhia would be an extremely difficult operation. Meanwhile, by keeping slow pressure on the Kherson front line and concentrating the deep strike campaign on Russian crossings, they made it impossible for the Russians to resupply such a large force. In October, Ukrainians finally began to make serious inroads into the Russian presence around the city.

After the collapse of the Russian positions in Kharkiv, part of the Kremlin's response was to try to raise the international stakes. The Russian occupation authorities organised a series of referendums in Kherson, as well as Zaporizhzhia, Luhansk and Donetsk Oblasts, none of which they fully controlled. They barely bothered to disguise how unfree and unfair they were. In Novopetrivka, where this book's story began, the locals said that even at gunpoint, only three or four people filled them out: 'They just claimed 90 per cent voted for them anyway, but nobody wants Russia here. It was all fake.'

But Putin also began to take belated but necessary decisions for the future of his fighting force. The first was to organise a partial mobilisation of young Russian men. The second was to appoint, for the first time, a commander to oversee the entire war effort. The new Russian chief, General Sergei Surovikin, nicknamed 'General Armageddon' for his scorched-earth tactics against the rebel-held cities of Homs and Aleppo in Syria, had a serious choice in front of him. Russian positions in Kherson were clearly unsustainable. But they were the Kremlin's biggest prize of the entire invasion and were now an official, legal part of Russia's territory. Russia had threatened to use nuclear weapons to protect its 'territorial integrity and sovereignty'.

Abandoning Kherson would admit the annexations to be the fictions that the rest of the world knew they were. The Russian military realised that their situation was only going to get worse here, not better. The Ukrainian Army was also threatening to push forward into the Luhansk region, approaching the towns of Svatove and Kreminna, the backbones of Russian logistics in the Donbas. In the end, Surovikin and his commanders decided to make a gambit, sacrificing Kherson for the sake of the rest of the Russian front line. His 30,000 crack airborne troops would end up being killed for nothing if they remained here, and they could be used to plug other gaps.

In a tense televised meeting with Russian high command, he announced their decision to leave the city and retreat to the left bank of the Dnipro. Unlike the messy and chaotic retreat in Kharkiv, it was done quickly and efficiently. By the time I got to Novopetrivka, as described in the Prologue, the Russians had managed to transport most of their equipment and troops back over the river, avoid Ukrainian capture or destruction and live to fight another day. Only their mannequins, the trenches they cut into the land and the mines and unexploded ammunition polluting the land remained. It was a decision that was humiliating for the Kremlin at the time. Igor Girkin, who had started the Donbas war in 2014, later fumed:

> Who made the 'Hard Decision' to leave Kherson uncontested – a territory of the RF [Russian Federation] and a capital of one of its subjects? Why are suggestions to 'freeze the conflict in the current positions' … not criminally investigated as an attack on the RF's territorial integrity? Or is Kherson no longer Russia? Who made that decision and on what basis?

But this decision looks prophetic and necessary in hindsight.

CHURCHILL

KHERSON, NOVEMBER 2022

Oleksiy Guzenko was dressed in his combat camouflage but holding a huge bouquet of flowers. A veteran of the first war in Donbas, he was a special forces soldier who had been involved in the battle to liberate Kherson. 'You can't walk one minute in Kherson without someone coming to hug you, give you flowers, ask you to autograph their flag,' he told me. 'The people here were waiting for the Ukrainian Army for so long. They were occupied for eight months by Terror Russia. They killed, they raped. [The victory] took longer than we wanted. Like all Ukrainians, I wanted it to take one hour. But it took eight months.'

'Kherson, Forever with Russia!' read one poster. 'Russians and Ukrainians are One People' read another. Now, gleeful citizens were pulling them down in their dozens. It was if the city itself had been let out of a cell and was casting down its shackles. Despite it being

November, it was a beautiful blue cloudless sky. You could see children playing down by the river. On the main square, children were handing out flowers to gleeful soldiers. 'For eight months this was a silent city ... [where] you feel you can be shot at any time. But the fear is gone. We can finally breathe again,' said Fyodor Lobyanin, a manager at an industrial plant in the city that the Russians had looted. The only thing puncturing this air of serene peace was the regular thumping of artillery in the background and the smoke rising from shell impacts on the left bank which silhouetted the children playing.

There was a huge contrast between Kherson and other frontline cities. Kherson International Airport in the town of Chornobaivka was smashed to bits, the wreckage of shells and aircraft dotted everywhere. But Kherson city itself was curiously untouched. The buildings had sustained the telltale broken windows, but the streets were not littered with debris or shell fragments. Soldiers had been able to precisely target them and almost entirely avoid civilian casualties among their citizens.

Everyone we met on the square and in the streets held the Russians in complete contempt. 'They are pure scum, dirty vile beasts,' said one woman. '[Russian soldiers] were buying toys for their children back in Russia. I said to them, "You bastards, you come here to destroy us and now you are buying gifts for your kids?"' Yet some interviews suggested that these opinions had not quite been uniform. When I asked one man if he knew anyone who had collaborated, he replied with a snort. 'Yes. She was my sister!' She had always been pro-Russian and had lived in the far eastern Russian city of Vladivostok. He said, 'She was actively helping them, telling them the names of people who worked for the Ukrainian government.' She had apparently fled with the Russians and he did not expect to ever speak to her again. Collaboration was and will remain a difficult subject.

The Russian foothold over the Dnipro was always precarious and the Ukrainian Army never far away. In the end, Kherson was liberated after only eight months – not a long time for anyone who wanted to hedge their bets. What the situation will be if the Ukrainians liberate cities like Kakhovka and Melitopol – now occupied for more than three years – is anyone's guess, but the Russians will have had much more time to integrate those cities into their economy and brainwash the inhabitants into believing that Russia is there for ever.

Then there is the question of what is collaboration really? Obviously, someone who gives away Ukrainian military positions, informs on their neighbours as being pro-Ukrainian or participates directly in an occupation authority is a collaborator. But what about a teacher who continues their job but teaches a Russian version of the curriculum? Or someone who distributes aid they receive from the Russians? What if those people are doing so at gunpoint? It is these difficult questions that the prosecutor's office was forced to deal with after liberation. I heard one case of a farmer who owned many acres of land, running a thriving trade of milking cows, ploughing sunflower and wheat and raising sheep for slaughter. Like many Ukrainians before the full-scale invasion, he sold his produce throughout Ukraine and Russia. When he was captured and his town was occupied, there was no way his products could reach Ukraine through the occupied territories. Some businesses, like factories, shut down completely and reopened when Ukraine retook the region.

'You can't just stop the running of a farm and then start them up again the next year. That's not how farming works! Are you supposed to kill the cows then resurrect them next year?' So, he continued selling produce to the only buyers who could take it – the Russians and the Luhansk People's Republic authorities. He remained pro-Ukrainian, he said, and never supported the Russian war effort. But he was tried for collaboration and spent a year in prison for it. This type of explanation would never fly for people like Anton, who considered any co-operation, even economic, with the Russian authorities as legitimising their occupation. These types of cases would go on to haunt the inhabitants of liberated territories for years afterwards.

But still this was a beautiful day in Kherson. The Ukrainian flags flying from people's hands, windows and lampposts could have been punished by imprisonment and torture just days ago. Zelensky stood straight as an arrow, his hands clenched, dominating the proceedings despite his miniature stature. He was flanked by some chief aides, including his chief of staff, the 'Green Cardinal' Andriy Yermak. It was a moment that we could only describe as historic, as if we were watching a triumphant General Charles de Gaulle returning to Paris in 1944. Occasionally, the comedian and showman in Zelensky would shine through and he'd flash a smirk.

He was taking an extraordinary risk being here: the city was still well within artillery range, and he was the Russians' highest-value target. But in his calculation, it was worth it. As detailed in Simon Shuster's biography, it gave Zelensky a chance to show that he was willing to take the same physical risks as the rest of his population. The contrast with Vladimir Putin, with his long tables to protect him from Covid-19 and compulsory quarantine periods for anyone in the same room as him, could not have been starker. Zelensky has many flaws, but his legendary physical courage is not in doubt. He was mobbed by an adoring crowd, delighted to see that their

President was there to support them on the most emotional day of their history. It showed the morale boost of leading from the front. It was the 'beginning of the end', Zelensky told us, deliberately emulating Churchill. But the liberation of Kherson was merely the end of the beginning. The Russian Army, humiliated and in retreat, would finally start taking the war seriously.

As our press bus drove back towards Mykolaiv, we stopped just outside the city to take photos. There was a structure that looked like a Greek amphitheatre with the name of the city in gold plate. It was the gate to the city, and it was a reporting tradition to take a photo to 'show you'd been there'. We dawdled here just slightly too long and suddenly an explosion smashed into the ground around a hundred metres away, kicking a huge plume of dirt into the air. 'IN THE BUS NOW,' one of the Ukrainian soldiers screamed at us, gesturing furiously. Then, another crack, this time from the other direction. It was a terrifying reminder that this city was still the heart of a war zone. But no one knew just how bad things were about to get.

WRATH OF GOD

KHERSON, JULY 2023

The Ukrainian Special Boat Service (SBS), trained by the British military, was conducting daring rescue missions. There were thousands of civilians living in Russian-occupied towns like Oleshky and Hola Prystan on the left bank of the Dnipro whose homes were flooding and were at serious risk of submerging. The Russian Army's 'assistance' to the people they considered their citizens, whom they had come to protect from 'Ukrainian Nazis', was to leave them to drown. The Russians had blown the Nova Kakhovka Dam just two days ago and large parts of the city were totally flooded. We were on a small rubber dingy following one of these rescue teams when we got caught right in the middle of the fire.

A Ukrainian volunteer organisation had set up a makeshift evacuation centre on a partially submerged street. Small civilian boats and rubber dinghies were leaving and returning every few minutes. 'We were on the seventh floor of our building,' said 84-year-old Antonina, who had just been rescued by a SBS crew. 'The flooding had reached the fourth floor and was rising' and her son had carried her down the stairs, then lifted her through a window into the arms of the Ukrainian soldiers waiting for her under heavy fire. A few minutes later, another boat dropped its cargo off. Two middle-aged women got off and were embraced by family members.

Ukrainian soldiers were tapping into networks of pro-Ukrainian partisans living on the Russian-occupied left bank. Usually, these people would be used to help Ukrainian artillery and special forces target Russian positions. Now they were being used as intermediaries to locate people who needed rescuing and to arrange a time and a place for such missions. It was a perilous job that involved dodging Russian troops and spending a long time searching the riverbank for the few places with patchy mobile phone service. But those unsung heroes were responsible for saving dozens of lives during these days.

It was as we were following the SBS that we were caught in the middle of the Russian rocket barrage. I was joined on the boat by my Dutch colleague Chris, *New York Times* reporter Brendan Hoffman and our unflappable driver Oleksiy. He was from Kryvyi Rih and had come down to Kherson to offer help. After the rockets stopped falling in the river, Oleksiy began to calm us down. The Russians were shelling the entire city, he explained, and we were actually safer on water than land. On land, the shell would cover an entire blast radius with thick pieces of red-hot shrapnel that would rip you to shreds. Here, they would go straight through the water to the bottom and the water resistance would stop the shrapnel shredding too far. The only real danger was from a direct hit, in which case we'd never know about it. He revved the boat's engine and drove us behind the hull of a large container ship. We heard the shells fall around us, but with seventy tonnes of solid steel between us and them, we felt safer. It was the closest I had come to dying in all my time in Ukraine and the most scared I had ever been in my life.

There was something utterly terrifying yet also liberating about being under shelling in a river. In a frontline city like Bakhmut, you could dive into a building, a trench or behind fortifications for cover. Here on the open water, I had to fight the instinct to dive into the water and swim. My body armour was lying against a tree on the riverbank. It was a conscious decision, because if the boat had capsized, the weight of my armour would have dragged me straight to the bottom. So all we could do was cover our heads and pray. By the time we made it back to shore, the evacuation centre was deserted, the civilians and soldiers packed into a bunker behind me. My phone lit up with a WhatsApp message. 'Leave Kherson IMMEDIATELY,' said the Ukrainian who had arranged my permissions. He was a tough army officer, his profile picture showing him smoking a cigarette with his arm around the actor Sean Penn. He'd seen the worst of the war, and this was a terrifying day even for him. We drove the long road back to Odesa, with the sounds of shells gradually getting quieter.

I could take comfort that at least one story from the day ended well. Chris's girlfriend said yes, and they are now happily married.

The Russians would shell the city for the rest of the day, hitting soldiers, civilians and rescue workers alike. They had been doing this for months after the liberation of Kherson.

The citizens of Kherson had decisively rejected the *Ruskiy Mir*, and they would have to be punished for it. The Russians had been pushed out of the city, but they had taken up positions just along the left bank of the Dnipro. Artillery generally has a maximum range of thirty kilometres. At their closest, Russian guns were less than a kilometre away. So they sat back and shelled the city with absolute impunity. Within two weeks, the Russians had killed thirty-two civilians, more than had been killed in the entire year to that date. In May 2023, the worst Russian strike so far, on a supermarket at peak shopping hours, killed twenty-three people.

This was, President Zelensky said, 'ecocide', which threatened to ruin the crops and farmland of the surrounding area for generations. On the ground, the mood was miserable and furious. A soldier with Ukraine's 122nd Territorial Defence Brigade, codenamed 'Mushroom', told me:

> The United Nations is a shitty organisation, they just take our money. And please quote me on that. It is an ecological disaster, but the United Nations, what does this organisation do? When the war starts, we think, this is a great organisation, they must save people from wars ... from things like this, but now we see that Russians do anything they want. They [the UN] just say 'that's awful' and that is all they do.

The motivations of the Russian destruction of the dam are still difficult to determine. They cared nothing for the lives of the Ukrainian civilians they affected, but they also washed away large parts of their prepared defensive positions. One theory is that they wanted to stymie a potential amphibious landing by Ukrainian troops across the Dnipro as part of the summer counteroffensive. The dam's destruction cost the Ukrainians $14 billion according to the government's Post-Disaster Needs Assessment. A million people lost drinking water, huge crops of wheat and sunflowers were lost and tens of thousands of homes were damaged or destroyed on the Ukrainian-controlled side alone. The damage on the Russian side, which is believed to be even more extensive, remains unknown. Yet Ukrainians recovered as they always did, and as the floods receded, they gradually rebuilt in between the shellings. The government tried to pursue Russia through international courts to be held responsible for the damage, along with its many other war crimes, but a Ukrainian lawyer working on the case admitted to me it was hopeless to expect justice through the international system. 'Whoever wins the war will force the other one to pay,' she told me.

By now, most of the city's population that had held on during the Russian occupation had left. A few determined stragglers stayed behind. 'I lived the whole period of occupation in Kherson ... After liberation, we were constantly attacked by various types of weapons. Artillery, tanks, [rockets], mortars, Shahed [drones],' says local Svitlana Horieva.

> But for me, there is nothing scarier and heavier than occupation. The terrible feeling of lawlessness. We were outlawed by the occupier ... We had no right to anything. At any moment, we could be killed and robbed. Any Russian on the street could have checked your phone ... They were kidnapping people on the street. A man could have walked into a store and never come back.

DRONE SAFARI

KHERSON, AUGUST 2024

In the dim light of the evening dusk, you could see the leaves slowly begin to fall from the tree. These leaves are Mother Nature's only protection against the enemy from the sky. You could make out the faint ring of artillery in the background or the quick acceleration of a solitary car, the distant barking of a stray dog, perhaps a little birdsong. There still wasn't much in terms of damage, but that added to the eeriness. The streets were mostly intact, but they were utterly deserted. It reminded me of a zombie movie, the opening scene from *28 Days Later*, where Jim wakes up and comes out to a London that is just empty, as if the people had been sucked into space. The grass on the sidewalks is a little overgrown, the unpruned branches just drooping a little too closely over the roads. Nature is beginning to reclaim the city. But as anyone who visits Kherson will note, the city is still rife with danger. And there is one sound that terrifies the few souls remaining like no other. It is a faint whirring, which sounds like a lawnmower crossed with a housefly: the sound of a drone.

'I wouldn't spend a moment longer in Kherson than absolutely necessary,' Paul Conroy said to me, labouring in emphasis over the last two words in his signature northern English drawl. It was August 2024 and we were sharing a dinner with some colleagues in Odesa, by then almost back to its typical bustling self. I had pitched the idea to Paul, who had taken shrapnel in the leg in Syria while famed *Sunday Times* reporter Marie Colvin had died next to him and who was not known for scaring easily. He had just spent five months living in the city. By his description, every few months seemed to bring a new depth to the horrors. I confess I had mostly forgotten about Kherson over the past year. The conflict had moved on, the action had shifted first to the counteroffensive in Zaporizhzhia and then to renewed Russian offensives in Kharkiv and Donbas. The south here was the most 'static' part of the front line, where nothing much of interest happened, and it had never been an easy place to work in at the best of times. I was also scared. I still occasionally saw that rocket flash past my eyes, heard the banshee scream my name. I had cheated death here once; did I really want to give it another crack at me? I'd heard terrifying stories from colleagues who had been there. One, Zarina Zabrisky, who also wrote for *Byline Times*, had written a searing collection of articles describing a 'hunting season' where drones and artillery would pick off civilians in the streets. But I also wanted to face my fears. I knew so many of those I had met had stayed come what may.

I knew I hadn't seen the story of the city through, so I packed up the car with my Icelandic colleague, Óskar Hallgrimsson, and we made the drive along the southern coast, through Odesa and to Mykolaiv. On the way, we passed row after row of freshly cut trenches, barbed wire and dragon's teeth fortifications. After recent Russian breakthroughs to the east caused by poorly constructed defences, the Ukrainian government had instituted a mandatory trench-building system. They had held off for so long because they believed it would be bad for morale, a sign that the Ukrainian Army was moving backwards, not forwards. Now, they were accepting the inevitable.

'Make sure to park your car under a tree,' Oleksandr Tolokonnikov, the head of Kherson's press office, had told us before we arrived. He met us next to the main city square, which had been so colourful on that fateful first visit, so full of life and pride and joy. Now, on this overcast, gloomy day, everything was in grey monochrome except for the small blue and yellow flag that still flew from the top of the city hall. There were no people walking through the square. One car drove past, going at extremely high speed.

'It's the drones,' he said.

We hear nothing. There is no warning. The drones are so high up that you don't notice anything until a bomb suddenly lands beside you and explodes. With artillery fire, there is at least a few seconds of a whistling sound or a distant explosion that you can react to – from the drone, you hear nothing until the bomb is right beside you.

The Russian commanders had designated a huge swath of the city as a 'red zone', where anything moving was considered a military target. While we were there, there was an average of 100 drone strikes per day, but as the year wore on, that number grew higher. September saw a peak of 330 drones, as the lack of foliage on the streets gave them better visibility.

'They can fly about 1 kilometre into the city, and venturing into that area is a complete death trap ... [The Russians] must drop the bombs before turning back across the river so that the battery has enough charge to get back,' Tolokonnikov says. How far away are we, I asked? 'About one and a half kilometres,' he said with a nervous laugh. Everything that they had planned to reopen after liberation – schools, the city university, local businesses – are closed. We found one cafe that had stayed open, its windows boarded up, shrapnel holes in its door. It was destroyed by an artillery shell a few weeks after our visit.

There is still a hint of civilian life left in the city, which has a fragile ecosystem all of its own. There is one major grocery store, its entrances hidden, which the remaining civilians visit in the morning. An open-air market still appears on Saturday mornings, but the more the leaves fall from the trees, the more it is abandoned as there is no longer any cover.

The few civilians I met there were downcast, most of them dreaming of better times. Liubov, a 71-year-old who we met tending to her watermelon garden, refused to leave her home even when it was almost entirely submerged by the flood. She slept on her roof for weeks instead. She yearned to reconnect with her family, who thought Kherson far too dangerous to live in. 'I hope the war ends as soon as possible, so I can repair my beloved home and reconnect with my grandchildren. They live far away from me. I want us to be together here – that's all I want, for everything to be good again,' she said. 'My husband is dead, and I am all alone here. My children are growing up without me, and I'm getting old without them.'

We did meet one old man of seventy-six, Alexei, who still talked about how he believed Ukrainians and Russians were one people, 'like siblings'. He spoke with pride about his thirty-year service in the Soviet Navy and expressed deep regret at the end of the connections between the two countries. I noticed this sometimes happened with military veterans in Ukraine; they pined for a lost time when their rank and years of service earned a respect that the new society only granted to the soldiers who were fighting the Russians now.

My colleague Caolan Robertson, who visited the town to film the documentary *Hunted in Kherson*, pointed out that 'everywhere else in the world, people look down at their phones. Here, everyone looks up, to check for drones.' He noticed that 'in London, we wait for the wind to stop and the rain to stop before we leave the house. In Kherson, they wait for the wind and rain to start, because the drones can't fly.' Interspersed with his interviews with civilians, he used drone footage published by the Russians themselves in his documentary.

Caolan's videos did prove one thing beyond doubt: this was a deliberate targeting of civilians. In Bucha, the Russians had shot civilians deliberately, that was clear. But as the pace of manoeuvre slowed, and they approached cities closer to the front line, they usually used artillery or airstrikes. These were clearly indiscriminate but often unguided weapons, and the Russians would always claim that they were hitting military targets. Sometimes, as in the strike on the Kramatorsk pizzeria, it was clear there were at least soldiers there, if not in numbers that would make it proportionate to aim a missile into it. In others, such as the strike on the shopping centre in Kirovohrad, there was no conceivable military utility. Still, getting to the level of proof needed in a war crimes tribunal was difficult.

But in the drone videos the Russians released, the operators can clearly see the characteristics of anything they were aiming at. Children in a playground park, civilians buying bread at a market or firefighters extinguishing the blaze from a previous strike. The Ukrainians had various methods to fight them – drones are too small and cheap to use traditional expensive air defence missiles on. I met 'Mushroom' again with a group of soldiers who drive around in jeeps with heavy machine guns strapped to the back. We meet under the ramparts of a residential house, out of sight of any drones. One of them shows me a bulky contraption that looks like a cross between an old wind-up camera and a blaster from *Star Wars*. It is an idea taken by the soldiers straight from science fiction, designed to shoot a radio wave beam to burn the circuits within a drone and cause it to crash down to earth before it hits its target. Often, they use small arms fire. 'Kalashnikovs are common, but a shotgun is best, as the scattering of the pellets means a higher chance to hit such a small target,' one of Mushroom's team explained to us.

They use electronic warfare systems where available, but these are expensive and unreliable – the Russians can shift the intercepted frequencies almost at will. Svitlana Horieva, one of the few Ukrainian journalists who still lives in the city, remains determined but fatalistic. She will stay in the city, until the very end: 'It is unbelievably scary, but you understand that staying in the city is your choice. Whatever happens, you are equal among your people, you have rights, you are in your own country. And you are free.'

AFTERWORD: REBIRTH
POSAD-POKROVSKE, KHERSON OBLAST, AUGUST 2024

The symbol of hope in Kherson was the simple little plastic wrapping. Coloured red and white, it would be wrapped in a neat bow on the letterbox or doorframe of the entrance to a yard. It was a sign left by DSNS, Ukraine's de-mining team, showing that the plot of land was cleared of unexploded ordnance and was considered safe to live in again. In November, I had never seen a town as minutely destroyed as Posad-Pokrovske. Lying on the administrative border between Mykolaiv and Kherson Oblasts, it was on the front line between Russian and Ukrainian troops for nearly six months. In that time, it had seen all the horrors of modern warfare. Tanks had rolled through it and traded fire, airstrikes had levelled houses that soldiers had used for cover and artillery had pounded each dwelling into rubble.

Yet here, outside the range of artillery and drones, life was slowly returning. About a hundred of the town's inhabitants had returned, they said. Builders were putting up telephone poles and wires; a couple of men were on top of their houses hammering corrugated iron roofs into place. 'Don't worry, it's clean here!' said Sergey Tabachkovskiy, a twenty-year-old who had recently returned to his town. He beckoned us inside his backyard to meet his family. We saw a group of teenage boys and girls walking down the street, laughing and stopping to take photos with us, shopping bags in tow.

Somehow, this destroyed town, just a few miles drive from the chaos of Kherson's flooding and shelling, was coming back to life. To be sure, this was barely a village, and there were scores of equally destroyed settlements that lay abandoned across Ukraine. No rational observer could believe that a place like this could be restored. But the resilience of the residents here, determined to thwart their grim destiny, was a ray of hope that Ukraine could be rebuilt and restored by its people, once it was given the time and peace to do so. On the paved street leading out of one of the villages was a hole made by a shrapnel burst, notable for the fragmentary marks that spread out in rings from the place of impact. Inside the mark left by the shell was growing a small tuft of greenery and the buds of a flower about to bloom.

CHAPTER SIX

FORTRESS OF REGRETS: THE MERCILESS MEAT GRINDER OF BAKHMUT

> 'What passing-bells for these who die as cattle?
> Only the monstrous anger of the guns
> ...
> No mockeries now for them; no prayers nor bells;
> Nor any voice of mourning save the choirs,
> The shrill, demented choirs of wailing shells.'
> – Wilfred Owen, 'Anthem for Doomed Youth'

FOXTROT UNIFORM

BAKHMUT REGION, DONETSK OBLAST, APRIL 2023

When I met Kateryna Petrenko in February 2022, she was wearing a patterned dress and heels, sipping from a tall glass of red wine, listlessly tapping at the laptop she'd perched on the table of a chic Kyiv cafe. When I saw her next, more than a year later, she'd traded the dress for combat fatigues and a ballistic helmet. Barely five-foot tall, sporting jet-black hair and a nose ring, her round face and dark eyes somehow filled out the headgear that could appear ungainly on men nearly twice her size. Strapped to her armour was a lookalike black-haired doll and two magazines of rifle ammunition. I clambered into the back of her armoured car as a cacophony of shellfire erupted in the distance and she turned, looked me in the eye and said, 'Tom, now we drive to Bakhmut.' Fifteen minutes later, we pulled up to a hedgerow where a platoon of Ukrainian soldiers had been holding the line against a Russian assault. But their luck was running out. Kateryna had been a writer in her previous life. Now, she'd joined the Ukrainian Army as a chaplain and press liaison and was here to help us tell the soldiers' stories.

Instead of a gourmet brew prepared in an Italian espresso machine, the coffee here was a bitter black sludge cooked in a rusty metal pot over an open-fire stove. The tree canopy around us was supposed to hide us from the enemy, but the foliage was thinning, the leaves and branches of the trees sheared by regular shellfire. The view from a spy drone bought off Amazon showed the fields around us pockmarked with craters. A viral photo taken from near here a few months previously showed soldiers caked in mud with destroyed trees around them and drew comparisons to the dugouts of Verdun or Passchendaele more than a century ago.

The Donbas could be beautiful at this time of year, with its gently undulating hills and patches of wild tulips and rose bushes that bloomed among the fields. The vast rows of yellow sunflowers and the backdrop of a clear blue sky were the inspiration for the two colours of Ukraine's flag. But any moment you took to admire the serenity of the landscape would soon be rudely interrupted by the sounds of a shell or a line of smoke rising from an artillery shell impact. Behind Kateryna, a Ukrainian artillery officer barked commands with theatrical vigour. When visiting journalists arrived, the soldiers liked to put on a show for the cameras, and Kateryna's visits provided a moment of colour in the monotony of their routines.

'Ready! Fire! Glory to Ukraine!' the officer shouted, swinging a large stick that looked like a baseball bat, as the cannon beside him burst into life. For a split second, a flash of flame engulfed our view, the gun's kickback blew dirt and leaves into our faces and a shell hurtled towards Russian trenches a few miles to our east. 'Hellish battles are going on, but we are fighting for every metre,' said Misha, the 32-year-old squad commander, as we huddled in a dugout command post. 'Of course, Russian guns can reach us here easily, but we are never scared when we are on our own land.' That bravado, tinged with fatalism, was common to troops up and down Ukraine's 1,200-kilometre front line.

Despite everyone having their own stories of sacrifice and heroism, Ukraine's soldiers began to blend in the mind after a time. Their bloodshot eyes, prematurely lined with permanent bags that had inked themselves into the skin like tattoos; their wrinkled, calloused hands thick with grime and gunpowder. Of Kateryna's civilian outfit, only her blood-red nails, which she had somehow kept perfectly manicured in the mud of the trenches, remained the same.

She said the war had turned her into 'a completely different woman'. Her wistful expression in the cafe had suggested more joy from the half-finished wine bottle next to her than the drudgery of her writing. But here on the front lines, she seemed fired up and full of vigour, confidently directing men twice her size. Like so many Ukrainians, she found that the struggle against Russia gave her a vital sense of purpose, despite the horrors. Shortly after the invasion, she'd written a report from Irpin, then recently freed from its weeks of Russian occupation, and what she'd seen haunted her. 'I began to cover the events of the war more, write about the crimes of the Russians: murder, torture, rape,' she said to an army interviewer. After that, Kateryna's old life was over. 'I could no longer walk in dresses, go to the cinema, wear heels... I had no energy to do anything in the capital,' she said.

By July, the Russians had captured Severodonetsk and Lysychansk at a huge cost in blood and treasure. In doing so, they had completed what they called the 'liberation' of Luhansk Oblast, while razing those cities to the ground. Now, they had to focus on neighbouring Donetsk Oblast, where the Ukrainians had been building strong defences ever since 2014. The Ukrainian lines here had mostly held since the start of the full-scale invasion and Bakhmut was the closest major city to where the fighting had come to a stalemate in the first war. Russian proxies had tried and failed to take the city in 2014. Now, they were back to finish the job. Bakhmut held no special strategic or even symbolic significance.

Journalist Chris Miller, who lived in the city from 2010 to 2012 as part of the US Peace Corps programme, described it as a beautiful town full of 80,000 or so rough but friendly people. 'The city was archetypically post-Soviet, with a handful of beautifully intricate buildings still standing from the pre-revolution period surrounded by prefab concrete apartment blocks,' he wrote in his book *The War Came to Us*. Much of its charm came from a patchwork of Soviet-era memorials that dotted the city:

> There was the decommissioned fighter plane, the battle tank atop its plinth and the sculpture of the soldier picking up a wounded comrade, monuments to the Great Patriotic War, as Soviets called the Second World War. Statues of Lenin and Artyom were used as meeting locations. 'See you at Artyom at 10 o'clock,' we'd say. Or: 'Under Lenin at seven.' The fighter plane would later become one of the most fiercely fought over monuments in all of Ukraine.

The residents spoke mostly Russian, with a thick lashing of Ukrainian words on top, a practice known as Surzhyk. They were disillusioned with politicians in Kyiv, but most had no desire to split from Ukraine. Parts of the city were captured by separatists in 2014, but they were chased out by forces loyal to Ukraine within a few weeks.

The city would come to take on a huge importance, and not only because it would turn out to be the longest and bloodiest battle of the war to date. It was also a hinge moment, where what was best for Ukraine politically and militarily would diverge, and many of Russia's advantages would become evident. It was where the morale and bravery of Ukraine's soldiers, formerly a huge advantage over their Russian counterparts, would no longer be enough to help them. Instead, Bakhmut would complete the transition to a withering war of attrition by artillery and drones. Here, Ukraine would sacrifice many of its best soldiers, while Russia disposed of the dregs of its jails.

Kateryna and her comrades belonged to an artillery unit in the 80th Air Assault Brigade, which had been fighting without rest for more than a year. Early in the war, they had performed miracles, embarrassing the Russian Army on several occasions. They had helped defend southern Ukraine in a crucial battle at the town of Voznesensk, which stopped the Russians from advancing on Odesa. Then, they had helped rout a foolhardy Russian battalion tactical group near the town of Bilohorivka further north of here, which had attempted to ford a waterway and catch the Ukrainians by surprise. The artillerymen had spotted them as they crossed and pounded them with shells. They left the Siverskyi Donets River running red with the blood and corpses of nearly 500 Russian troops.

The artillery gun Kateryna was showing us was a Soviet-era D-30 howitzer – a model from the 1960s. It was a dependable workhorse, something like the AK47 of artillery pieces.

Ukraine was preparing for a major counteroffensive and was training new brigades with fresh soldiers to participate in this. The country was hoarding its advanced western-supplied tanks and long-range rocket launchers for this upcoming strike. Brigades like the 80th were battling it out with antique Soviet-era kit, hand-me-downs from the days when Russians and Ukrainians had expected to fight on the same side. This meant that the soldiers remaining to defend Bakhmut were the most experienced and hardened fighters of the Ukrainian Army. In addition to the 80th Air Assault, the 93rd Kholodnyi Yar Mechanized Brigade and the 4th Tank Brigade, some of Ukraine's most bloodied units, were all in this battle. Between them, they had defeated regular Russian troops all over the country. But in Bakhmut, they faced a more dangerous enemy, notorious for its ruthlessness and for how cheaply it valued life.

ALL THE KREMLIN'S MEN

Few slogans are as honest or succinct as: 'Our business is death, and business is good' – the tagline of the Wagner Private Military Company. Few unit symbols are as gruesome or iconic as the sledgehammer the Wagner mercenaries used to beat a deserter to death. For the war that was born of the dreams and fantasies of President Putin, it was ironic that its biggest battle would be fought mostly by an armed force not under Moscow's official control.

Regular Russian units had taken such a battering in the war's first months that the task of capturing Bakhmut had fallen to the Wagner Private Military Company, led by a man equal parts cruel and charismatic. Yevgeny Prigozhin commanded a grudging respect even in Ukraine. Putin, and his succession of hapless military commanders, such as Valery Gerasimov and Sergei Shoigu, were figures of ridicule for having bungled the invasion so badly. But Prigozhin, an ugly, bald stump of a man who had served a long stint in prison and slaved away as a hot dog salesman before becoming Putin's chef, was a self-made man and an effective warrior. Like Zelensky, he earned the esteem of his men by frequently appearing next to them near the front lines. In the court of Putin, he was Thomas Cromwell, the low-born fixer who climbed from obscurity to wield vast and unaccountable power as the king's right-hand man.

Prigozhin spoke with candour about battlefield conditions and clashed frequently with Russian high command, a rare privilege in such an autocratic country. His forces recruited their shock troops mainly from prisons, promising them clemency if they survived six months of brutal combat. Wagner commanders would send the troops as part of what they called 'meat storms' to probe and test Ukrainian defences, before Wagner's elite units would attempt to storm and capture those positions. It was the beginning of a change towards tactics that used Russia's structural advantages, particularly its much larger population, to great effect on the battlefield.

One Ukrainian officer described a 'meat storm' to the *New Yorker*: 'Part of the group is destroyed, others are wounded, and, instead of evacuating, the rest continue with the storm – this is completely unreasonable.' The threat of being shot from behind by blocking units meant that, 'if they move forward, they at least have the chance to live another day', the officer said. 'If they go back, they're dead for sure.' It was 'not so much a lack of fear but, rather, the total devaluation of life'.

Some analysts believe the Wagner Group's fearsome reputation is not entirely deserved. Michael Kofman says:

The Wagner Group was not especially effective, despite being mythologised as such. Its main advantages were that the Russian airborne covered its flanks to prevent counterattacks, that it was granted access to convicts from the Russian prison system to use as expendable assault infantry and, most importantly, that Russian forces enjoyed a fires advantage of 5:1 for much of the battle.

WAITING AND WATCHING

'Do you want your children to live or die?' Bryce Wilson had taken to yelling in exasperation at terrified families huddling in basements or stairwells. These harsh tactics looked callous when directed at a traumatised population. But these methods saved lives, as I witnessed when we were in the town of Soledar. With a prewar population of 10,000 people, this salt-mining settlement just north of Bakhmut lay near a key supply route. It was August 2022, shortly after the battle for these settlements had started in earnest. The Russians were trying to dislodge the Ukrainians from their weaker defences here, to go around Bakhmut from the north and trap its garrison inside the city. As ever, they were raining terror down on the local population. But many of the civilians remaining did not want to leave, no matter how dangerous their conditions became. Here, I saw a window into a totally different side of Ukrainian society than that represented by attractive, social media savvy young people waving European flags on the Maidan. Instead, these were the run-down industrial towns that survived on digging for coal and iron, where late Soviet-era rock music played on the radio, whose parks were littered with statues of Russian writers and monuments to the Red Army. The townsfolk were often more nostalgic for Ukraine's past than they were optimistic about its future.

Bryce was a tall stocky Australian, with strong square features, short cropped hair and piercing light blue eyes. He'd lived in Ukraine on and off since 2015, first dabbling in journalism and now running evacuations. Soon after I accompanied him on this mission, he would join the Ukrainian Army. He adored his adopted country and talked of buying a farm in Donbas to retire. A despairing girlfriend back in Melbourne had recently demanded that he choose between her and Ukraine. He chose Ukraine.

In the centre of Soledar, we saw Sasha and his mother Elena swilling from a bottle of vodka in the late afternoon while battle raged around them. Sasha was shirtless, showing off his significant bulk as the flab of his stomach flopped over his shorts. The 24-year-old's arm was in a sling, and he was wearing a makeshift eyepatch of dirty cotton wool crudely stuck on with Sellotape. Despite his drunkenness, he was friendly enough, and he spoke clumsy but understandable English, picked up from his teenage years playing video games like *Call of Duty* and *Counter-Strike* with young Americans online. He didn't know it, but he was dying. One of our team members, a former British Army combat medic named Darren, examined his injuries and turned to us, saying, 'If he doesn't get to a hospital within forty-eight hours, he's going to die. The wounds have gone septic, and he will probably lose the arm and the eye.' We convinced him to come with us only by promising that we would drive him back to Soledar, despite the danger, as soon as his wounds had been treated. When the doctors in nearby Kramatorsk immediately bundled him into an ambulance to send him to a bigger hospital for treatment, he cursed Bryce, saying he had kidnapped him and broken his promises.

Was it worth it, I asked Bryce, risking yourself for people who still held you in so much contempt? 'It's always worth saving someone's life,' he said.

But sometimes people won't leave without certain things they're attached to. One old man wouldn't leave without his fishing rods. Another bloke made us turn back because we'd left his cooking equipment behind. The Russians shelled within a few dozen metres of us on the way. The closest I came to dying was for some idiot's fucking George Foreman grill!

By this stage of a battle, large global NGOs would go nowhere near frontline towns, saying they were simply too dangerous. The Ukrainian Army and local police forces would occasionally help with evacuations, but their focus was the war effort, not reluctant stragglers. Instead, the job of evacuating remaining civilians and delivering supplies to those who stayed was taken up by a variety of Ukrainian and foreign volunteers. Braving the shellfire to drive back and forth from frontline towns was the easy part. The hard part was convincing people to leave. There was a great deal of mutual mistrust between those who stayed and the soldiers, journalists and volunteers on their missions.

The soldiers knew that their enemy was not just in front of them, however. There were also plenty who remained far behind the trenches. They are not just in danger from enemy soldiers – they also face an enemy within. Once, when we sat down for a meal in a civilian home in the city of Kostyantynivka, Matthew, a medic with the Third Assault Brigade, confided that many of the locals in the area still see the Ukrainians as the enemy. 'These women are some of the only civilians we trust here. Too many of the people still here are waiting for the Russians. I can't understand this mindset.' The Russians offer the locals as little as $100 for information on both potential civilian targets and Ukrainian military positions. Matthew recalls once opening his window at a base and seeing a civilian filming the soldiers on his phone from outside. He tells me: 'I nearly shot him in the face right there.'

People had various motivations for staying. Often, they were pensioners with nowhere to go and deeply attached to the houses they had usually lived in their whole lives. They would sometimes extend that suicidal stubbornness to their whole families, many of whom would be kept in danger by a single member, who refused to leave. A lot were what the soldiers contemptuously called '*zhduniv*', after the Russian word for 'waiting'. The Donbas had always had the most Russian-friendly sentiment of any of Ukraine's eastern regions and many of the locals genuinely believed their lives would be better under Moscow's rule.

Bryce was particularly enraged by the plight of the youngest here, often kept in extraordinary danger by their families who refused to let them leave. 'I can understand if someone doesn't want to leave. But keeping your children here is murder,' he told me.

One of the people straddling the two Ukraines I came to know was Anna Demidova. The 28-year-old was living in Berlin and working as a make-up artist for film and theatre productions. But her family was from Kostyantynivka, a city of around 60,000 in the heart of Donetsk Oblast, a short drive from Bakhmut and a staging area for Ukraine's military. Interspersed with film premieres were desperate phone calls to her family as she tried many times to convince them to move to safety. They rebuffed her for months, until finally agreeing to move after the situation became dire. She still tried to understand the way of thinking among many older people here. 'After the end of the Soviet Union, our cities in this region were neglected and people felt abandoned,' she said. 'So, they were susceptible to propaganda.' Russian TV channels and radio stations were officially banned but easy to tune into. The economy declined steadily after Ukrainian independence in 1991, and many of those born in the Soviet era became wistful for those days. 'I would always hear the older generation saying how things were better in Soviet times – that life was stable, people had better values and that we got everything for free.' When the first war broke out in 2014, there was a receptive audience for Kremlin narratives.

These could take on truly dark and twisted dimensions. When we had taken one woman and her daughter to an evacuation hub in a small church in Kramatorsk, she burst into tears. She explained she had been shocked to see warm food, sleeping bags, priests and humanitarian volunteers asking about their needs. There were people in the basement communities she lived in saying that the rescuers were going to steal their children, sell them into global slave rings.

'These narratives seem so ridiculous to outsiders, but people here take them deadly seriously. The choice to come with us is literally life or death,' Bryce reflected.

'You're like an acorn, green and strong,' one of Kateryna's military instructors told her when she first reported for duty. 'But this war is going to fuck you up.' She had tired of her job in Kyiv and began taking courses on everything from battlefield medicine to explosives disposal. By October 2022, Kateryna had a choice to make. She had started the process to enlist in the army, but she also had tickets to France, a chance to leave the destruction behind her. The train west would take her to the galleries and boulevards of Paris or the promenades of the Riviera; the train east would take her to the blood and tears of the trenches of Donbas and Kharkiv. She went east.

Her best friend was killed the day she deployed, which she took as a sign that her rightful place was with the soldiers. She absorbed a fatalism that day that never left her. After arriving in Kharkiv, she was given a position with the 80th Air Assault Brigade. As women were not usually assigned to combat roles, she was designated as a military chaplain, as well as a press liaison. The 80th had just played a major role in pushing the Russians out of the city of Kupyansk, but rather than savouring their victory, they were immediately dispatched to reinforce Ukraine's crumbling defences in Bakhmut. She would arrive with the men around her in a city that was wrecked beyond repair. The streets were all dotted with the signs of war – sandbags, tank traps and shrapnel debris. At any time, three or four towers of smoke would be rising from fires caused by shelling. The crack and rumble of artillery could be heard all around, day and night.

In January 2023, the battle reached its climax. In the middle of a central street, an old lady's body lay prone, kept from decaying by the winter frost. The body was wearing a thick coat and grey skirt, and a curved walking stick lay next to her. The buildings on all sides were destroyed, with rubble and broken glass carpeting the streets. Inside one derelict hotel, the windows and doors were all blown out, but a disco ball hung from the ceiling, a reminder of happier times. Most of the few hundred souls who remained lived their lives in basement shelters.

Not everyone who stayed in Bakhmut did so out of stubbornness or pro-Russian beliefs.

Some did so out of a sense of public duty. One of the few civilian institutions that was still working was the fire department, although with only three of its original fifteen employees still there. I asked one of them, Nikita, why he hadn't left Bakhmut, and he shrugged and said, 'Then who else is going to do this job?'

'As long as we have even ten people remaining here, their lives matter,' said Sergey Chaus, the acting mayor of nearby Chasiv Yar.

I was constantly taken aback by the care I saw Ukrainians and volunteers give the most vulnerable here, bringing food and medicine under mortal danger. Some rescuers paid the ultimate price for this care. After the deaths of two volunteers, Chris Parry and Andrew Bagshaw, in the town of Soledar, I wrote a piece for the *London Evening Standard* that raised my concern, based on my time in Donbas, that many volunteers were going to the most dangerous places in the world with little training or language skills and taking on extremely risky tasks, sometimes solo. I knew some people were giving these two the riskiest missions in places where even the Ukrainian Army feared to enter, knowing that they would take on almost any level of danger.

My article, written in the fog of war that followed their disappearance, was controversial among the community of journalists and volunteers in Ukraine. In his biography of Bagshaw, with which I was not involved, New Zealand writer Philip Matthews strongly criticised my decision to write about them. Across four pages, he critiqued the 'tone and timing' of my piece and quoted friends of the pair who were 'furious' at my decision to raise these issues at such a sensitive time. Our views on the situation differ substantially.

Yet his wider points – that I had got the tone and the timing of this article wrong – were reasonable. I did wade into this debate before the dust had settled, the facts of their death came to light and loved ones had had time to grieve, and I should have given more space to the moral calculus. After a year of reporting on some of the war's most difficult topics, the deaths of so many people begin to blend into one. It wasn't until my friend Arman was killed on his mission in Chasiv Yar that I understood the pain of a single death in the war, a young life, the most promising of all our colleagues, snuffed out by a split-second decision, by rolling the dice once too many times.

More to the point, I feel that the real story that neither I nor others truly explored was the fact that major international aid organisations have shirked their duty, despite being the recipient of billions of dollars' worth of aid in donations and government funding. I barely ever saw any of the well-known names near the front lines, whether distributing aid or helping evacuate or support the vulnerable and wounded. This was left to volunteers of varying capacities but all operating on a shoestring budget. Much was spent on comfortable offices and flash four-wheel drives for well-resourced and remunerated staff who often did not travel far from the relative safety of Kyiv. Matthews declined to comment for this book, other than to acknowledge some factual errors in his account, which he described as 'extremely minor'.

War can be an extremely cruel force, and many will die despite taking all reasonable precautions. Had I reflected more deeply on the situation, I would have written a more sensitive article, in tune with the pain and loss, that gave greater emphasis to the complexity of Parry and Bagshaw's situation and included examples of the many lives they had saved. Yet I would not have changed my essential conclusions about their situation.

SALT IN THE WOUND

It was a cold day in early March, and a shivering middle-aged soldier with a walking stick limped past a coffin, his arm supported by a young companion. Next in line was a young blonde-haired girl wearing military camouflage with tears streaming down her face. A black flag with a white Ukrainian trident embossed on it lay over the young man's corpse, his hair and beard neatly trimmed. The bottom half of the coffin, where his body lay disfigured, was obscured with bouquets of red, white and orange flowers. The crowd, which covered half of Maidan Square in Kyiv, had come to mourn Dmytro Kotsiubailo, callsign 'Da Vinci', killed in action at Bakhmut. He was twenty-seven years old.

The crowd repeated a chant, bitterness and anger dripping from every voice. 'Glory to Ukraine. Death to the enemy, death, death, death… Glory to the hero of Ukraine.' He had founded the 'Da Vinci Wolves', one of Ukraine's most fearsome battalions, and was awarded the 'Hero of Ukraine', the country's highest military honour for his exploits in the first Donbas war. Every so often, the death of one of these young men or women would capture the nation's grief at the loss of so many of their most promising youth. 'We see our friend groups more regularly at funerals than at weddings,' one young Kyiv resident said. These public outpourings of grief served to jolt the residents of the capital out of their complacency if they dared to ignore the war that raged out of their sight.

Even by the standards of Ukraine, the beginning of 2023 was a time of appalling bloodshed. According to leaked documents from Wagner, that January saw the most soldiers killed in action in total between both sides of any month in the war. The director of a Ukrainian field hospital near Soledar said that they were overwhelmed with dead and wounded during this period, treating up to 200 patients per day, a colossal number. Maimed men would constantly be rushed in on stretchers, having been shot full of morphine, before the medical staff would strip off their clothes and try to sterilise and clean the wounds and staunch the bleeding. But overwhelmed by casualties, the best they could do for many was to ease their passing. Finally, Ukrainian defences cracked in Soledar, and Wagner forces poured into the city. They gradually gained ground to the south of Bakhmut as well, until they had the city surrounded from three sides.

The Ukrainian high command and political leadership then had a difficult decision thrust on them. General Zaluzhnyi, the head of the armed forces, wanted to withdraw from Bakhmut. He had sound military reasons for wanting to do so. Rob Lee, a respected scholar who had predicted the invasion, shared his own fears. 'I just got back from Bakhmut,' he told me that February. 'Bakhmut is no longer a good place to wear down the Russians. It is an exceedingly difficult place to defend... It lies in a punchbowl, with high ground all around it.' While Ukrainians controlled the flanks around Bakhmut, they had the advantage over the Russians. But now the Russians held the high ground and could pound the hapless defenders below them with artillery.

Before January, the Ukrainians could have been killing as many as five to seven Russians for every loss of their own. Now, the 'attrition ratio', as military strategists refer to it, was as bad as one dead Russian for every dead Ukrainian. Ukraine, Lee said, would be better advised to make an orderly withdrawal from the city to the higher ground behind it, where they had a well-prepared defensive line and better terrain. The battered Russians would be in no shape to give chase. Few Ukrainians, especially in the military, were airing their doubts publicly, but everyone reporting from the scene returned with the same scepticism.

But Zelensky was unwilling to have Ukraine give the Russians anything they could claim as a victory. He was caught in a bind partially of his own making. He had staked personal credibility on the city holding. After visiting the troops in Bakhmut, he carried a Ukrainian flag signed by the defenders to the floor of the US

Congress, where he received a standing ovation after he called the battle 'Ukraine's Saratoga', the decisive battle of the American War of Independence.

The President was a perceptive reader of public moods, especially those in foreign capitals. He knew that he was selling a vision of Ukraine as the plucky underdog hero that had the momentum over the aggressor. As an actor, he was aware of just how fickle a crowd could be, particularly a crowd like this, which he relied on for tens of billions in military hardware. He did not want to risk Ukraine's international perception as the winning side. He chose Bakhmut as the literal hill, or in this case valley, to die on, and his decision would come at a huge cost. Thousands of young Ukrainians would die in the battles to follow, often as quickly as they arrived in the city.

Yet in one way, he was right to worry about perception; the same fickle crowd of congressmen who deified him on this visit would block aid to Ukraine just a year later once Ukraine's winning streak came to an end. Putin, who had the luxury of ruling a dictatorship in a country that produced most of the weapons it needed, could afford to play the long game in Ukraine without worrying nearly as much about public opinion or international support. The fact that his supporters were other autocracies, particularly Iran and North Korea, only reinforced this.

Still, stories of Bakhmut's notorious 'meat grinder' began to eat away at morale in Kyiv, particularly among the young men Ukraine needed to convince to join the fight. A soldier who returned from Bakhmut to Kyiv showed a carousel of photos of the men he'd trained with and just pointed, saying, 'This guy's dead, this guy's dead, this guy's in a wheelchair.' He'd been disillusioned about the war effort and said he'd warn anyone thinking of signing up not to do so. 'They'll be wasting their lives. In Bakhmut, the life expectancy is a few days.' It heralded the start of a recruitment crisis that would severely affect Ukraine's combat power in the year to come.

It was little comfort that the Russians were also taking huge losses. A leaked internal report from Wagner showed that they recruited nearly 50,000 prisoners, around 17,000 of whom were killed storming the trenches in Bakhmut. Thousands more Wagner mercenaries, as well as Russian regular troops, were churned up by the meat grinder.

For Ukraine, there was another terrifying factor to the calculus. Wagner and the other Russian forces arrayed alongside it may be taking terrible losses, but many of them were the dregs of Russia's jails. Prigozhin had specifically targeted maximum security prisons housing Russia's most violent and anti-social prisoners with promises of absolution. The Ukrainian forces that were bleeding out in the fields and on the streets in exchange were the country's most talented and patriotic, its future leaders and innovators.

One Russian Telegram channel covering the war reported at the time of their shock at the human quality of the Ukrainian troops they were killing: 'Among those liquidated: a librarian … a sound engineer, head of [a regional branch] of the European Solidarity Party, an economics professor, a choir soloist, a producer, a history teacher.' I was reminded of the National Guard unit I had met on the front lines near Izium, which contained a similar collection of talent. There were two lawyers studying for their PhDs, a member of the President's personal security unit and a philosophy professor who now serves in Zelensky's Cabinet. Possibly most crucially, these were often Ukraine's most motivated and experienced troops. The troops the Russians lost were, by contrast, a gallery of its most vile criminals.

Men like serial killer 'Denis', notorious for chopping extremities off his victims, or 'Roman', who murdered his mother and sister, only to be buried in an 'Alley of Heroes' back in Moscow. If they survived, some men like drug runner 'Igor' would return to Russia to stab six of his townspeople to death. The death of these men was, if anything, a positive for Russian society. Not everyone agrees that this trade-off wasn't worth it. Vadim Adamov, a tall, blond-haired Ukrainian drone pilot with Ukraine's 93rd Kholodnyi Yar Brigade, said, 'We killed them over and over again. It must have been at least five or six to one. It was worth it in the end.'

To help prove his point, he sent me a documentary he had helped film for German TV channel WELT, despite being an active soldier. His film followed him and two of his comrades, Mykhailo Alekseenko and Yuriy Samanyuk, as they set up positions to scout with Mavic drones to direct artillery fire and drop homemade bombs on the Russians. The men were shown smiling, smacking each other, cracking jokes as they snuck into abandoned houses to set up temporary bases. By the end of the Battle of Bakhmut, both Mykhailo and Yuriy would be dead. I remained sceptical of the defence of the city to the end. Prigozhin had been candid about his war aim, which was the destruction of as much of Ukraine's army as possible. Bakhmut was simply the battleground to do it.

THE BUTCHER'S BILL

Before they fired the next round, the gunners of the 80th Air Assault Brigade showed me the name and message they had written on the shell casing in black ink: 'For Chuba Sasha, we won't forgive, 12 April 2022'. Winter bled into spring, and the men and women in Bakhmut bled with the seasons. On every street, in every burned-out and bombed apartment building, in every ripped-up treeline and churned field, both sides paid their appalling butcher's bill. Yet the onslaught, of expendable convicts who fought with firing squads at their backs, proved too much for Ukrainian defences in one village and city block after another. Wagner forces were gradually pushing them back until, by the time I visited Kateryna's unit, they were desperately holding on to their last positions and supply routes.

'The strategic goal of the 80th is to make it impossible for the Russians to surround Bakhmut or cut it off,' Kateryna said. By then, the lifeline to Bakhmut they were guarding was nothing more than a series of muddy dirt tracks, hidden from Russian sight yet perilously within artillery range, turning every resupply effort or medical evacuation into a deadly gamble. The Russians controlled nearly 80 per cent of the now ruined city, and the Ukrainian strategy was getting harder to understand. Kateryna found it hard to accept so many needless deaths: 'For now, I cannot accept the fact that they died. I still feel their spirit and strength.' It was in Bakhmut that I suffered my own greatest personal loss of the war. On 9 May, my friend Arman Soldin, a journalist with Agence France-Presse, was killed by Russian artillery fire. He was born and died in war. His family fled Bosnia for France in 1992, and he'd lived in London before coming to Ukraine shortly after I arrived.

His eulogies were a torrent of praise, for his character, his humour, his smile. His charm and striking good looks left behind more than a few broken hearts. Fluent in five languages, an accomplished writer and videographer, he had an extraordinary talent for humanising the stories of people affected by the war. Shortly before his death, he became locally famous for a short video where he rescued a wounded hedgehog he found in a trench and nursed it back to health. Arman was almost constantly at the front line and in one of the last videos I made of him, he spoke with wide-eyed wonder about the jets and helicopters flying overhead and firing at the Russians.

Wagner would capture the last street of Bakhmut in late May. Observers were and remain split on its significance. On the one hand, it ended up being the sole significant gain of an entire Russian winter offensive. Moscow's forces had tried to capture towns like Kupyansk, Avdiivka and Vuhledar with no success and huge losses. In Vuhledar in particular, the Russians had been routed so badly as to cause a rare public scandal about the waste of troops inside Russia itself. Ukrainian casualties rose as Ukrainian forces were outgunned and ran low on ammunition. At this stage, western assistance became crucial. Various types of tube artillery and long-range precision-strike systems entered the war. Buoyed by mobilisation, the Russian military launched its own winter offensive in late January by way of a series of localised attacks across a broad front.

The Institute for the Study of War, a well-known think tank which tended to put a gloss favourable to Kyiv on its reports, described it as a strategic victory for Ukraine. It said:

> The Ukrainian defense of Bakhmut was a strategically sound decision as Ukrainians would benefit from exhausting Wagner forces ... The Russian military command continued to pursue a relentless assault on Bakhmut after the city lost its original operational significance and failed to adjust its military objectives appropriately ... Ukraine thus now has the initiative [and was now poised to begin its long-awaited counteroffensive].

Yet the Ukrainian assault would fail, and it seems the protracted defence of Bakhmut was a contributing factor. Some analysts, like Lee, have suggested that Ukraine could have retreated safely, rotated its best units and prepared them for the counteroffensive. This could have given the offensive a much better chance of success. Even worse, the waste of life in Bakhmut damaged the reputation of the Ukrainian Army in the country itself. The commander in charge of the defence of the city, General Oleksandr Syrskyi, is still known as the 'butcher of Bakhmut'. He now commands the entire Ukrainian armed forces, and many soldiers are yet to forgive him.

By contrast, Russian commander Sergei Surovikin's decision to withdraw from Kherson with his forces intact looks wise in retrospect. It was a temporary humiliation. But it allowed the Russians to shore up their defences and wait for their losses to be replenished through Putin's mobilisation order in Russia. Prigozhin would become disillusioned with the war. Barely a month later, he would shock the world by denouncing the Kremlin's motives for invading Ukraine. It was not about the protection of Donbas, he said, instead about the lust for power and greed of politicians in Moscow. He would then lead Wagner troops on a mutiny he called the 'March of Justice', where they captured several major Russian cities, and he could easily have taken his men to the gates of Moscow. He inexplicably called it off at the last minute, and his fate after that was obvious. Cromwell met his death by the headsman's axe. Prigozhin suffered a much more modern form of execution. His plane exploded in the sky.

Zelensky called Bakhmut the 'fortress of our morale', but for every side of the battle, it became a melancholy, haunted place, a fortress of regrets and bitter endings.

As I left Bakhmut's trenches, I reflected how the war had turned Kateryna from the shy, sullen-looking young woman from the cafe in Kyiv into the confident warrior in front of me. Occasionally, she still posts an Instagram story from a fashion shoot a few years ago, interspersed with selfies from the battlefield, fundraisers for military gear or obituaries of fallen comrades. She became my mental image of how the war had refashioned Ukraine's young people. But the tragedy of Ukraine's iron generation was that many of them, she reminded me, would never see the free society they had fought so hard for:

> It would be right to meet the end of the war, together with my brothers-in-arms. I wish I could. If I don't get wounded or die, then I'll go to my friends' graves and mentally say to them [what] I haven't said in my lifetime. I don't think about the end of the war – where I will meet it or whatever.

For me, it was a westbound train back to Kyiv, the comfort of a stiff drink and a warm bed. I would sleep soundly knowing that the capital's advanced air defences could shoot down any incoming missile. For her, a night on a dirt-strewn mattress in a trench beckoned, with only the protection of some wooden slats and a few feet of mud.

I'm not sure she would have had it any other way. Kateryna dropped me back in a local town and headed back to the front. Reflecting on Bakhmut later, she said, 'It seems to me that few of us will live to see our victory.'

CHAPTER SEVEN

IN THE MOOD FOR LOVE: KYIV IN THE BLUR BETWEEN PEACE AND WAR

> 'In Donbas everything is black and white.
> In Kyiv it is always shades of grey.'
> – LIEUTENANT YULIA MYKYTENKO

> 'I should like to bury something precious in every place where I've been happy and then, when I was old and ugly and miserable, I could come back and dig it up and remember.'
> – EVELYN WAUGH, *BRIDESHEAD REVISITED*

CUT YOUR TEETH

KYIV, MARCH 2022

The train meandered slowly into the empty station. I walked the empty streets alone and full of fear and awe at the deserted streets of the capital, until I arrived at the thin glass door and Rosa was downstairs to meet me, her face as white as the single white sheet draped over the prickly mattress awkwardly jammed into her corridor. Rosa's windows were taped up. One of the biggest dangers from an explosion is that the shockwave shatters the glass, sending deadly sharps through the room and giving you lacerating wounds. It was the first of my regrets in the war. The shame had gnawed at me for days while I was in the safety of Lviv knowing those I cared about had braved the Battle of Kyiv. I decided to return. I sheltered that one night and we heard the faint rings of explosions, far enough in the melancholy distance that they sounded almost like church bells.

'On the last Sunday in March, the city was flooded with the rays of the midday sun,' Rosa said.

> It was a city I did not recognise, empty, silent, frightened. It was frozen in anticipation. My friends lent me a car, and I drove around the city, skirting past endless checkpoints. While driving, I saw a place I had dinner with a friend six hours before the war, a courtyard with a bar where we danced until dawn all weekend and an office where we discussed projects and planned months ahead. Past a church where our friend got married, the platform from which we loved to watch the city fall asleep ... But that day, I needed to return home before the curfew.

But Rosa stayed in Kyiv, against all my predictions, and I think even hers. 'My decision to stay in Kyiv seemed insane,' she said.

> I started to prepare for anything. I arranged a safe place to sleep in the corridor of the apartment and made a supply of food. Nervously, I packed a backpack just in case; there was very little space. I prepared a base and food for the cat. I made sure that I was ready to leave my house at any moment.

The winds of early spring were cruel, the streets cold and empty.

Yet as the Russians withdrew from the city outskirts, the darkness seemed to recede with them, the first rays of spring's sunshine disinfecting and illuminating the great city, which seemed to come roaring back to life. Anyone who has lived in Kyiv will tell you that spring is its most magnificent season, and that spring of 2022 was a garden of otherworldly delights. It was as if the city's residents had been in hibernation, and they were awoken from a slumber with a new appreciation for the splendour of life. The fortress that was the centre of the city had melted away with scarcely a trace. If an alien were to have been parachuted into the centre of Kyiv, they would have found little sign that there was a war on at all. Only the poster draped over the city hall that said 'Free Mariupol Defenders' or the occasional discarded detritus of fortification would give it away.

Truly happy memories are fleeting and rare, but that sun-filled day in early May, when couples walked dogs through Taras Shevchenko Park, the ice-cream vendors filled our scoops to the brim, the old men in the corner laughed and slapped their cheers while playing chess, stands out as a day that was like a flawless gem.

I heard a tune waft from a set of speakers lying on the steps of the statue to Shevchenko, Ukraine's national poet, his visage still mostly boarded up to protect him from any flying debris. The tune was *Cut Your Teeth*, a collaboration by Kygo, one of my favourite DJs, and Kyla La Grange, a tropical house song I had first listened to lying on a beach in Thailand, a sound that calmed me instantly. Katerina Rybkina was watching her younger sister lead a dance class. 'It is amazing to be back outside safely,' she said, inviting me to dance.

There was still a pain behind her eyes, a slight quiver to her smile and I asked her about her worries. 'Our family is still in Zaporizhzhia and 80 per cent of this is occupied by Russian fascists.' This was a common refrain in Kyiv. You may not see the war on the streets, but it still loomed over the city. Any conversation would turn quickly to a beloved brother or husband fighting in an infantry trench, a daughter clad in gloves and aprons at a field hospital stitching up the wounded near the front line, or relatives living under Russian occupation.

Veronica, a friend I'd met in the days before the war, had left for the safety of western Ukraine but was miserable from the start. 'I wanted to return from the first day,' she says. Her return in April was

> euphoric ... All my friends were there to meet me, and I cried with happiness to see people so dear to me. The first days I literally hugged the walls of my apartment. We can live almost the same lives as before the war but with a few restrictions. Kyiv is almost the same as always. There are a lot of people and cars everywhere. Cafes and restaurants are back open.

Almost, was the operative word. There was still a curfew, then set at 11 p.m., which curbed any nighttime revelry; it avoided the authorities having to deal with late night drunks and also gave the military the cover of darkness to move military assets.

In these early blissful months, Kyiv was mostly spared the bombing campaigns that hit other areas in the country. There was a smattering of tourists, and Kyiv's most popular hostel, Dream, began to fill up with an assortment of adrenaline junkies, wannabe soldiers and foreign volunteers of various stripes, sizes and levels of competency.

But what I felt most in the Kyiv of those months was what I'd felt in Oxford: a sense of purpose and belonging. In Dream Hostel's living room is a 'wish board', which used to hold people's dreams of love, travel and adventure. Now, the wishes are markedly different: 'I wish to kill a Russian soldier with a knife' and 'I wish to kill a Russian soldier by drowning him,' were a few of the choice ones. As the city became safer, and no more disasters struck, those who had left Kyiv for safety began to return, first as a trickle and then as a flood as the summer months wore on.

'My mum was begging me to wear this ugly sweater she unburied in the old grandpa's wardrobe ... Another ugly thing she made me wear was the bitter taste of embarrassment and guilt, and it will not save me when my heart gets frozen.' Marta, a 29-year-old friend of mine, had been miserable for every minute that she'd spent in Poland. 'It was the worst ever in my life,' she told me, saying she felt an extraordinary sense of having abandoned her loved ones. 'I felt horrible mentally; the feeling of guilt would never leave me all that time ... I wanted to punish myself for not being in Ukraine. There was always a feeling, regardless of being safe, that I am not where I am supposed to be.' She was overcome with a deep depression that only abated on her return to Ukraine and says she will never relocate again. 'I am not scared anymore,' she said. She has come to trust that the country's armed forces can keep her and the rest of the country safe. Of the 5 million people who left Ukraine, perhaps half returned within a year.

Others ping-ponged between a foreign home overseas and their native Ukraine. Yet one constant stood out among their stories. Those who had returned were invariably happier than those who stayed abroad. By experiencing the physical dangers and deprivations, they seemed to share a sense of community with other Ukrainians that those who left lacked.

Anastasia Alekseyuk from Bucha seemed noticeably frustrated with her situation when I visited her in Belgium. She had constant problems with her residence status and still suffered from trauma-induced flashbacks from the first days of the war.

Others had problems with their hosts. Some well-meaning families who took them in experienced a mismatch between their expectations – desperate refugees in rags – and the regular people who turned up at their door, some of whom were wealthy, often dressed in expensive clothes with designer accessories. I remember one conversation with a friend who had moved to London whose host family had expressed shock that she had been spending time going to shows and getting her hair and nails done. They thought she had treated the whole experience like a big holiday. 'What, do they just expect me to sit around and mope in my room all day!' she exclaimed with exasperation.

Ukrainian women with children had concerns about uprooting their lives. A friend in Germany, recently married, told me: 'I want to come back to live in Ukraine. But I also want my children to grow up with their grandparents, somewhere safe.' She could rely on her husband's family if they stayed and she didn't think it was safe enough to return. After time abroad, her children would learn new languages, make friends, settle into schools. For women who didn't yet have families, there were a series of emotions – shame, loneliness, regret – that they regularly described to me, which appear to affect those who had stayed in Ukraine or returned to the same degree.

I never met one woman who regretted her decision to return. Most men could not leave, as the conditions of martial law prevented any man aged eighteen to sixty from leaving the country.

Kyiv became the unofficial capital of the free world, and it became a magnet for politicians looking to make a name for themselves. Amazingly, so much in Ukraine continued to function smoothly.

IN THE MOOD FOR LOVE

The next time I arrived in Kyiv's imposing central station, I noticed the special arrivals and departures board next to the main staircase. It lists mock train services to various cities currently under occupation, including Donetsk, Luhansk and Sevastopol. Several of the liberated cities, such as Kherson, are lit up, while the other ones wait for the Ukrainian Army. The one at the bottom reads '*peremoha*', the Ukrainian word for victory. Only when the trains have run to the last currently occupied city will this light be switched on and the celebrations begin. Having lived in England, where a few inches of snow could delay trains for hours, it was amazing to see a train in Ukraine get hit by a rocket and only arrive fourteen minutes late. If Ukraine was a body, the railways were its arteries, carrying white blood cells in the form of weapons and ammunition to the front line. The trains also transported millions of refugees in the other direction. 'When there is a total mess in the country, people need something stable, something predictable, and we can give that to them,' says Oleksandr Shevchenko, a spokesperson for Ukrzaliznytsia, the state-owned railway company that controls most of Ukraine's trains. Ukrainian railway services have remained one of the minor miracles of the war.

The railways have more than just a utilitarian function, however. They are essential elements of Ukraine's diplomatic outreach. With all flights into Ukrainian airspace suspended for the foreseeable future, foreign dignitaries are ferried via train across the Polish border straight to Kyiv. Just before the war's first anniversary, these trains took US President Joe Biden back and forth on his historic visit to Kyiv.

Ukraine uses these trips as part of a charm offensive, what former Ukrzaliznytsia CEO Alexander Kamyshin nicknamed 'iron diplomacy'. 'Most of the time a world leader spends in Ukraine will be spent on the trains,' Shevchenko pointed out. 'I think Biden spent three or four hours in Kyiv. But he spent more than twenty on the train. We are the first and last thing that all of them see about Ukraine, and you cannot make a first impression more than once.' Each visit is carefully personalised, and they try to match the hospitality to the diplomatic needs of the moment.

'When the President of Finland came, this was shortly after they had announced the delivery of Leopard tanks to Ukraine,' Shevchenko said. 'So we all decorated the compartment with leopard colours and dressed with leopard spots on our clothes. Similarly, when the government was lobbying Germany for IRIS-T anti-aircraft guns, we put vases of iris flowers in the German President's compartment to remind him of our needs.' I was disappointed that no New Zealand Prime Minister had bothered to make the journey. Ukrainian officials were dismayed by the refusal of Jacinda Ardern, with her worldwide star power, to visit Kyiv.

Later that summer, I got the chance once to relax in the Carpathian Mountains, shortly after I returned from Donbas. I walked in the gentle peaks near the village of Yaremche, savouring the Hutsul hot springs, the delicious home-cooked borscht and hearty portions of chicken and thick-cut local potatoes, so fresh they seemed to have been dug up yesterday. The peaks were a place of solitude and respect, where the locals considered their surroundings almost living spirits. Some mystical traditions have a concept of a 'thin place', where the veil between the physical world and the spirit world becomes frayed and connection with nature, mystery or God is enhanced. I've always had a slightly superstitious side to my character, and I felt this connection, a sense of serene calm that I've barely experienced before and since. In between the horrors of war and bombing, this tiny piece of paradise stood as the one place the god of war seemed barred from entering. Like all such places, it was not meant to last.

24.02 DÉJÀ VU

KYIV, OCTOBER 2022

'It's 24.02 déjà vu,' Genia Aslanian texted me after the missiles smashed into Taras Shevchenko Park, cracking the facade of peace and beauty that had reigned in Kyiv since the spring. The numbers, representing the date the full-scale invasion had started, were seared into the mind of any Ukrainian, shorthand for all the death and destruction that followed.

It was just over six months since the liberation of Kyiv, and reality was bound to collide with the dreams sooner or later. We'd had a taste of it in early October, when the new Russian field commander, General Surovikin, had switched strategies. He was determined to wage war against not just the Ukrainian armed forces but the will of the Ukrainian civilian population to resist. The Kremlin also began a strategic partnership with Iran, buying the infamous Shahed kamikaze drones. We came to know their sound very well in Kyiv, as dozens could be launched against the city in any one night. From a distance, it sounded like the irritating buzz of a housefly; the closer you were, the more it sounded like an enormous lawnmower. Then, in November, shortly after the Ukrainians had recaptured Kherson, Putin had lashed out in fury, launching eighty missiles through the length and breadth of Ukraine, killing nineteen people and injuring hundreds. Many people have often wondered why Kyiv doesn't look like Aleppo or Gaza. The answer lies in the skill and dedication of the capital's air defence teams.

We would also get used to the sounds of the US-donated Patriot missile system that moved throughout Kyiv. It made an almighty crack, like God's own personal cannon, when it fired, followed by a rippling crash that echoed across the skies when it inevitably hit its target. The Ukrainians used it with such skill that it was able to take down missiles that were thought to be impossible to intercept. While they could protect the skies over Kyiv, however, it was much more difficult to protect critical infrastructure.

There was a perverse and brutal military logic to the Kremlin's strikes against civilian targets. As the war dragged on, Russia began to reintroduce its air force, particularly its fleet of fixed-wing aircraft, which began to be equipped with long-range glide bombs, and its fleet of KA-52 Alligator helicopters, which it would use against advancing Ukrainian troops in the 2023 counteroffensive. By striking civilian cities, Russia forced Kyiv to ration its limited air defences. It could choose to cover its major cities, critical infrastructure or major frontline fighting points – but rarely all at once. The more Russia struck, and the more varied the targets, the less protection Ukrainian troops could count on while they were on the front line.

Ukrainians had generally come to adopt a fatalistic mindset towards death. Early in the war, everyone would race for a shelter at the first sign of an air raid siren. But as war and regular life dragged on, what people called their 'war–life balance' took over. People would check Telegram channels for information about what the alert was, and everyone had a different risk level. If it was just drones, they usually left it alone. Missiles, especially if fired in significant numbers, sometimes warranted a trip to the shelter based on one's mood or risk appetite. I occasionally wandered down to a Metro station during an air raid, more out of boredom or curiosity than sense of danger. People's responses varied in different cities, different time periods and according to personal risk level. In fact, every aspect of war itself became normalised the longer you stayed.

I remember once having lunch with a colleague from a major national broadcaster. She had spent only a brief time in Ukraine and showed me a photo she had taken and was shocked by, of a destroyed house. I feigned interest, but I had seen so many destroyed buildings it made absolutely no emotional impact on me. Later, when I embedded with Ukraine's Third Assault Brigade, I excitedly showed one of the soldiers the video Nick Fisher and I had taken in Kharkiv, of Grad rockets flying over our heads. He shrugged and said, 'Nice video, but I see that shit every night guys!' I took his point. The first explosion or air raid siren you hear is usually terrifying. The fiftieth, not so much.

Of course, all this calm obscured a desperate and difficult effort by Ukrainian authorities to make life liveable. Mustafa Nayyem remembers

> every single power station that we saved, each electricity terminal, distribution station. It required various forms of protection, of air defence, coverings and nettings to protect from the missiles and drones. It was some of the most difficult work; and it is the work I am the most proud of.

The missiles were usually shot down, and if they impacted in a city like Kyiv that was well defended, they would kill usually only one or two people. Others, especially those that hit more lightly defended cities, caused mass devastation. My friend Roxy reflected on the futility of trying to truly celebrate Christmas among all of this: 'We will not be able to rejoice knowing that our soldiers are now in the cold trenches and that some of them will never return home.'

CULTURE WAR

KYIV, DECEMBER 2022

Christmas has been a solemn affair in Ukraine since 2022. 'My grandmother told me that when she was a little girl, her family celebrated Christmas in secret,' said my friend Roksolana Oliyarchuk.

The Soviet authorities forbade celebrating Christmas and observing any Ukrainian traditions. Under threat of arrest, people gathered at the festive table behind tightly curtained windows and by candlelight. They were brave enough to follow their traditions, preserve them and carry them through the generations, and thanks to this, I know what Christmas is.

Some again were forced to suffer in the frozen candlelight, as Russian missile strikes knocked down power stations and electricity grids throughout Ukraine. But they persevered. The figure most associated with Christmas in Ukraine is Mykola Leontovych, who composed the well-known 'Carol of the Bells' but was killed, as so many Ukrainians were, by the Soviet Cheka, the shadowy secret police that would become the KGB. There was at least one major change, as many Ukrainians switched from celebrating Christmas on 6 January, according to the Russian Orthodox calendar, to focusing on the date that we are familiar with in the west, 25 December.

What Russia's relentless assaults did do, however, is push Ukrainians further away from any association with the culture of the *Ruskiy Mir*. Nowhere was this more evident than in the domains of religion and language.

The grand marble courtyards and golden domes of the Kyiv Pechersk Lavra are impressive. Yet the monastery is surprisingly empty, and the chill in the air is spiritual, not just physical. For this is also the centre of a hidden battle for Ukraine's identity and, for the parishioners here, the country's very soul. 'It took a while to get the smell of the devil out of here,' said a priest at the Lavra, who had been present for the visit of Russian President Vladimir Putin in 2013.

Now, it is clean and quiet, and eerily so for a place that was once a centre of community life. Some of the priests here, along with the head of the Lavra, were arrested by Ukrainian Security Services on suspicion of spying for the Russians. It had once belonged to a branch of the Ukrainian Orthodox Church that was still connected to the Moscow Patriarchate. Many priests had angrily repudiated Putin's actions – remember Father Vasili in Kharkiv in disbelief at how Russians were bombing a city with such close connections.

The Moscow Patriarchate itself called this a blatant attempt to suppress religious freedom; many right-wing influencers in the United States, most notably Tucker Carlson, climbed on the bandwagon, saying that Zelensky and his government were 'persecuting Christians'. The truth, according to those involved, is much more complicated.

Maksym Ostapenko, the new general director of the Pechersk Lavra, welcomed me into his office. He showed me a number of documents that Ukrainian police had found when they had raided the Lavra. These included signs and symbols supporting President Putin, signage implying Crimea was part of Russia and lists of phone numbers, some of which he said were directly linked to the Russian military. These cases are currently winding their way through court, and the priests have strenuously denied all charges.

'You need to understand, for Russia, the church is not about religion. The church is another way to maintain political control over the population. Through propaganda, through influencing the population to support the Russian regime. Nothing in Russia exists outside of the control of the state.' He had good evidence for this claim. Patriarch Kirill, the head of the Russian Orthodox Church, had described Putin as a 'miracle of God' and publicly supported the invasion by blessing soldiers who were travelling to fight in Ukraine. Russian troops had already destroyed hundreds of religious institutions, mostly churches but also synagogues and mosques like one I'd seen in Bakhmut, since the invasion began. When I left, there was a small group of five protesters, holding signs and chanting hymns against the takeover of the church. No one paid them any mind – they looked like a relic of a former era.

Language was a trickier question. Rosa grew up speaking Russian in Kherson and still spoke it with her family. In Kyiv, Russian had been the language of business before 2022. Even in the weeks before the invasion, eight out of ten conversations seemed to be in Russian. These days, it's closer to half – and in polite society, it's rude to address someone in Russian unless you know them already.

Still, people slip up. I still catch friends who'd sworn off Russian speaking it casually in front of me, assuming I wouldn't understand. Others say it is the language that comes to them in a rage, that they swear in. On the front line, where a miscommunication can be life or death, most Ukrainian troops still speak Russian. In Kyiv, it's a social faux pas.

I've learned passable Ukrainian, more than most foreigners, but I'm far from fluent. It has a rich linguistic variety – my favourite new word was *zmyrytysya*, which means 'to make peace with'. You can hear the word *myr*, peace, buried like a splinter.

Most language teachers in Ukraine no longer want to teach Russian. 'Our rule is that if you were learning Russian with us before the war [we can continue lessons]. But we want to only take new students for Ukrainian now,' said Natalia from my language school. It was, she said, their way to 'decolonise' the rest of Ukraine. This also rubbishes one of the key propaganda lines that the Russians used to justify their invasion: the idea of the 'persecution of Russian speakers'. It is true: some in the Donbas wanted more educational options in Russian. But this is so far from the Russian fantasies of pogroms or re-education camps.

One Russian speaker from Odesa told me: 'I love Ukrainian, and I hope everybody eventually speaks it. But Russian will always be my mother tongue. There are just some feelings, some subtleties that I can't express except in Russian.' There was never discrimination against Russian speakers in public, although there were some cumbersome rules restricting the use of Russian in public institutions. Nobody was ever persecuted for speaking Russian with family and friends, colleagues or even on the battlefield. Among native speakers, attitudes to continuing to speak Russian are mixed, even now.

'We are just like the Irish,' said Denys, a staff member at a cafe in Dnipro. 'They speak English, but that doesn't mean they want to be part of England!'

Russian wouldn't be banned, like Russian propaganda claimed. Just left to die out. 'I grew up speaking Russian, along with everyone else in Mykolaiv,' my colleague Natalia said. 'But my future children... I don't even want them to know that language or this country exists.'

DANCING AGAINST DESPAIR

IRPIN, KYIV OBLAST, MAY 2023

Kyiv had mostly escaped the destruction, but its suburbs had taken the full brunt of the early Russian invasion. I was therefore shocked when I returned to Irpin to find it almost unrecognisable. I was shown round by an old friend. 'It is amazing to see you guys again,' said Oleksiy Ovchynnykov, who had finally left his home of Slovyansk to set up his dance studios in the Kyiv region. After months of driving supplies to soldiers on the front line and risking his life, he was beginning to rebuild his businesses. His dance studios in the Donbas were no longer viable. Some had been shelled, some were under occupation and no one in the Donbas was in the mood for dancing.

So his wife, Nastya, and he had moved to reopen them in the Kyiv region. They specialised in ballroom dancing but also cycled through ballet and swing dancing. When I visited, Nastya was teaching a group of young children hip-hop. The town's recovery seemed miraculous, and if not for the occasional bits of shrapnel or a broken window or two on every apartment block, it would be hard to know there had ever been a battle here. More than two-thirds of the city's buildings had been damaged, but Irpin and Bucha had been the subject of a major reconstruction effort.

'When we came here, the city was very destroyed,' Oleksiy says. 'But Slovyansk was also destroyed in 2014, so I knew Irpin would rebuild, like Slovyansk did.' Further away from the front lines, we had a chance to reflect on the causes of the war and how Ukrainians felt towards Russians after these years of fighting. For Oleksiy, the fault lay with the Putin regime for sure, but responsibility was shared with ordinary Russians. 'I can't see how Russian people saw this and approve of what is happening,' he said.

When Ukrainians had leaders who wanted to be dictators, like in 2004 and 2014, we rose and overthrew them. In 2012, when

Russians protested Putin, they had their chance to overthrow their dictator. But they did not try hard enough, and now Ukrainians pay the price for the Russian people's failure to do so.

Walking through Irpin's parks, seeing the rebuilt buildings, happy families strolling through the grass while children played safely in playgrounds, you could see so clearly what the Ukrainians were fighting for.

Oksen Lisovyi was one of the few who had swapped his combat fatigues for a suit. When I met him in Kyiv, he seemed wistful. He still held gravitas, but he spoke of yearning to be working directly with young people, whereas his new job as Minister of Education and Science afforded little of that. But President Zelensky had insisted he return from his service to serve in his Cabinet, and this was not a call he could turn down. One of his most pressing concerns was to get children back in physical classrooms. 'These young people have lost a lot,' he has said. 'A year and a half in Covid-19, then a year and a half in the war. Adolescent loneliness is catastrophic.' The ministry under his guidance began allowing educational institutions with shelters to resume in-person lessons. Schools and teachers have always played leading roles in helping their community adapt during times of crisis.

Oksana Minikova, a teacher from Zaporizhzhia, described how her pupils adapted during the war: 'We changed the education process. In the morning we spend ten to fifteen minutes speaking about mental health and focus on each pupil personally – every pupil has an opportunity to share how they feel today and ask for help.' As Zaporizhzhia is still bombed regularly, classes are held in cramped, clammy basements. The war, Oksana says, has robbed many of Ukraine's youth of a real childhood. 'Children became more serious.

They were pushed to grow up so quickly. But they still dream about their future – [many] want to become doctors, engineers or join the military.' In Kharkiv, the Passengers in the Metro stations have been replaced with classrooms. This is the only place safe enough for a group of children to gather.

ET IN ARCADIA EGO

KYIV, JULY 2024

Jay and I lay on our couch in our underwear, drenched in sweat, our exhaustion barely relieved by a pitiful wind from a weak ceiling fan. We reflected on the irony that Ukraine's worst power outages had in fact come during the hottest summer in living memory, a heatwave that went up to forty degrees. Ever since the war had started, we'd been warned to expect the harshest of winters, when the power grid would collapse and people would freeze in their houses. Instead, it was the heat that was defeating us. Then the crash and boom of the missile that smashed into the centre of Kyiv, blowing its target to rubble. It was a children's hospital.

It was a stark reminder that the war was not something anyone in Ukraine could ignore for long. Kyiv had begun to feel less like an enchanted garden and more like a bubble, where you could be shrink-wrapped away from the realities of war and chaos that were just an overnight train ride away. Feelings of defiance and camaraderie that were so ubiquitous in Ukrainian society had changed to grim resignation, and fractures were beginning to form. There were those who wanted to talk about making a deal with the Russians, and those who were determined to fight to the bitter end. There were the tensions between the women who moved abroad and knew the war mostly from television and those who had remained, who felt they had suffered in a way their compatriots had not. Most of all, there was the conflict between the men who had fought and those who had not. In Ukraine, which had never conquered its issues with endemic corruption, there was usually a way for those with money or connections to avoid military service.

Music festivals even returned. At Atlas Weekend, once Ukraine's largest, we interviewed the frontman of a well-known Ukrainian band, who said all the usual lines about the importance of supporting Ukraine. But I asked him and his bandmates, well, what about mobilisation here? Are any of you considering joining, now that the army desperately needs more men? After all, alongside performances from Ukraine's biggest stars, like Nadya Dorofeeva and Boombox, were recruiting stands for the Third Assault Brigade and video game demonstrations of drone warfare for anyone interested in enlisting.

There was a brief and uncomfortable silence.

'Oh, we feel we do our best to fight here, on the cultural front line.' The next day, the band's PR manager called us, pleading for us not to publish that line. 'It might sound very disrespectful to the war effort,' he worried. The term had meant a shared sense of struggle among all parts of society in Ukraine. Yet as the war ground on, it now sounds like stolen valour, artists pretending they were fighting the war without actually risking their flesh in the horrors of the trenches. I heard many soldiers say that they felt unable to relate to the people in Kyiv, whose lives were occasionally interrupted by an air raid siren but who could otherwise ignore the war. Some felt angry about the young men in bars and cafes living their normal lives – others said that they were fighting precisely so that other Ukrainians could have the freedom to live their lives how they chose.

Genia was furious at many of her colleagues. More than half of her male colleagues at her IT firm had illegally left the country since the beginning of the full-scale invasion. She called them 'arrogant pricks' and listed the various ways men can pay to get out of military service. First, some of them pay doctors to certify them as disabled – a clinic in Odesa, for example, became notorious for diagnosing men with spinal injuries that exempted them from military service. Others try to sneak across the border. The going rate for a smuggler to take someone into neighbouring Poland or Romania is $5,000. It is a similar amount to bribe certain NGOs to certify a person as a volunteer bringing in humanitarian aid. This gives the man permission to leave the country for a limited period, although there is no way to force him to return to Ukraine. 'Corruption will destroy the country faster than Russia,' one young woman told me.

Forced mobilisation tended to happen outside of Kyiv, however. While it was a wartime necessity, the Ukrainian authorities were aware of how bad it looked and did not want to do this in front of the prying eyes of the numerous western journalists and aid workers who lived in Kyiv. Once, when I stepped off the train in the western city of Chernivtsi, I was immediately accosted by a mobilisation squad, presumably with the goal of sending me straight to Bakhmut. The moment they saw the colour of my passport, New Zealand black instead of Ukrainian blue, they shooed me away without a second thought.

By the end of 2023, I began to hear more and more people express pessimism about the war effort. Genia was always worried sick about her husband, who was an officer in the Ukrainian Army. He had proposed to her by text, to make sure they could organise a shotgun wedding – 'the Vegas thing', as she described it – in the ten days or so leave he got from the front that year. She picked out her ring, dress and shoes in a quarter-hour shopping trip and then went straight to the registry office where they got married in the presence of a celebrant. It was not the wedding she'd dreamed of, but it was still a fairytale, as she'd managed to marry the man she loved against all the obstacles the Kremlin could throw at them.

She was one of the lucky ones, and her husband has since survived his stint on the front line and lives back with her in Kyiv. But for many people, their lives remain in a state of suspended animation. Birth rates in Ukraine, already low, collapsed after the invasion. How could you have children if you didn't know if your home would be safe or under occupation? Marriages remained small, subdued family affairs, and large celebrations or parties were particularly frowned upon. Really, the only community events where large groups gathered were memorials for fallen soldiers. 'We have more reunions at funerals than at weddings', was one post I saw on Instagram after Kyiv buried a young man in his mid-twenties.

Rosa was always worried about her family. She was from Kherson, where her mother lived under occupation; her father was a shipman and had been lucky enough to be out of port when the invasion began. 'I am very lucky; I have not lost touch with my family and friends,' she said.

> However, since the beginning of the conflict, I have not been able to be with them. Access to them is blocked, and I do not know how long it will last; it is heartbreaking and the cause of much pain. Courtesy has become a measure of love and care between everyone far and wide. Of course, war is one of the worst things that a person can experience and go through. No one is ready for that. It causes huge amounts of stress that reveal a different side to people. I don't know who I am anymore. Who am I? Is a question I ask regularly now.

To represent what the war meant for her, she supplied me with an artwork of a winged serpent, the missiles and drones that fell with malice and poison on the guilty and innocent, young and old alike. It reminded me of flicking through my phone, which is always such a strange experience in Ukraine – your friend's holiday snaps, drinking champagne on beaches in Croatia or Bali, next to a soldier's dispatch from a boiling trench – when I came across an image that had been shared widely. It was the skull of a Russian soldier, taken by a colleague of mine, Nikoletta Stoyanova, his jaw wide open, as if in the moment he screamed for his life.

Et in Arcadia ego. Even here, I, Death, hold sway. It is a common trope in literature, to represent the overarching power of death, even in places that are supposed to be filled with joy. It is the epitaph written on the skull in *Brideshead Revisited*, the line written on the judge's axe in *Blood Meridian*, and I now know that much about the joy of Kyiv in that grand spring and summer was ephemeral, perhaps entirely illusory, like the joy of Oxford for Charles Ryder and Sebastian Flyte and for me during my four years there was partly a trick of the mind. I realised that a door was now closing, or the enchanted garden of Kyiv had been a trick to begin with, a desperate attempt to push away the reality of war, whose tendrils managed to sneak in through the cracks in the wall regardless of what mere mortals could do.

Rosa decided to leave in the end, to start the life abroad she'd dreamed of before the war. I took her on one last outing to mark our goodbye. It was the opera – I'd sung well as a child, and my father and my grandfather had both been professional singers, so it remains my favourite fancy date place, a chance for both parties to dress up and feign sophistication.

The show was the Italian classic *Rigoletto*, and people arrived dressed in anything between their evening best and casual work wear, with a few military uniforms visible in the crowd. We were given directions for a bomb shelter in case we needed it, but we were able to watch the story of the wicked and rakish duke, the vengeful hunchback and the tragic soprano without interruption.

Later that night, Rosa lay with her head on my shoulder and put on the film *In the Mood for Love*, Wong Kar-wai's doomed love story of Chow, also a journalist, and Su, a secretary. Their drama could seem mundane compared to that of a war, merely being the realisation that their respective partners are having an affair, but something about the tragedy of unconsummated passion fit the melancholy vibe of life in Ukraine's capital.

Rosa left the next day to start a new life in Spain, where she moved to the warm, lively southern city of Seville; she had stayed in Kyiv when it was at risk and left when it was safe to start a new life – but one that she had chosen on her terms, not to live as a refugee but a free woman. Like Kar-wai's doomed couple, wreathed with cigarette smoke and bathed in the red hues of Hong Kong's neon lights, Rosa and I were never to see each other again.

CHAPTER EIGHT

SEE NO EVIL, HEAR NO EVIL, SPEAK NO EVIL: THE RUSSIANS AND HOW THEY RULE

'We've committed half the crime but paid the full price.'
– Alexander Dugin

GOODBYE LENIN

SUDZHA, KURSK OBLAST, RUSSIAN FEDERATION, AUGUST 2024

'We're in Russia.'

A smile flickered across Vadim's otherwise stoic face as he hoisted his rifle and peered through the bulletproof windscreen. Through the slits between the huge metal armour, we could see the broken barricades and pummelled buildings of the former border checkpoint that had been obliterated in a hail of artillery shells about two weeks ago. There was a cacophony of different languages going on between the small team of international correspondents. The backseat of the Turkish armoured vehicle was a Tower of Babel; we went between English, Spanish, Ukrainian, Russian, Arabic, Latvian and German, all of us repeating Vadim's words hurriedly into our phones or cameras like they were an incantation. No one could quite believe we were here, me least of all.

In June that year, I'd received a notification from the Russian Embassy in Wellington, New Zealand's capital. 'In response to the politically motivated sanctions ... introduced by the Government of New Zealand as part of the collective West's Russophobic campaign,' it began, in the outraged language beloved of Russians, 'entry to the Russian Federation shall be additionally closed in perpetuity to thirty-six New Zealand citizens ... shaping an anti-Russia agenda in that country.' There I was on the list: 'Number 17, Tom Mutch, photojournalist, *New Zealand Herald*', just below our Deputy Secretary of Defence and an army major in charge of the Kiwi troops training Ukrainian forces. It was a 'badge of honour', my colleague Colin Freeman of the *Daily Telegraph*, who was also on the list, had told me. It meant that my articles had angered the right people.

Now less than two months later, I jumped out the back of a Ukrainian troop transport and onto the main square of the small Russian town that had been thrown into the centre of the war. Having nearly been killed by Russian troops on several occasions, it was satisfying to be giving a middle finger straight to the Kremlin.

Every window in the stucco art deco city hall was blown out, shrapnel and explosive marks all over its exterior. In front was a plinth that had once held a statue of Lenin. His head had been blown off, and his name scrawled out and the word 'faggot' in Russian scribbled below it. As part of decommunisation, statues of Lenin had been torn down all throughout Ukraine and the former Soviet bloc – but none as humiliating as this. The streets were full of broken glass and branches from blown-up trees. The wall of one house was graffitied 'Ukraine Above All'. The streets were almost completely quiet, except for the crack of artillery and drone fire in the distance.

Many major media outlets declined to send correspondents. After the recent arrest of Evan Gershkovich, a *Wall Street Journal* reporter, everyone was scared for the safety of their correspondents. The Russians had threatened all sorts of retaliation against anyone who 'violated their borders' by going into Kursk. They would be considered enemy targets.

On 6 August, Ukrainian forces launched a surprise offensive into Russian territory, aiming to throw yet another spanner into the works of Putin's war machine. After two weeks of intense fighting, the Ukrainians had advanced nearly twenty-five miles into Russia proper, controlling around 750 square miles of territory. The Ukrainians were delighted to be able to finally turn the tables on their oppressors. 'Kursk, Belgorod, Bryansk [Russian border regions], they are all Ukraine!' one soldier told me, tongue half in cheek. There was a clear Ukrainian heritage here – some of the civilians mixed many Ukrainian words into their speech.

I had a different reason for joining this mission. What I really wanted to know was what did ordinary Russians, who had lived next to the war against their peaceful neighbour for more than two years, really think? I was finally able to peer through a window into the mysterious Russian soul.

DISTURBIA

DONETSK, MAY 2011

A young woman with a shock of bright red hair and a black and grey dress strode out onto the star-shaped stage to raucous cheering. In 2011, Rihanna was at the height of her powers. Donetsk is now so associated with war and destruction that it is difficult to remember that this was once a flourishing city. Yet her haunting 'Disturbia' lyrics presage the future the city was to face. This ground was designed as the home for Shakhtar Donetsk, Ukraine's best football club. It cost more than $300 million to build and held 52,000 fans. In 2012, it was one of the stadiums that hosted the Euro football championships, where Wayne Rooney headed the ball in at point-blank range to score the only goal in England's 1–0 victory over Ukraine. Donetsk's supposed 'pro-Russian' population came out in their tens of thousands to cheer for the west's biggest cultural events.

The Donbas was caught between the parallel evolutions of Ukraine and Russia after their independence. Russia experienced a similar trauma to Ukraine at the end of the Soviet Union. It also suffered a severe economic crisis. Life expectancy and economic output both plummeted. Moscow and St Petersburg were taken over by mafia gangs and basic foodstuffs disappeared from supermarket shelves. But unlike Ukraine, which was finding its feet as a young, independent democracy, Russia also suffered a humiliating loss of prestige. Vladimir Putin inherited a demoralised nation and so his personal reputation became intertwined with Russia's rebirth on the world stage. So, there was little serious pushback to his stripping away of political liberties and centralising power in Moscow – or when he began to blatantly rig elections to stay in power.

As Putin consolidated domestic control, there evolved an unspoken but well-known social contract between the state and its citizens – that if you never get properly involved in politics, never cross the authorities' red lines, you are free to eke out a living. Meanwhile, all former Warsaw Pact allies moved as quickly as they could to integrate themselves into western institutions, particularly the EU and NATO. Many of them had been subjugated by the Russians multiple times over recent centuries and were desperate to get under the NATO security umbrella while Russia was too weak to prevent this. This is very different to the 'alliances' built by the Russians in Europe after the Second World War, which were enforced by the barrel of a gun.

The Donbas always had an uneasy relationship with the rest of Ukraine. Residents distrusted Kyiv, which they saw as a faraway city, and Viktor Yanukovych's overthrow in 2014 was taken particularly harshly in Donetsk. He may have been corrupt, but he came from a hardscrabble youth in a Donetsk coal-mining family and had been in jail. Yet there was not enough separatist sentiment here for a successful uprising. That required an outside spark.

On 12 April 2014, a gang of fifty or so masked men stormed the building of the Interior Ministry in the city of Slovyansk in the Donetsk region. They had a mix of odd and amusing codenames, including Baloo, Chamomile, Motorola, Fang, Mute and, most infamously of all, Strelkov. He was a former FSB colonel, who had also fought in Transnistria and the Balkans, had raised a small private militia from irregular Russian forces that had taken over the Crimea. It was Strelkov who had fired into the air and later said, 'I pulled the trigger that started the war'. They were Russian ultra-nationalists, and his writings leave no doubt as to what they were after. Ukraine, Alexander Zhuchkovsky said, was a fake state: 'Ukraine as an idea and Ukrainian nationalism as a political project were purposefully created to subvert and weaken both Russia and the Russian people.' He claimed that Ukraine had 'illegally separated from Russia in 1991' and made no claim that they would stop at the Donbas and let Ukraine go its own way. No, he wrote, they were 'irridentists' and 'Russian irridentism is the struggle of the Russian People to reunite the Russian lands of Ukraine, Belarus, Kazakhstan and the Baltics into a single Russian state'.

An English colleague of mine, Joel Gallagher, worked as a security adviser in Donetsk shortly after the war, and I relied heavily on him for the following account of the first war in Donbas.

On 2 May, Girkin and his rebels got an unexpected and terrible boost from events elsewhere in Ukraine. Pro- and anti-Maidan groups had been clashing regularly in cities throughout the south and east of Ukraine, particularly on the streets of Odesa. Then, one street fight got seriously out of hand. The two sides began using guns and Molotov cocktails. When the pro-Maidan camp gained the upper hand, the pro-Russian group retreated into a temporary base in the trade union centre, but the fighting continued, and the building caught fire. Forty-two Russian supporters were burned alive, with hundreds more injured.

The exact bomb that lit the blaze has never been identified. But the horrific videos seemed to confirm the messages the Russians were pumping throughout eastern Ukraine, that fascists and murderers were targeting Russians and burning them alive. Several Donbas pro-Russian fighters cited this as an event that radicalised them.

'I thought we'd be left alone,' one soldier recalled.

> I never thought [Kyiv would] go this far. This country was always a fucking madhouse, but in 2014 the lunatics started running the asylum. To us, Kyiv and Lviv might as well have been a foreign country at that point. Surely, there was a way to resolve this by sitting at a table, but it's all pointless now. Once they spilled our blood on the streets, there was no going back.

They became convinced that the only way to save Russian speakers in Ukraine was the creation of a Novorossiya state from Donetsk all the way to Odesa and joining with Transnistria.

Not everything they were saying about 'Ukrainian fascists' was propaganda. Far-right parties had little effect on electoral politics in Ukraine. But they did have influence on the battlefield. The Ukrainian Army was in such an unready state that pro-Ukrainian forces were heavily reliant on irregular militias, most notoriously the Azov Battalion. During its founding, many of its members were openly neo-Nazi and would wear patches and armour covered with Nazi insignia. You can still occasionally see this legacy on the battlefield today. In November 2022, on my way to Kherson, I passed a pair of Ukrainian tanks, one of which had just detonated a mine and was lying in ditch while its crew were trying to repair it. The other, idling next to it, was flying a large flag of the *Sonnenrad* (black sun) and had an eagle reminiscent of that of the Third Reich below it. Another, I spied, had the same eagle with a Ukrainian trident below it.

Ukrainians would react uncomfortably if you brought this up. 'It is trolling,' was a way they defended it. More realistically, the answer came from the fact that the Germans were seen as the ultimate anti-Soviet, anti-Russian figure, which became understandable when Ukraine was fighting for its national existence.

Azov was disbanded as an independent force and incorporated into the Ukrainian armed forces. The core of what remained of these battalions was destroyed or taken prisoner in the Siege of Mariupol, and you'll hear whispers that the Ukrainian authorities were not altogether unhappy to have this thorn in their side removed. After months of fighting, the once beautiful city of Donetsk was a shell of its former self. More than half the population, especially those holding pro-Ukrainian views, had fled. Joel told me: 'Theft, banditry and casual death were common. I can recall staying in hotels with blood on the walls and 9mm shell casings on the floor, barricading the door and praying to make it through the night.'

Tanya Azuaje, the OSCE monitor I met in Mariupol shortly before the war, described the whole city as something of a theme park of rebellion:

> You had these weird dystopian things everywhere. There was a boardgame shop that had things made out of bullets from the war. Roses made of corrugated iron or metal from weapons. They even sold a monopoly game that was Donetsk themed. One of my biggest regrets is not buying this! There was Donmac, this McDonald's copy from Donetsk. There was a restaurant that I told you about, it was rebel themed, DPR flags, Russian flags but also Confederate flags, native American symbols, all these strange things just fighting against the bigger man or the colonial order.

Across many of the streets and billboards were the words 'Donbas is Russia', written over and over again.

Even Strelkov, who became deeply disillusioned with the Kremlin, noted that the separatist regions had become dystopias. In 2023, he founded the 'Club of Angry Patriots', which wrote a Grand Remonstrance against the Kremlin. 'Why were', he asked, 'outright crooks and fraudsters put at the head of the People's Republics of Donbass, who discredited the ideas of the Russian Spring by the very fact of their presence in power?' He went on: who was or will be held responsible for the fact that instead of a 'showcase of the Russian World' in the Luhansk/Donetsk People's Republics, for eight years there was a 'lagoon' where people lived much worse than in the Russian Federation and worse than in 'Ukraine'?

This became much worse, because of the comparison with nearby Crimea, the crown jewel of Putin's conquests. 'We're Moscow's whore or mistress!' another pro-Russian fighter, codenamed Jurgoz, laughed loudly.

> When I saw what happened in sunny Crimea, I thought that Russia would do the same for us: annex us and keep those Ukrainian bastards away from us like a big brother ought to do. Little did we know that pretty Crimea was like the Kremlin's wife, and we're like its bit on the side. The wife gets all the jewels and expensive meals, and we just get fucked!

Jurgoz didn't know it, but he'd stumbled upon one of the truths about the Kremlin's designs for Donbas. The Donbas was merely a means to control Ukraine; Putin cared little about the people for their own sake. If they could be shoved back into Ukraine under the Minsk Accords, they could be used to control the whole country's directions of travel. And when Putin wanted a war to control Ukraine, the simmering Donbas conflict was a convenient excuse. Even his speech on 21 February 2022 recognising their independence was mostly a diatribe against Ukraine itself; the self-declared republics were merely an afterthought.

The annexation of Crimea and the war in Donbas had another effect. They pushed the people of Ukraine firmly away from Russia. Previously, they had not seen the need for NATO membership. Now, it was a national priority in the face of an invasion from an aggressive neighbour. And, as Strelkov acknowledged, these were ugly, repressive places ruled by bandits.

Ukraine, on the other hand, had taken a light touch with the parts of the Donbas region where they remained in control. They didn't ethnically cleanse them of Russians, as many feared, or take steps to ban the Russian language or even dismantle monuments to the Second World War and shared cultural heritage.

In occupied Crimea, the situation was glitzy from the outside. While the peninsula was cut off from the world economy by sanctions, the Kremlin and friendly oligarchs aligned to it poured enormous amounts of money into the area. They built glitzy resorts and infrastructure projects, like the enormous Kerch Bridge to the Russian mainland. In one extraordinary show of bathos, a pro-Putin biker gang called the Night Wolves staged an elaborate rock opera in 2015 recreating Second World War battles with fireworks and lasers and then compared it to the ongoing war in the Donbas. The performance, which is on YouTube, is even more bizarre than words can do justice.

They did this alongside stamping out any dissent against their rule, especially from the indigenous people of the region. The Crimean Tatars had a peculiar and tense but mostly respectful relationship with the rest of Ukraine. 'Ukrainians didn't really care about us,' said one Crimean Tatar friend of their experience after 1991. She didn't mean it negatively. The Soviet Union had deported almost all of them after the Second World War and had crushed their language and traditional cultural institutions. So, to be left well enough alone was a significant upgrade.

Nariman Dzhelyal, a member of the Mejlis, the elected representative of the Crimean Tatars that was disbanded by Russia, told me how he had been arrested on blatantly ridiculous charges of planting explosives to destroy a gas pipeline. With his kindly smile, tufts of white hair and oversized glasses, Dzhelyal is one of the gentlest men I have ever met – the planet's least convincing terrorist.

After being released in a prisoner swap, he said that anyone who spoke out for the cultural rights of Crimean Tatars or continued to say that Crimea belonged rightfully to Ukraine was punished. Organising political activities became impossible, and anyone politically suspect was likely to be prosecuted under bogus 'terrorism' laws.

When the Russians had the Ukrainians in their cells, they would tell them what they really thought. Maksym Butkevych, a Ukrainian human rights activist and former pacifist who was taken prisoner in the Luhansk region in 2022, explained that most Russians he met, even those who were anti-Putin, hated Ukraine. 'The Russians slept through the period when it stopped being fashionable to be an empire,' he said. 'And there is no Russian Empire without Ukraine. In prison, after talking to civilians, to Russian nationals, to guards and to interrogators, it's clear they want to destroy liberal values, and Ukraine is just the first stage for them.'

Butkevych said that even a prisoner who would be critical of Russian propaganda, saying it is all nonsense, would change their tune when the topic became Ukraine, saying:

> Ukraine does not exist; it is a fake state. Ukrainians are spoiled Russians who should be reminded they are Russians. If they don't think they are Russians, they are broken and need to be fixed. Ukrainians who don't want to be part of Russia are by this very fact Nazis.

Those I have met from the Donbas who fled seem to have the most difficult time of any refugees abroad. Anna Razumna, a 25-year-old who grew up in the city of Donetsk, moved to Kyiv in 2021 after doing her high school and bachelor's study under occupation.

'Most teachers supported Russia. After the Maidan, one said it was good that we were going towards Russia. They were the ones that didn't have the money to leave, so they stayed and tried to survive, following the rules.' Razumna had lived in Russia and hated it, so was never able to believe what she said was the Russian propaganda that would come from over the border. 'I was living in Russia for a year, and I didn't see anything good that was supposed to be there. There was a lot of lies and disrespect.'

Hanna Demidova had a similar experience in Kostiantynivka, which remained under Ukrainian control. Yanukovych, the pro-Russian President deposed after the Maidan in 2014, was considered a local hero, despite his notorious corruption. 'There was obviously a pro-Yanukovych propaganda, it was so strong. All these people saying that Yanukovych is a person from Donetsk ... he is our man, he is from Donetsk region, he is a simple person, he is the man to vote for.'

Many parts of Ukrainian culture were denigrated in this region. 'You can't speak two languages at the same time,' Anna Demidova, from Kostiantynivka, once said to me, mocking her choice to speak Ukrainian instead of Russian. 'Ukrainian was "peasant Russian". I completely switched to Ukrainian, I love it. It had become the cliche that Russia is cool, that we are a *"malorossiya"* [little Russia], but it wasn't something somebody told me, it is a vibe.' People had a tendency, she explained, to be ashamed of their Ukrainian heritage. She noted that Russia was seen as 'cool' or 'modern' in the way that French culture was seen as sophisticated.

'After 2014, when it was changing, it was a breath of fresh air. Why should we be ashamed! We have such a culture! Especially when I was educated in Ukrainian literature and Ukrainian culture.'

After the Russians took over the capitals of Donetsk and Luhansk in 2014, the occupied regions had very little connection with the outside world; nor were they officially integrated into Russia. They were stuck in a no man's land, no international recognition, under a corrupt, authoritarian government, where the majority of the population sank into poverty. While occupied Donetsk was poor for most people, this of course did not apply to everyone, especially those who were in highly placed positions in the Russian-backed government. 'The top people in Donetsk government were living like kings,' Razumna, who lived in Donetsk until 2021, told me. 'They had huge cars, villas ... one got a new tiger as a pet!'

The war itself slowed down. 'I woke up from shooting once and went on to my balcony and saw they were shooting rockets from the middle of the civilian apartment block!'

While many other refugees had mostly supportive families back home, many of those from Donbas have families with very different political views. 'My grandmother would start sending me messages, saying Ukraine is fascist, Nazi, that Ukrainians are devils and demons that needed to be killed,' Razumna told me. 'Do you think it is normal, for Christian people to be saying that?'

'GOOD RUSSIANS'

KAZBEGI, GEORGIA, OCTOBER 2022

The new refugees were swarming though a chasm between extraordinary snow-capped cliffs overlooking the border between Georgia and Russia. A small monastery dotted the mountaintop, and the greenery stretched as far as the eye could see. Of all my assignments, this was the most beautiful by far. Russians, mostly young, upper-middle-class men, terrified of being mobilised, were pouring into the safety of Georgia, a country which Russia had also invaded and currently occupied 20 per cent of. My translator Lia was a curious mix of almost the entire Soviet Union. Half Estonian, half Georgian, she had grown up in Moscow and got involved with Alexei Navalny's anti-corruption foundation. After the war began, the Russian authorities stopped brooking any kind of dissent.

So, we stopped young men coming across the border and asked them for a brief chat about why they were leaving and what they thought of the war. One young man said:

> I think my actions will tell about it. I quit my job, broke off many connections there, people with whom I really had been in touch for a long time. Many do not understand. The seriousness of the actions that are happening there. Those who do understand are taking some specific actions. It is difficult to explain to people who have not lived in a totalitarian and militarised country. That you cannot just go to a rally. When this whole story [mobilisation] happened, I deliberately changed my route from work and drove through the city centre. I expected to see people there who would not like THIS, who would protest. I did not see anyone. Maybe in the evening a couple of dozen people gathered in the square, but most people agreed with this.

'What can we call you? What is your name?' I asked the young man.

'Patriot of Russia,' he said from behind his helmet. That said it all to me. I'd stopped him, and he told me he wanted nothing more than to denounce the Putin regime to the world. As soon as I stuck a camera in his face, he cowered and begged not to be shown. We came to the agreement that he could stick his motorcycle helmet on and cover his face. Tens of thousands of Russians crossed this border, flights to Istanbul and Yerevan were booked out for months, when Putin announced his mobilisation. Theoretically, anyone in the Russian military reserve, which covered most young men, could be mobilised.

Lia's friend Muta, from Moscow, had opened a shelter for Ukrainians and Russians both, refusing to discriminate. Like many of the Russians I had met in Georgia, she was deeply, genuinely depressed about the hellhole their country had fallen into. 'Why does everyone think that all Russians support the war?' Muta asked me.

'Well, we don't see any evidence that you don't!' I said. 'Even here in Tbilisi, where you are safe, why don't you have social media posts every day? Why don't you have a protest in front of the Russian Embassy every day saying, "Not in our name?"'

'Well, nothing would change. It wouldn't affect anything – we would just be ignored and our families punished,' she told me.

I remember asking Lia about her cousin who had fled and spent three days in a freezing car on the border. 'It was like hell on earth,' he apparently said. For someone who was supposedly anti-war, I couldn't understand how he could compare his experiences to the genuine hells on earth in Mariupol, Bakhmut, Bucha or anywhere the Russians had gone in Ukraine. It was the exact same attitude as the poor despairing civilians I'd seen in Sudzha: there is nothing we can do, the government has all the power, the poor people have nothing. Russian propaganda had been entirely effective in politically neutering everyone in the country. It was the direct opposite of the Ukrainian mentality.

It also showed one other thing that Ukrainians came to deeply dislike about Russian liberals. They almost always saw themselves as just as much the victims as Ukrainians. An old Oxford colleague of mine, Polina Ivanova, had written a fascinating essay about how the pressures of war had crushed Russian theatre. She talked about how government and social pressure had gradually coaxed the most supposedly liberal sector of Russian society, the theatre community, into supporting, or at least acquiescing to, the war. A few are forced to leave Russia because of their anti-war stance. But Polina's protagonist, Oleg, had wound me up the wrong way. At the end of the article, after he's moved from Russia to Bulgaria, to escape arrest for his stance against the invasion, he speaks. 'Because, shit, I left everything behind. I have nothing left … That's the most horrible thing. It makes you think, then, well, what was all this for? You're sitting alone in Bulgaria. What for?' Oleg says. 'It's quite frightening to end up nowhere, to jump into nothingness.' Oleg, by his own admission, had a house, money and the safety of his family. Thousands of Ukrainians have none of these, and I felt like Oleg still managed to shine the spotlight on his own suffering rather than that of those who genuinely have nothing left. I thought of Helga, fleeing Mariupol after seeing the corpses of her neighbours and friends, knowing she'll likely never see her home or family again. That is a real 'jump into nothingness'.

The Kremlin's first priority, after launching the largest European land war since the Second World War, should presumably have been to win the war. In fact, it was to maintain social stability. So, Putin ended up treating it like the war campaign of a feudal king of old, a crusade which made the war the king's private business. He would use the country's treasure and raise his own army from prisons or occupied territories, and his underlings would compete for his affections. But the ordinary people, as long as they kept their heads down, would be allowed to continue their normal lives mostly unmolested.

A few drinks in, Russians could be bolder about their opinions. 'You know Zaporizhzhia and Kherson, we all know they voted to be Russian,' slurred one drunk young man to me in a bar in the Armenian capital of Yerevan. The referendums had been so fatuously rigged that I couldn't believe anyone would take them seriously, but he did. 'Yeah, I know!' I shot back. 'If it is so important they are Russian, you should be taking up a gun and going straight to the front lines there!'

According to one friend who visited Moscow several times during this period, next to nothing about everyday life has changed. There is a McDonald's substitute, more Chinese cars on the road and a few patriotic recruitment posters. But outside of the border regions that occasionally see shelling, there has been little effect on the average Russian.

'A few stores closed because of sanctions, which is frustrating but not that bad,' Yuliya, an eighteen-year-old high-school graduate, told the *New York Times*. It was a curious mix of messaging. On the one hand, the Kremlin declared that this was an existential war for the Russian nation, that they were fighting Nazis and Satanists. But on the other, it wanted to wage this war with as little domestic blowback as possible. Russia's liberal opposition was cratered; its popularity destroyed by infighting, an exodus of dissidents to other countries and a relentless propaganda and lawfare campaign by the regime. So, the only real opponents of Putin were not those who wanted to stop the war. They were the ones who wanted the war to continue as hard and as fast as possible. They also ranted about corruption in the elite and the lifestyles. As Yevgeny Prigozhin put it in an interview shortly before his death:

Lavrov's daughter lives in London! I told them, 'Have you no shame?' What about Shoigu? What about the shameful behaviour of his son-in-law and his daughter? What are they spending these large amounts of money on? Are they using their own money? But no money for supplies! Talking about how they are against the SMO! We didn't come up with this SMO. It was not our idea. But we have to see it through to the end. They have lost their goddamn mind. They go to UAE to shake their asses. The kids of the elite are beyond saving. Consider the 'Navalny effect'. Whenever someone stole something, Navalny would raise a stink. And so, these corrupt officials would think twice before running with their stolen money. Now that he sits behind bars, and everyone thinks that all is going well, there are no controls on bad behaviour.

Luc Oerthel, a French journalist in Armenia who was covering the conflict in Nagorno-Karabakh, was shocked to be asked by a colleague also living there if he wanted to be an 'international observer' for one of the referendums that was supposed to pave the way for the incorporation of occupied areas of Ukraine into Russia. Oerthel flew to Russia with a camera and a team of misfits and oddballs. They included a Brazilian economics undergraduate, a general of the Myanmar military junta, western employees of Kremlin-controlled TV channels and a few pro-Russian activists from Zimbabwe and Togo. The group gathered at a conference in Moscow, and Oerthel says, 'You can't make this up.' Speaking in appalling French, the conference organiser told the observers that Russia had nothing to do, he claimed, with even organising the referendums! It was all a local initiative, so desperate were the occupied populations to join with Russia.

Later, they were taken to the Russian-occupied Kherson region. One observer says, without a hint of irony, 'They are expecting 100 per cent turnout!' Another leads the crowd in chanting, 'Long live Russia, long live President Putin!' Remember that international observers are expected to be non-partisan, independent professionals. They then fly to Simferopol in Crimea and are divided into groups, where they are then driven into the town of Skadovsk in the Kherson region in the company of Russian special forces. The deputy head of the Kherson occupation authorities, Kirill Stremousov, openly admits that heavily armed Russian soldiers were going door to door supervising people as they filled out their ballots. Oerthel and his fellow 'observers' were taken to 'observe' empty ballot boxes in a school and shown that they had a curtain in front of them as 'evidence' the vote was free and fair.

Oerthel was then taken to St Petersburg to witness the votes being 'counted', where it is just an endless count of 'yes'. In the end, more than 90 per cent vote to join the Russian Federation, and the Myanmarese military 'observer' gets up to give a speech congratulating President Putin and the people of 'Donetsk and Luhansk'. Despite the general's presumably heartfelt pleas, even the thugs of Myanmar's military junta didn't recognise the annexations. Only North Korea and Syria did.

Repression in the occupied areas became harsher after annexation happened. 'Serhiy' was just thirteen when Russian police in the occupied Ukrainian town of Vasylivka arrested him. They had watched the teenage boy, already tall and broad shouldered, going up a hill in the city five times a week and suspected him of spying. He managed to hide his phone as they approached, and as they could find no incriminating evidence on him, they eventually released him. According to his teacher, who now lives in the Ukrainian-controlled city of Zaporizhzhia, what he was doing was benign – he had been looking for an area with stable mobile internet reception so he could continue to study online with his classmates in the Ukrainian school he was enrolled in.

'When the war began, all of Serhiy's values were re-evaluated,' his teacher told *New Lines* in an interview. Before the war, he saw school as an unpleasant duty, and he didn't want to go or do any lessons.

> But when regular things that we take for granted in regular life, such as friends, going to school and doing lessons and learning from a teacher, became difficult and disappeared, he realised what an opportunity they were ... He changed his attitude. He understood how much Ukrainian school is necessary for him, how many important things they learn and gather for their future life.

She refers to the children who continue their education as 'little heroes' for playing their part in preparing to build the future of Ukraine.

But for the Russians, with their increasingly fragile hold on occupied regions in southern and eastern Ukraine, this seemingly harmless activity is considered a grave challenge to their authority. In Vasylivka, the experienced teachers had mostly been replaced by pliant Russian collaborators, and the students' phones began being regularly searched for any pro-Ukrainian material.

Most ominously, the Russians began visiting the houses of parents of school-age children late at night. After searching their properties, they would warn that any parent who allowed their child to stay in school in Ukraine or refused to send them to the new Russian schools could be 'deprived of their parental rights and have their children taken away from them', said Serhiy's teacher.

According to Ivan Fedorov, the exiled mayor of the occupied Ukrainian city of Melitopol, these threats have been carried out.

He said that one woman was deported to Russia, along with her children, because occupation authorities discovered they had been studying at a Ukrainian school.

But it is what the Russians make the children do outside the curriculum that is the most unsettling. They have instituted a mandatory youth organisation, Yunarmia or 'Youth Army', where children have to wear paramilitary uniforms and patrol the streets, putting flowers on First World War graves. They were also forced to write letters to Russian soldiers, thanking them for 'liberating' them from Ukraine.

One of the teachers shared with me the link to a pro-Russian Telegram channel, which is full of photos of glum-looking students writing the letters and then displaying them. It claims that 'the children are congratulated by representatives of other regions of Russia … All letters are united by one phrase: we believe in you, our dear defenders! Victory will be yours!' But the bags under their eyes, worried frowns and unconvincing smiles make the photos look like stills from hostage videos.

THE Z FACTOR

In May 2023, a small group of Russians launched the 'Angry Patriots Club'. The founding was barely covered in the western press, receiving scant mention on a few blogs. It was headlined by Igor Girkin, the instigator of the first Donbas war, who was joined by some of the veterans of that conflict, and they were here to protest the war. They were not against the war itself, of course, but the absolutely bungled way the Kremlin had handled it. To give the devils their due, they were some of the only people in the country willing to call the Kremlin out on its lies and propaganda. They made a list of the thirty-nine most serious failings of the war, demanding answers from the government. Russian writer Anatoly Karlin translated some of the highlights:

> Who answers for allowing Ukraine eight years to arm and consolidate itself – when in 2014 the new Kiev regime's authority rested on a thread, and all Novorossiya lay bare for the taking after Crimea?
>
> Why were criminals and fraudsters allowed to take power in the People's Republics, transforming what should have been a showcase of the Russian World into a midden heap? Who was behind the killings of the 2014 resistance heroes?
>
> Why were SMO plans built on assumptions fully detached from reality? Who misinformed the President?
>
> Why were Ukraine's decision-making centres, telecoms, air defence, transport infrastructure etc. not destroyed nor even significantly damaged?

Karlin had been a staunch pro-war Russian nationalist at the start of the war. When I met him in London in 2024, he had become disgusted with the Russian regime because of its mix of brutality and incompetence. It was a 'kakistocracy', he said, rule of the least competent. He'd written a long essay, 'The Z of History', where he explained the corruption, rot and intellectual incoherence at the heart of the Putin regime, which he said was reduced to 'inane drivel about the holy war against the Gay Satanic Nazis'. He was convinced that as soon as Russian nationalists stopped being useful to Putin, he would have them jailed or killed. 'Any prolongation of the war is programmed to be an unmitigated negative sum horror,' he wrote. 'The war is degenerating into the cyberpunk man and drone equivalent of the Early Modern "push of pike" that will programmatically involve ever more brutally coerced manpower.'

One of the other pro-war figures to challenge the Kremlin's line was Yevgeny Prigozhin, still Wagner chief at that time. Prigozhin became more and more disillusioned with the Ukraine campaign and was convinced that his men were dying for nothing. In one interview, he said:

> We came, rudely, trampled all over the country, searching for Nazis, pissing everyone off, got to Kiev, shit our pants and then left. The same thing happened in Kherson, Izium, Liman, and we keep shitting our pants.
>
> What really happened though? Russia decided to make Ukraine the cause célèbre of the world and legitimised their country. The whole world now knows and supports their cause. This is 'de-Nazification' apparently. As for de-militarisation, well the people of Belgorod know how well it is going.

He would soon denounce all the reasons the Kremlin had given for starting the war and lead a rebellion almost to the gates of Moscow.

One of the people who joined the Wagner rebellion was Sever. Despite being initially euphoric during the Russian invasion of Ukraine in 2022, Sever soon began to grow disillusioned with the often disastrous military choices, logistical nightmares and territorial losses coming from decisions made in Moscow. When the Prigozhin-led Wagner rebellion erupted in the summer of '23, Sever threw his weight behind it and expressed full support for a regime change that would, as he described it, 'put a real warrior in charge and rid us of these pen-pushing faggots'. Prigozhin might have originally been a chef by trade, but his regular presence on the battlefield was well respected by ethnic Russians in the Donbas. In contrast to Putin's swanky offices in Moscow, Prigozhin was certainly winning the lion's share of alpha male attributes.

But when the rebellion fizzled out, many of those who'd initially backed Prigozhin saw the writing on the wall and slid into the shadows, praying that their disobedience to the Kremlin would go unnoticed in the overall fog of war. Sever, though, was a stubborn miner and refused to pipe down, often airing the same grievances even after the leader of the pack, Prigozhin, was out of the picture. Following a heavy drinking session with some former comrades in the suburbs of Donetsk, Sever was never seen again.

'Who the fuck is this?' an unknown voice barked back at me when I tried to make contact with Sever's old phone in 2025. A former friend of his informed me in coded lingo that 'Sever is gone, man; you can say that he ran with a rabid dog and got bit. That's it.' The call was then abruptly terminated.

PEACEFUL PEOPLE

We were in a school basement in Sudzha, the biggest Ukrainian-controlled city in Russia's Kursk Oblast, listening to the sound of shelling growing closer. There were Russian drones flying overhead, and the Ukrainian soldiers escorting us were growing nervous that they could spot us and we would become a target for artillery fire. Around us were twenty to thirty bedraggled and frightened civilians of various ages, who had moved their sleeping bags and personal amenities down here to shelter from the incoming storm. The basement smelled terrible, full of body odour and mildew. It was a familiar scene that could have been in any of the Ukrainian towns that have been systematically levelled by the Russians during their invasion. Back in the school, there was a sign next to the door of the basement that said 'Peaceful people'. It was written by the local residents – it meant not only that they were civilians but that they had nothing to do with Russia's wider war against Ukraine. The remaining residents told us that the city authorities had simply fled the Ukrainian advance, organising no evacuation or assistance for their civilians. Those who had their own vehicles had since left for the regional capital of Kursk.

Nikolai, a middle-aged man bringing supplies in and out of the basement, maintained that ordinary Russians had nothing to do with the war and should not be blamed. When asked what the people living so close to the war zone thought of the situation in Ukraine, he said, 'We are small poor people, we don't know what to do, whatever we do will not help. We don't watch TV or this propaganda ... But, these are the masters of the country, they are doing this war, not us. We are not guilty.' He didn't vote in elections, he said, because 'I'm not going, because nothing will change so why should I waste my time?'

Now, the locals are on their phones, playing games, scrolling TikTok and waiting out the war until the fighting in this region stops. Like so many Ukrainian civilians, they are trying to survive day by day. 'Oh. Not political!' Vadim, the Ukrainian officer in charge of leading me around Kursk, said with a smirk. It is a pointed barb at the fact that many Russians who claim not to support the war say they are not political people and should not be blamed. The Ukrainians think that this political apathy is what has allowed Putin to get away with his invasion. Nikolai put a hand over his brow before saying, 'We are poor and no one cares about us, you understand? Poor, unwanted!'

'There are good people everywhere and there are bad people

everywhere. We all want one thing – peace. Nothing can be stopped here,' one woman said. 'This is a useless conversation. We are not leaders, we are nobodies and nothing, they abandoned us because we are old. If I were the leader, this wouldn't be happening.'

There it was again, the same as with the Russians I had met in Georgia. The total abdication of responsibility, the total adject acceptance of their own powerlessness, the learned helplessness that you would never see from Ukrainians.

'You see, they're lying, they're all lying. Who should you trust? You can't trust the TV either.'

The argument continued back and forth between the commander and the civilians.

My Ukrainian friends were scathing about these people. Tetiana Drobotia, a Ukrainian journalist from Zaporizhzhia, told me this was typical of the Russian mindset that took no responsibility for their country's atrocities:

> I just listened to that recording you sent and honestly, I'm so angry. They look nice, but when the conversation goes deeper, they are so absolutely Russian! Only on the third year of the war when there was shelling, they went to the basement. But other than that, they did not care about this!

We asked Andrei, one of the Ukrainian soldiers stationed here, if he had sympathy for the civilians sheltering ironically from the shelling of their own army. 'Honestly, not really. I am from Mariupol, so after seeing what happened in Bucha and in my home city, I maybe feel a little sympathy for them, but they are very low down my list.'

The most honest Russians, even the right-wing nationalist ones, admit their real motives. One pseudonymous Russian blogger

'Rurik Skywalker' wrote: 'At the most fundamental ... the Kremlin's SMO [special military operation] isn't about biolabs, Donetsk, Kherson, Odessa, nazis, NATO rockets, Ukrainian shells, FSB roadside bombs, or the fanciful notion that Ukraine was about to commit national suicide and ground-attack Donbass. It isn't about any of this small fry stuff.' Strelkov said, 'The Russian invasion ... was about retaining control over Ukraine's direction of travel, and the Donbas was simply a potentially useful tool in this.' For his insolence, Strelkov was arrested by the Russian authorities and now sits in a cell, doomed to rot in prison.

Rihanna had finished her set to a standing ovation, and she pranced off the stage as a bevy of fireworks exploded over the stadium's roof. 'Thank you, Ukraine, I can't wait to come back again,' she shouted, as she waltzed off a stage that now lies abandoned and overgrown, where the turnstiles that welcomed her thousands of spectators have been wrecked by shellfire, and the only fireworks that can be seen are the flames of rockets being fired from their launchers in the dead of night.

That is the *Ruskiy Mir*.

AFTERWORD: MAN OF THE YEAR

STEPANAKERT, NAGORNO-KARABAKH, OCTOBER 2020

It was the 'first video game war', the terrified soldiers in Nagorno-Karabakh said. Pop their heads out of a trench or jump in an armoured car and they'd be struck by a terrifying pinpoint strike from up to 30,000 feet in the air. Their foes were using new Bayraktar TB-2 drones, made in Turkey and bought for the express purpose of righting what Azerbaijanis said was a great historic wrong. I watched one strike a field near the town of Martuni – no warning, just a huge bang and a plume of dust where the target had been. The Ukrainians cursed their opponents for not fighting 'like men', but armed with antiquated artillery and assault rifles, they were no match for their enemy's technological might. They might as well have been cursing the wind for blowing.

For more than twenty-five years, Armenia and Azerbaijan were engaged in an on-and-off conflict over the enclave of Nagorno-Karabakh. Nestled in the mountains of the Caucasus, this mostly ethnically Armenian region had been part of Azerbaijan under the Soviet Union but had declared independence in the early 1990s. Local militias, backed by the Armenian Army, had decisively defeated Azerbaijan in the fighting – thousands on both sides were killed or ethnically cleansed. But in the years after, the oil-rich dictator Ilham Aliyev in Baku prepared ruthlessly, modernising his military and building crucial alliances with Turkey and Israel while Armenians rested on their laurels.

In 2020, the war was over in forty-four days of bloodshed. The Azerbaijanis captured back large swathes of territory, both in Nagorno-Karabakh itself and the provinces around it. But they stopped short of capturing the capital of Stepanakert and agreed to leave this and other large population centres in Armenian hands, for the time being. It was the Russians who brokered the deal – they'd historically had a friendly relationship with Armenia, and a hot war in their backyard was not something they wanted to deal with at this point.

For Armenia, a small country in need of protection, whose people were victims of a genocide by the Ottoman Empire during the First World War, siding with Moscow is understandable. There is ironically a precedent here in Ukrainian history – the nationalists who preferred the Nazis after the Holodomor genocide by the Soviet Union.

Armenia begged Russia for protection, and Moscow sent nearly 2,000 peacekeepers to protect the people of Nagorno-Karabakh. The Karabakhis at first saw the Russians as their saviours. Russian soldiers guarded Armenian communities and escorted worshippers to ancient Armenian churches that had ended up on the wrong side of the front line. They ensured the flow of people and goods to and from Armenia via the Lachin corridor. On the road from Armenia to Stepanakert in 2021 was a huge photo of Putin, with the words 'Man of the Year' written below it.

Then, Putin invaded Ukraine. All of a sudden, events in what he saw as this backwater were of no concern. As he lost more and more land in Ukraine, the cunning Aliyev realised he had a unique opportunity. So, he started his own hybrid warfare campaign, using food as a weapon. He cut the supply corridor from Armenia, causing huge shortages of food and fuel throughout the region. His soldiers slowly took pieces of territory in the grey zone, including in Armenia itself.

As he expected, the Russians did not react, despite their promise to protect the people of Karabakh and their treaty alliances with Armenia. Bogged down in Ukraine, they had no appetite to stand up to Azerbaijan or for another war. They wanted to wash their hands of Karabakh.

In September 2023, Aliyev decided to finish the job. He launched a lightning offensive against what remained of Armenian-controlled Nagorno-Karabakh. This time, the war was over in a single day. Videos of Azerbaijani soldiers decapitating and murdering soldiers and civilians in areas they had captured in 2020 gave the Armenians an idea of what was in store for them. So, the entire population, just over 100,000 people, were forced to leave their ancestral homes. The Russian peacekeepers stood by and watched. This is how the

Ruskiy Mir treated people who genuinely begged for its protection – it abandoned them as soon as they became inconvenient to Russia itself.

The country has announced its withdrawal from the Collective Security Treaty Organization, the Russian version of NATO, passed legislation to apply to join the EU and invited American and French military co-operation on its soil. Putin might have secured either support or acquiescence from his citizens for his war in Ukraine – but some of Russia's oldest allies are finally turning their back on him.

CHAPTER NINE

THE LONGEST DAYS: UKRAINE'S FAILED COUNTEROFFENSIVE

'Our landings in the Cherbourg-Havre area have failed to gain a satisfactory foothold and I have withdrawn the troops. My decision to attack at this time and place was based upon the best information available. The troops, the air and the Navy did all that bravery and devotion to duty could do. If any blame or fault attaches to the attempt it is mine alone.'
— General Dwight D. Eisenhower

AUCKLAND TO ANDRIIVKA

ANDRIIVKA, DONETSK REGION, AUGUST 2023

A young man emerged from the basement bleeding lightly from his stomach and limping. Two Ukrainian paramedics were helping him make the journey to our waiting ambulance. With his mohawk, pierced ears and tattoos, we called him 'Cossack' because of his similarity to the seventeenth-century Ukrainian swashbucklers.

Smoke was rising from all sides from the recent Russian shelling salvos all around us, although the countryside was eerily quiet. He was still grinning and excitedly sharing a story as he entered the ambulance with us. 'They only killed their own,' he would later relay to us from the relative safety of a nearby hospital. 'They fired at our positions, and the only person they killed was one of our prisoners who we had captured a few days ago.'

Knowing it wouldn't be long until the artillery battle resumed, we hightailed it. Normally, injured soldiers are transported from the front in an armoured medevac vehicle. But casualties had been so high today that they had run out of suitable vehicles, so the medics had to take a chance on the open road to the trenches in a soft-skinned ambulance. Cossack told us it had no way of stopping an artillery shell.

A few miles in front of us was the town of Andriivka, which Cossack's brigade had been fighting towards since the beginning of Ukraine's counteroffensive in June.

Matthew, a medic with Ukraine's Third Assault Brigade, took us in his ambulance to watch medics picking up soldiers like Cossack from the front line and delivering them to hospitals for emergency treatment. The day we visited was the day they had finally reached their goal of taking back the village of Andriivka, which had taken more than two months. Its capture allows Ukraine to threaten one of the key supply lines into Bakhmut, a major step to encircling Russians inside the city. 'We know the price; every kilometre is paid for with the blood of our guys,' Matthew told us. They had smashed the remaining Russian positions in the village with artillery before infantry units moved in to mop up the last pockets of resistance. Before the war, in a different life, Matthew was an interior designer. Constantly concerned for the safety of our team, and never comfortable with a weapon in his hands, he is not a natural killer, but a determined doctor. 'We need you to stay safe here – the world needs you to show what fucking Russians do on Ukrainian lands.'

When we arrived back at a designated evacuation point, the

location of which we were asked not to identify, it was a blur of movement. Several armoured vehicles had brought injured men from other parts of the front. The Russians had learned that the Ukrainians had completely taken Andriivka, and they had blasted the town with a mass artillery barrage in revenge. Matthew, along with the rest of his unit, has fought in and around Bakhmut since January this year. It is an entirely volunteer unit, with little fancy western kit such as Leopard tanks or Bradley Fighting Vehicles. Old Soviet-era equipment, including T-72 tanks, is constantly trundling down the road next to us. At night, we see flames bursting into the sky in front of us as a Grad rocket launcher fires towards Russian positions. Yet the brigades here have achieved some of the counter-offensive's most notable successes, and the fighters believe that their extensive combat experience matters more than whatever weapons they receive.

It was a day of celebration – the Ukrainians having finally taken the objective that had eluded them for so long with heavy fighting. Now, they expected to press on much more quickly and even retake the city of Bakhmut entirely. Instead, this was to be their last hurrah.

I was glad I was able to help these guys just a tiny bit. I'd been involved in helping load and drive a series of ambulances from New Zealand that had passed their mileage straight to the front line. 'We call these Ubers for the wounded,' said Matthew, nodding towards his ambulance that had been brought by New Zealand charity Kiwi Kare (Kiwi Aid and Refugee Evacuation).

'If soldiers are injured on the battlefield, their location is relayed via walkie-talkie. A vehicle is called, and it reaches them and gets them out of danger and into our hands to a safer place,' he explained.

Tenby Powell, the founder of humanitarian charity Kiwi Kare, said the idea to bring New Zealand ambulances to Ukraine was sparked by his work last year bringing in European ambulances, many from Poland. He contacted Hato Hone St John, which he described as 'a dream to work with'. His experience both in business and as a colonel in the New Zealand Defence Forces with former deployments to Israel and Lebanon gave him a unique advantage when operating in a war zone like Ukraine.

The ambulances were donated at the end of their New Zealand lifespan when repair costs had become too high. For Ukrainian soldiers, accustomed to decades-old Soviet-era ambulances, they are a dream to drive and operate.

In Kyiv, six of the ambulances were painted black and green to disguise them from the prying eyes of Russian observation drones that look for targets all around the front line. They also had Māori names painted on them including Rangatira (leadership), Kaitiaki (guardianship) and Wairua (spirit). They had been blessed by an iwi in New Zealand before leaving to grant those driving and riding in them safe passage.

After that, it was time for the Ukrainian soldiers to take the wheels and deliver them to the front lines in the east and south of the country where they met Matthew and their other drivers. Yet while individual Kiwis have made significant contributions to the war, it has faded from public view in New Zealand. New Zealand is yet to send any military weapons or supplies to Ukraine, no New Zealand Prime Minister has visited the country and the subject was barely raised on the campaign trail for the 2023 election.

'While it seems that NZ is far removed from Russia's war of aggression in Ukraine, the reality is it impacts everyone around the world ... Commodity pricing, wheat, grain and fuel,' Powell highlights. 'But the real reason we need to support Ukraine', he says:

is our shared values. At its most fundamental, this is a fight for democracy, in the sense that a much larger aggressor is seeking to take away Ukraine's sovereignty and we should all be concerned about that. This is a reshaping of the world order, and we should all be very concerned about that because the new alliances could very well clump together … It will be of no surprise to me if this spills over to the rest of the region … It is both the economic issue and the moral issue.

KA MATE

SALISBURY PLAINS, ENGLAND, NOVEMBER 2022

The New Zealand soldiers lined up in formation, legs akimbo, clad in camouflage and thumb their chest, '*Ah ka mate, ka mate, ka ora, ka ora*' or 'it is life, it is life, it is death, it is death'. The haka, made famous by the New Zealand Rugby team, is a war dance, and you slap your own chest to indicate that you will live and point at your enemy to let him know he will die. It was being done to greet a series of visiting dignitaries. The crack of rifle fire echoed over the Salisbury Plains, and in the background, we could hear the whir of helicopter blades as a large dark green military helicopter carrying the Defence Ministers of New Zealand and the United Kingdom landed. I was proud to see my country doing its part. Here, about 130 Kiwis had been training greenhorn Ukrainian troops in the basics of combat. My countrymen were impressed. Nathan, one trainer, said that the Ukrainians were far more impressive than the Afghans or Iraqis he had trained on previous missions. 'They're really hungry to learn; they have a passion and a thirst for knowledge.' In between breaks, the recruits would come to the instructors and bombard them with questions and demand explanations and extra rehearsals of what they had been learning. Nathan said it was astonishing that 'we haven't had people pulling sickies or trying to get out of the field. They hate it if they have to leave for some medical thing. Whereas back home, if things are going hard, you might get up and say, "Oh, I'm feeling sick today."'

After Ukraine's stunning success in Kharkiv and Kherson, many in the west had finally come around to the possibility of Ukraine not just keeping itself alive but even winning territory back, possibly kicking the Russians out of the Ukrainian territory they had stolen in 2014. There was one military objective over all others. The only real prize the Russians had captured – outside of some ruined husks of cities in the Donbas – was the land bridge running to occupied Crimea via southern Donetsk and Zaporizhzhia Oblasts. An attack here could potentially cut off the Kremlin's access to Crimea.

Ben Wallace, then UK Secretary of Defence, was about as gung-ho as it gets about Ukraine's chances. He said that in recent conversations with his Ukrainian counterparts, which were on a weekly basis, he'd urged them to 'keep up the pressure'.

The Ukrainians were taking an operational pause, but he seemed to think this was unwise. 'Given the advantage the Ukrainians have in equipment training and quality of their personnel against the demoralised, poorly trained, poorly equipped Russians, it would be in Ukraine's interest to maintain momentum through the winter. They have 300,000 pieces of arctic warfare kit, from the international community.' The British had always been the most bullish about Ukraine's chances. The US, by contrast, was beginning to show a note of caution. Mark Milley, chairman of the Joint Chiefs of Staff, had said that Ukraine should consider negotiating, now that it was in its strongest battlefield position yet.

Vitaliy Krasovskiy, the defence attaché in London, who works on liaising with foreign militaries, was full of praise for his British counterparts, saying that British commitment went 'well above' that of most other countries. He noted that officials at the UK's Ministry of Defence were 'extraordinarily committed', often working regular overtime and weekends at key points of the military campaign. 'If our armed forces need a particular vehicle or piece of weaponry, the Brits will search through the military catalogues of different countries and find what we need,' he added, citing the Australian Bushmaster as an example. The difference, he explained, was that while the US saw Ukrainian success as in their own interests, the Brits had a passionate emotional attachment to a full Ukrainian victory.

He also mentioned former UK Prime Minister Boris Johnson's early and regular trips to Kyiv to meet with Zelensky as an important factor in boosting Ukrainian morale and demonstrating international support. While Johnson is mostly disgraced in his home country, he remains a folk hero in Ukraine, appearing on murals, T-shirts, coffee mugs and beer cans.

Despite the professionalism of the western trainers, and the thoroughness of their instruction, they privately admit there is a gaping hole in their ability to teach. 'Quite frankly, we've never fought this kind of war before,' one instructor said.

Western militaries' major combat experience in recent decades has been fighting counter-insurgency battles against the Taliban in Afghanistan. But this was a war being fought largely through massive artillery barrages from a powerful state military, which western soldiers have almost universally never faced.

One trainer told me:

They are practising artillery on the light fire range at the moment, and we do fire manoeuvre ranges as well as battle simulation. We'll have loud bangs that simulate artillery. We have exercises where we bring in amputees and dress them to make it look like that amputation was caused by artillery and make the recruits responsible for treating that individual.

He is confident that despite the short training time, 'after five weeks, they come out combat capable. They can shoot straight, communicate and medicate.' There were already some grumblings that not all of the preparations were going right. One of the Ukrainian soldiers on the base complained that when they were on the battlefield, reconnaissance drones were the big new thing, and so learning to navigate through binoculars and maps seemed completely anachronistic.

Cutting the land bridge was a daunting prospect, with considerably different battlefield contradictions from either Kharkiv or Kherson. Kherson had been a particularly tough nut to crack. Ukraine was fighting well-trained Russian airborne who were well dug in and took heavy casualties at first. It took months to make a breakthrough – and that was only because the Russians had their backs to the river.

Russians had mobilised 300,000 additional troops, and while the process had been bedraggled and chaotic, bringing in a lot of low-quality troops, it allowed them to plug the gaping holes in their front line. This situation would not be replicated in Zaporizhzhia. General Surovikin had invested huge amounts of work in building an extensive fortifications network stretching across Zaporizhzhia, where the Ukrainian Army was expected to come from. To make matters worse, the outlines of the Ukrainian plans were leaked to the Russians months in advance, so they knew exactly where, and close to when, Ukraine would attack.

To counter the Russian advantages, the Ukrainians and their supporters in the west embarked on a campaign to get Ukraine an extraordinary number of armoured vehicles and the latest western tanks, along with F-16 fighter jets and long-range missiles like the Army Tactical Missile System. The exact process of what was delivered when is a complicated and dull affair but suffice to say that the timelines were far too slow. There was a large delay caused by the international effort to convince Germany to allow the transfer of Leopard tanks to Ukraine.

But there were larger strategic errors as well. The Russians had begun ramping up their own industrial production for artillery shells and drones and importing extra weapons from North Korea and Iran.

It was reasonable to think that Ukraine could establish an advantage in artillery fire and the risk of a Russian counteroffensive was low. Western support, which has been essential to Ukraine's war effort, was also likely to peak in summer 2023. The United States was burning through its stockpile of ammunition, while European states had failed to ramp up munitions production in 2022 and were just beginning to make the required investments, with lacklustre results. With elections looming in 2024, the political headwinds in western capitals also suggested that funding to support Ukraine would decline following this operation. The US borrowed ammunition from South Korea, and other western countries made efforts to contribute as part of a crash train-and-equip programme for Ukrainian forces. All told, the west trained and equipped nine brigades for the offensive. Ukraine would field several additional brigades from the armed forces and National Guard, organised under two corps, and a reserve task force.

D-DAY

ORIKHIV, ZAPORIZHZHIA OBLAST, JUNE 2023

In the trenches, the rats are the apex predator. 'There are many rodents that cannot be stopped. They climb and gnaw on food, and you can't eat it, so you discard it,' said Bogdan, a medic fighting in the sweltering trenches of Zaporizhzhia. 'But these are trivialities, everyday occurrences.'

Artem, a soldier who fought in this region, said:

> We had no cover. We had no artillery at that distance. It would reach their positions up to a point, but after that it just could not. Our drones helped destroy the infantry. In order to continue, we needed to pull up the artillery and pull up the allies, and that way we could move on.

Orikhiv looked for all the world like a quaint English country town. Roses, poppies and other spring flowers bloom, and the green hills are adorned with small, charming stone houses. Each house has a vegetable garden and vines growing on nets that creep up the walls. The town, which was once a centre of agriculture in the Zaporizhzhia region, housed about 14,000 residents in rural bliss and prosperity before the war.

In the eastern part of the country, it was difficult to get answers about whom people openly supported. Whether it was fear or something else that controlled that fear is hard to say, but in Orikhiv, people were singing and shouting patriotic slogans, and there are

Ukrainian flags all over the walls. One middle-aged woman shouted at us with a big grin: 'We love Ukraine; it's our home, and we will win the war!' Here, people speak a lot of Ukrainian, even though Zaporizhzhia was previously a predominantly Russian-speaking area.

When the offensive started, the Ukrainians made the slightly puzzling decision to attack on three axes. The first was from Orikhiv down towards Tokmak; the second further east from Velyka Novosilka down towards Berdiansk; and the final one towards Bakhmut, to try to fix Russian forces in their positions. It went pear-shaped on day one.

One major report noted:

> Equipped with advanced American weapons and heralded as the vanguard of a major assault, the troops became bogged down in dense Russian minefields under constant fire from artillery and helicopter gunships. Units got lost. One unit delayed a nighttime attack until dawn, losing its advantage. Another fared so badly that commanders yanked it off the battlefield altogether.

Artem, a soldier speaking to me from a rehabilitation centre in Kyiv where he was learning to use prosthetic limbs, agreed:

> By the book, that's how it is supposed to be. We should have air support. But in Ukraine, there is a different type of war. We can't [even] provide air defence because they'll shoot it down. They carried me five kilometres because there was no way to get there by car.

The soldiers talk little about the pain they experienced, explaining it by being in a state of shock. 'I do not remember my pain; I only remember that I really wanted to drink. I had very big cramps, and somehow, I immediately realised that I was seriously injured. My legs were completely cut. Without the tourniquets, I would have bled to death,' Artem said. Both his legs were amputated, when I met him. He had learned to walk with his hands, drive a car, even workout; at one point, he lifted his torso up with a handstand. His unit was attacking Verbove, a small village, the second stop on the long way down towards Melitopol. It was supposed to be captured within the first four days of the operation. It was three months in, and the Ukrainians were only just knocking at the door.

Artem said that the difference between training and real combat in Ukraine was huge. The instructors who taught them how to fight usually did not participate in active combat themselves. Ukrainians understood this during training, but they didn't think the difference would be so drastic. 'They taught us from a book. But real war is different from a book. In reality, you have to build a shelter from improvised materials and no one brings you anything.' A significant difference in the training was also the reconnaissance by FPV drones. 'It is something that the Ukrainian Army already does, but the information as such was not widely taught.'

The war found Artem in Zaporizhzhia. He was originally in construction in a peaceful life. When the full-scale invasion began, his desire to volunteer arose immediately, although he did not have any prior military experience. At some point, he felt he was not brave enough to go to the recruitment office alone and voice his desire. After receiving a call and a special letter, he joined a special reconnaissance battalion. In the Zaporizhzhia direction, he worked as part of an assault group. The attack at Verbove looked like a normal working day. The soldiers were gathered near pickup trucks. In the morning, they were told about the area and given points along which they had to move. Artem had a map to lead his group. He recalls that it all happened around 10 September because on the 11th he had already been wounded.

When Artem and his team were in position, the Russians began to fire on them. Artem and his comrades tried to retake the position. They were fired upon with artillery and drones dropped grenades on them. After Artem was wounded, he waited for another three hours for help. Of the twenty-seven people, five died and twenty-two were injured. After his group faced losses, another one came to help. The Ukrainian Army took Robotyne and advanced towards Verbove. The main problem was that there was less ammunition. Artem was fired at by a drone every twenty seconds, and this was the case for three to four hours. He says it is a miracle that he survived.

Several Ukrainian soldiers complained to me about the lack of aviation. 'NATO would never do an operation like this without air superiority,' they said. Western experts tend to disagree. Justin Bronk, an airpower expert at the think tank, said this was unrealistic: 'The F-16 is an extraordinarily complicated airframe. The training pipeline is years on end, and this is for experienced pilots that can come off Soviet craft. They are combat inefficient for their first two years of service.' I'm not sure this debate will ever be fully resolved, but it continues to this day.

It wasn't all a catastrophe, however. In the Black Sea, things were looking better than ever. I remember in April 2022, when a long queue and an excited line of people were still a rarity in early spring anywhere in Ukraine, which made the huge line snaking outside the post office even more of an eye-catching moment. Everyone looked cheerful to be there, as if standing in that line was their patriotic duty. They were looking to buy a stamp destined to be an instant collector's item. On it, a Ukrainian soldier was facing the flagship of the Russian Black Sea Fleet, the *Moskva*, and giving it the middle finger. Early in the war, a Ukrainian garrison on the tiny but strategically important Snake Island in the western Black Sea had told the *Moskva*'s crew the impeccable line: 'Russian warship, go fuck yourself.' That statement had turned prophetic, and the Ukrainians had sunk the *Moskva* with a homemade Neptune cruise missile. Now, the pride of the Russian Navy was a rusting hull at the bottom of the ocean. I spoke to one tourism company which said that they planned to offer dives to the wreck site when the war ended.

This was just the first triumph in one of Ukraine's most successful campaigns of the entire war. On paper, the Russians dominated the sea theatre. Most of the Ukrainian Navy had been seized in 2014 when the Crimean Peninsula was taken, and this should have been an easy part of the battlefield for Moscow to keep. Instead, the Ukrainians devised a new strategy, based on naval missiles and strike drones, to deny the Russians access to the sea. In September 2023, they struck Russian naval bases and the fleet headquarters in the city of Sevastopol. Some attacks in this period used sea drones, others long-range British Storm Shadow missiles. They destroyed submarines, landing ships and dry docks, making the use of the port in wartime impossible. So, the Russians were forced to withdraw their naval assets further east, to ports such as Novorossiysk.

This may have had a serious military effect if the Ukrainian counteroffensive had got near Crimea, but alas, it didn't, so we will never really know. Despite this, the fact that it was part of the strategy that allowed Ukraine to create a sea corridor to export grain meant that it was essential for the Ukrainian economy, not to mention for other parts of the world that relied on Ukrainian grain. It was also a major morale blow against Russia. One of the reasons Crimea had originally been so important for the Russians was because of its location as the port of the Black Sea fleet.

LOVE'S FRONT LINES

SLOVYANSK, DONETSK OBLAST, SEPTEMBER 2023

Stanislav's and Oksana's eyes had a few more bloodshot lines running through them and deeper and darker bags under their eyes than when I met them a year ago near Izium. The cheerful gaiety and excitement they had in doing their jobs and the spring in their step had faded, and they walked as if their shoes were full of lead. Yet they still held each other's hands. The casual nods and eye contact showed that they were still as reliant and close as they had been. A few months ago, I'd seen a photo of Stanislav in a wheelchair on Facebook and texted Oksana to ask what had happened.

'[My husband] led an assault group to storm the Russian positions along the Izium highway and he was wounded. A mine had blown up and he had been hit several times with shrapnel,' she replied. 'He is now in hospital and was operated on today. Part of the mine fragments were removed, but the other part can't be removed for now.' She is remarkably zen about nearly becoming a widow. 'It is intense here, but we move forward,' were her last words to me before heading back to the front line.

They were together on the front line again, although working a bit further back: Stanislav as a drone pilot, Oksana in logistics administration.

'The counteroffensive is going well,' he said, in that unconvinced, downcast tone that I'd heard from soldiers up and down the front, but he admitted what he feared most is a longer war. 'Everyone who wanted to fight signed up long ago,' he says from a cafe in the city of Slovyansk. 'If the Russians wanted to, they have millions of men they can mobilise. We are at our total limit.' That they were together at all was a miracle. 'He went offline for around five hours, and I nearly smashed one of my potted plants with anger and worry,' Oksana said.

Stanislav did say that another major boost for Ukrainian forces has been the arrival of US-made cluster munitions. The weapons are highly controversial because they leave bomblets that can fail to explode and remain a hazard to civilians for decades after the conflict is over. Ukrainian soldiers do not take this argument seriously. 'I've seen them working, and as soon as we fire, the Russians scatter, they hide,' said Stanislav. Before their arrival, Ukrainian forces were losing ground in this region to a Russian offensive. Now, this has largely stalled. The casualties they were taking were substantial, and Ukraine was quickly running out of combat-capable infantry with the training necessary to sustain their offensive.

GUARDIAN ANGELS

The medical staff shout '300s! 300s!' as they race out from their clinic to meet incoming ambulances, donning surgical gloves as they run. Code '300' is shorthand for wounded soldiers; they're trying to keep those injured troops from becoming '200' – dead.

It is around 10 a.m. in the Donetsk region of eastern Ukraine and a beaten-up old ambulance creaks up to the makeshift clinic's doorway to unload two soldiers critically injured during a frontline assault raging just four miles away.

The medical team throws open the doors, loads the casualties onto stretchers and carries them into an operating theatre. The patients are wrapped in gold-foil blankets, one bleeding so profusely from the abdomen that he immediately gets most of the doctor's attention.

The battlefield heroics of Ukraine's soldiers are well documented. Less well known are the doctors, nurses and paramedics who risk their lives to save the injured. Troops call them 'guardian angels'. We were granted access to one of these frontline medical locations, known as stabilisation points, in a village close to the heavily fought-over city of Bakhmut, on the condition we did not reveal its exact location.

Pumped full of morphine by battlefield paramedics to dull the pain, the injured men do not shout or scream, just make the occasional low moan. The medical team – consisting of at least one surgeon, an anaesthesiologist and a few nurses – loads the badly injured man into a surgical room and gets to work, stripping off his clothes and trying to sterilise and clean his wound and staunch the bleeding. After his condition stabilises, they stretcher him back outside and into an ambulance waiting to take him to a medical hospital in the nearby city of Kramatorsk.

There were between ten and fifteen of these field hospitals set up around the various front lines in Ukraine's south and east regions. All are within Russian artillery range. Just a few days before we visited the clinic, a rocket landed in the courtyard, though no one was harmed.

In the background, we can hear consistent shellfire and can see the vapor trails of 155mm shells. *'Nashi'* ('ours'), the medics said as the shots ring out. A soldier accompanying us said that they are probably from US-provided M777 howitzers that have been making a difference in the fight. While Ukraine has spent much of the war outgunned by Russian ordnance, almost all the artillery we hear seems to be coming from Ukrainian forces, who are slowly gaining the upper hand in this theatre. An hour or so later, I speak with the less badly injured of the two men. He introduces himself as Alexei, and he explains that he was injured by a rocket-propelled grenade fired by a group of Russian soldiers who were counterattacking a trench position the Ukrainians had captured near the town of Soledar, outside Bakhmut.

Being injured by small arms is an exception on this battlefield, where the doctors say around 80 per cent of casualties are caused by enemy artillery. On the southern front lines, where the Ukrainians are going up against heavily prepared Russian defensive lines, many casualties are from minefields. A report from the Center for Strategic and International Studies called these 'the most extensive defensive works in Europe since the Second World War'. Last year's Ukrainian counteroffensive successes in the Kharkiv and Kherson regions had given rise to hopes that they would be able to make a quick push to the sea to cut the Russians' land bridge to Crimea.

To save its equipment and, more importantly, its manpower, Ukraine had turned to a strategy of attrition, attempting to use its advantage in precision artillery to wear away at Russia's ability to wage war. The constant artillery exchanges mean that thousands of soldiers have come through this medical facility. 'At the beginning of June, there were days when there were 120–130 patients per day because of the combat units' activities,' said Oleh Tokarchuk, a 47-year-old doctor from the small town of Kolyma in the western Ivano-Frankivsk region of Ukraine. That's twenty to thirty more than they have staff or operating theatres to cope with, he said.

It is strange, the level of normality that can exist so close to the world's fiercest fighting. Despite our proximity to the front lines, there was perfect mobile internet connectivity. In lulls between patients, one nurse is using a computer to play the video game *League of Legends* and another is scrolling Instagram and TikTok. In the small village where the hospital is located, a few civilians remain. A small shop remains open, and I can still pay for my Red Bull and chocolate bar with Apple Pay.

In the relative calm of a building on the outskirts of the city of Kramatorsk, we were received by a group of medics working at the stabilisation point who had rotated out for a day's rest. Lyuba, who asked to only be identified by her first name, had worked as a civilian doctor for eight years. Originally from the city of Chernihiv in northern Ukraine, she enlisted as a volunteer in March 2022 and regularly works near the front lines, together with other top-flight doctors. 'We are professionals – we don't have paramedics who had two- or three-week courses and ran to the front line,' she said. 'There is always a senior doctor in a brigade with a nurse, a driver and a guard in dangerous zones.' The life-threatening cases they deal with often require specialist surgery that would tax the best western hospitals, like the soldier who arrived unconscious with a traumatic brain injury.

'He got a bullet in his eye because of close combat. It was very difficult because the bullet was in the skull,' she said. Because of the surgeon's skill, they were able to operate and save the soldier's life. In some cases, they would treat people who see them as their sworn enemies, like the pro-Russian civilians in some of the Donbas villages. Ukrainians refer to them as those who are 'waiting for the Russians', she explained. They were treating one such man when he woke and realised that everyone around him was speaking Ukrainian. 'He started swallowing his blood, screaming that he wouldn't allow us to collect his blood because Banderovtsy [Ukrainian nationalists] would use it for experiments! It was terrible,' she said. 'The funniest thing was that when he was calmed down, he was moved to a hospital for civilians staffed by Polish doctors. Our guys laughed that when he wakes up, he will see the NATO army!'

Once, Lyuba said with a shudder, they even had to treat a wounded and abandoned Russian soldier, but they saved his life, not just out of a sense of professional duty but knowing that he could be valuable in an exchange for captured Ukrainians.

For medic Tokarchuk, what keeps him going is a sense of deep gratitude to the soldiers on the front line.

'Medics do a very important job, but it's nothing compared to what the guys in the trenches are doing,' he said. 'So, when one of them comes here and I can save the life of this hero lying on the table in front of me, it's an honour.'

HARD LANDING

KHERSON, AUGUST 2024

Speed is of the essence for Galina and her crew on their missions. They only have a few minutes to pack their boats with food, ammunition and supplies before they are inevitably spotted by Russian drones and pursued with artillery just like I had been in Kherson over a year ago. Short and stocky, with shoulder-length black hair, she was the only woman in a unit of thirty men from Ukraine's 123rd Naval Infantry Brigade rapid response unit. Every night, she and her comrades would undertake one of the most daring and secretive missions in Ukraine. They would drive motorboats to the occupied left bank and ferry out civilians who had agreed beforehand to a meeting point, or they would resupply and evacuate soldiers who were holding the tiny Ukrainian footholds in the Russian-controlled area of Kherson.

Speaking from a long-abandoned apartment complex on the

edges of Kherson, its windows long blown out and its chipped paint and wallpaper long coating the floor, Galina and Serhiy, one of her comrades, told us they had made dozens of trips back and forth across the Dnipro River, now subsided from the height of the torrents after the flood but still widened significantly.

Galina had been a peaceful citizen, a teacher in the town of Beryslav before the war, but her anger at the way the Russians had killed and looted in her town meant that she had 'no other choice' than to join the army to fight. The Ukrainians were attempting a fourth axis of advance after their initial three to the north had flatlined. By landing troops across the river, they could avoid the dug-in defences in Zaporizhzhia. Ukrainian Marines had been well-trained for landing under fire and river warfare by Ukrainian special forces. If they had landed in force, they could have been able to either attack the Russians on the Surovikin line from the south or even drive straight to the Perekop Isthmus that leads to Crimea. That was optimistic, to be sure. They tried to cross the river to the eastern side in several locations but were only able to establish a reliable beachhead at the village of Krynky. It was delayed after the destruction of the dam, meaning that it could not be synchronised with the other prongs of assault towards Russian lines.

Operational security from the Ukrainian Army had often been tight, but in Kherson, it was taken to the next level. Access to the front lines was vanishingly rare and senior commanders would almost never comment on the situation. One Ukrainian media outlet described its frustrations when reporting that story:

> The first Ukrainska Pravda source, a wounded marine who introduced himself as Monk, was so concerned about the privacy of the conversation that he contacted the team from different

numbers almost every time before the meeting … We are ready to give the floor to the military who planned and commanded the operation, in particular to Lieutenant General Yurii Sodol, the former commander of the marines, who has so far ignored our requests for comment.

It was a terrifying operational concept that felt like a replay of the D-Day landings at Normandy.

HOLY WAR

SDEROT, ISRAEL, OCTOBER 2023

'*Tzeva Adom*' ('red alert'), a slightly robotic-sounding voice projected out, followed by the familiar wail of a siren. After Ukraine, where an air raid siren either comes well before the missile or sometimes doesn't portend anything at all, it was fascinating to see the missiles themselves fly up from Gaza, streak towards us, only to be shot out of the sky at seemingly the moment before impact. As soon as the homemade Hamas rockets were taken care of, sites of the beleaguered Palestinian territory lit up with various shades of red and yellow, like a fireworks show. It was in fact part of one of the most contentious slaughters of the twenty-first century.

But what happened here also blew Ukraine off the front pages and out of the minds of western policymakers. Truth be told, some were waiting for this. The war had now dragged on for nearly two years, and genuine interest was waning. When I first started reporting on the full-scale invasion, in 2022, everything was new and shocking. The defence of Kyiv and the discovery of the Bucha massacre gripped the world. We watched in horror as thousands were slaughtered in the Siege of Mariupol, as millions of desperate refugees fled to the border and the kind-hearted Europeans willing to take them in. The battles in Kharkiv, then Kherson, then Donbas seemed endless.

In 2023, the conflict had slowed down, and the big news one week would be a missile strike at a city that had been hit dozens of times before or the news that Wagner had taken an extra street in Bakhmut. If this sounds callous, like treating war like a TV show or a football season where you are cheering for a team rather than real people's lives, that is because that is just how the human mind works. Now, the media and foreign politicians' attention was taken up by the appalling carnage both in Israel and in Gaza, much of which fell on civilians on either side. Everyone knew how awful the carnage in Mariupol had been, but there was little footage.

It was raw, horrific and unimaginably brutal. I remember peering through the wreckage of Kfar Aza, a peaceful kibbutz by the Gaza border where militants had slain more than a hundred civilians in cold blood and dragged others off to months of dreadful captivity that included reports of torture, starvation and sexual abuse. Turn 180 degrees and I could see smoke and flames rise from Gaza, as the Israelis undertook a brutal revenge bombing that spared neither guilty nor innocent. TV channels were filled daily with the unending sight of women and children in body bags, dismissed by American and Israeli officials as unfortunate collateral damage that they were doing anything to avoid.

I never got over the Gaza fence, but colleagues who did said that it was more destroyed than anything they had seen in Ukraine. Few of them believed the Israeli and American denials, and the credibility of the west was severely dented. Why, many in the global south asked, should we condemn Russia for its depravity in Ukraine, when we are watching what looks like equal barbarism being cheered on in Gaza? Looming in the background was the possibility of a wider regional war, drawing in Lebanese Hezbollah and possibly Iran, a near nuclear power. It made me yearn for the geopolitical simplicity and moral clarity of the war in Ukraine. Frankly, the war in Ukraine had got stale, and people were ready to change the channel.

Zelensky, to his credit, greatly understood this aspect of the war; but it would also lead him to take some arguably stubborn or even pig-headed decisions. One was to even continue the assault at all after it became clear it was a busted flush.

BLAME GAME

VELYKA NOVOSILKA, DONETSK OBLAST, OCTOBER 2023

'Give us the shells, and we can finish the jobs ourselves' is a refrain heard throughout the front lines, where Ukrainian soldiers I met recently discussed the need for aid and its impact on morale.

At a dugout a few kilometres away from Russian positions, we watched as a Ukrainian artillery brigade repelled an assault on their trenches after being issued an influx of shells. I was at the town of Velyka Novosilka, where hardened, weary soldiers paused from the front lines and discussions of war to play with 'Starry', a blue-eyed grey kitten the brigade rescued during operations in the nearby town Staromaiorske.

Just months earlier, these same soldiers had fought like hell to pry the town, located in the Donetsk region, from Russian control. It's now almost jarring to see them – muscular, bearded and battle-scarred – reduced to coos and smiles while watching Starry catch mice.

'Some in the west have no idea what we are facing here,' said Alexander, an officer with Ukraine's 121st Territorial Brigade. 'Comrades of ours were at NATO training in Germany, being taught how to operate tanks ahead of the counteroffensive. One soldier asked the instructor what to do if you encountered a minefield. "Oh, you just drive around it."'

This anecdote quickly became a running joke among soldiers on the front line, where, just weeks later, Ukrainians on what would be a failed offensive encountered minefields hundreds of kilometres wide, with as many as five devices per square metre.

Another officer was kinder about his instruction but noted the extraordinarily limited time the Ukrainians had to imbibe it. 'The training was very intense. Since we arrived late, they gave us an extra hour of sleep, and the training started in the morning. [But] in six days, we covered all the theories that NATO artillerymen go through in half a year.'

But what was clear was that as the offensive failed, a great blame game was starting between Ukraine and the west as to who was ultimately at fault for Ukraine's worst battlefield loss since the start of the war. The truth is, there is enough blame to go all around. The west, particularly the US under the Biden administration and Germany under Olaf Scholz, had always dragged its heels on giving the most powerful weapons when they could make the most difference, fearing crossing a Russian 'red line' and 'escalating' the conflict. This was a pattern that would become noticeable. Rather than pouring weapons into Ukraine from the start and mobilising their industrial bases to produce the necessary level of artillery shells and armoured vehicles, they remained in a sort of stasis. The war was important for the west but not existential – and it showed.

A lot of equipment that would have been useful at a particular time did not arrive until well after it could have made its biggest impact. Ukrainian sources still maintain they could have used ATACMS, a long-range missile system that the United States eventually provided, to hit Russians at their bases before they were able to cut down advancing Ukrainian troops. They note that mine-clearing vehicles arrived in much smaller numbers. They also grumble that it was madness that they were never provided with F-16s to give air cover, which the US or other NATO forces would never do.

It should be noted that the Ukrainians made several crucial errors. By attacking on three different axes, they diluted their firepower. They put pressure on three different parts of the Russian line, none of which broke, rather than concentrating against a single weak spot. As Michael Kofman told me:

> Ukraine lacked an advantage in correlation of forces. They took the riskiest and most difficult route for the offensive. The plans were leaked on Telegram about a month before. Not by us. But it was clear the Russians knew the thrust of Ukrainian plans pretty well. It was the most anticipated vector. You, me and everyone between DC and Moscow knew where it would take place.
>
> The new brigades were undercooked; they gave everything to new brigades with a lot of mobilised guys in them. We know now that you can't train brigades and expect them to be combat effective in three months.
>
> It would have been better if they'd expanded experienced brigades and given them western equipment. Where Ukraine ended up about three and a half months into the offensive is where they expected to be on Day Two. So, it wasn't close.

Some grudging credit must be given to General Surovikin as well. He made a difficult and humiliating decision to pull his forces out of Kherson and then spent much of the winter on the construction of a trench network, not any great military charge that would allow him to win glory. The Russian fortifications were extensive, extremely well prepared and full of all of the worst types of traps and obstacles you could think of.

UPGRADED

'Your father is dead.'

When the commander called, Angelina Alexandrova felt the world collapse. Her father, Vyacheslav Alexandrov, was a 46-year-old Ukrainian soldier from the central city of Kryvyi Rih. He had been in a trench assault in the Donbas region of eastern Ukraine, and his callsign had been reported dead. A few hours later, a call came from a member of his unit. There had been a mix-up. Her father had been hit in the assault but was alive. A soldier with a similar callsign had died. It was another family whose life would fall apart. Vyacheslav would make it.

Vyacheslav is recuperating in Lviv, a city in western Ukraine near the Polish border, far from the front lines. Despite the distance, the city has been struck by missiles several times since Russia's invasion began, killing civilians. But it has escaped the devastation seen in eastern cities like Mariupol, Kharkiv and Bakhmut. The cobbled streets, considered Ukraine's most beautiful, are full of bars, clubs and restaurants – a welcome respite from grinding combat. It's ideal for the convalescence that wounded heroes need. More than 5 million Ukrainians who left their homes to flee the war have passed through the city, and many have moved here permanently. In response to the increasing influx of refugees who already put heavy pressure on the city's healthcare system, the city administration built a special centre for individuals injured in the war: the Unbroken Centre.

According to the doctors working at the Unbroken Centre, more than 25,000 people lost limbs in the war in Ukraine – around forty people a day on average. Individuals like Vyacheslav receive integrated treatment from a wide range of medical staff members, including physiotherapists, orthopaedic surgeons, rehabilitation counsellors, psychiatrists and prosthetics specialists – with the goal of ensuring that instead of seeking help abroad or at multiple hospitals across the country, Ukrainians could receive treatment in one centre. But as the war rages on and more people need care, hospital resources diminish. It is impossible to determine exactly how many people have been injured in the war in Ukraine. But recent estimates put Ukraine's 'irrecoverable' casualties – that is killed, badly wounded and missing in action – at 300,000, with the Russian figures around twice that. A significant portion of the population is still under Russian occupation, and the status of healthcare services in the occupied areas is unclear.

When I visited Vyacheslav in early October, he had been in the centre around three months. We're waiting in a basement room when a technician arrives with the prosthetic leg. He assists Vyacheslav with the buckles and straps and attaches it to the amputation point around his knee. Vyacheslav settles in at the end of two bars for support, but when he tries to step forward, he grimaces and wobbles. Eventually, Vyacheslav drags himself a few paces forward.

We met Artem at a similar hospital as well. One of the great challenges of the war will be reintegrating the tens of thousands of men with various disabilities, amputations, traumatic brain injuries and PTSD back into regular society. Many of them disliked the situation in Kyiv, believing that they no longer belonged here. This applied to injured and uninjured alike. When I interviewed soldiers who had returned for one reason or another to Kyiv, one constant refrain is that they would ask how it was possible to return to service. Genia said that her husband, despite now working in an important position in the military, felt guilt for having left his colleagues behind on the battlefield. Others disliked the pleasant and mostly undisturbed nature of life in Kyiv, believing that the people here would never understand their sacrifices. When I first spoke to Vyacheslav, he expressed a desire to return to family life. But when I followed up with him about two months later, he said he believes there is still a position for him in the army. He has a long way to go before he's fully recovered. But he wants to be back on the front lines, piloting attack drones, he says, supporting his country.

At the Unbroken Centre we met Serhiy, who had stepped on a mine near Bakhmut. His injuries were light, relatively speaking. His left leg had been blown off below the knee, but he had mastered his prosthetic limb, having learned to sprint and jump rope with it. 'I'm not disabled,' he told us. 'I'm upgraded.'

CHAPTER TEN

THE DOLDRUMS: UKRAINE'S WAR OF ATTRITION AND THE RISE OF THE DEADLY DRONE

'This war has enough dead heroes.'
– CORTANA, *HALO: COMBAT EVOLVED*

LOVE IN A HOPELESS PLACE

KUPYANSK, KHARKIV OBLAST, FEBRUARY 2024

In the black of night, I descended the chiselled stone steps of the farmhouse and suddenly I was fourteen again, it was 3 a.m. and Shaun, Zhou, Russell and I were sitting around on a series of couches with crisps and energy drinks and Xbox controllers in our hands, staring at screens frantically clicking buttons and watching the characters exploding in pools of blood, except my high school friends had been replaced with tall stocky Ukrainian men in camouflage with drone command sticks in their hands and the faint figures writhing in pain were real men. The Russians here were being sacrificed in their tens of thousands on the plains of Donbas, for a tree line here, a flyspeck hamlet there. But they were slowly making their way forward, assisted by the deteriorating ammunition situation and general exhaustion of Ukrainian forces.

Five kills in a row were a 'killing spree', ten a 'killing frenzy', two in quick succession a 'double kill', three a 'triple kill' and so on, and these terms – once used to convey a youthful pastime – became very real descriptions of maiming and killing.

Fighters would go on to gamify the process, even having leaderboards for the best pilots. One of the top would have been Serhiy Pixel, an avid video-gamer turned drone pilot with Ukraine's 80th Air Assault Brigade. Kateryna Petrenko and him formed what she called a 'soul bond':

> He had been with the controller since childhood. He played all these games – *Red Dead Redemption, Cyberpunk 2077, Halo*. He was also a programmer. The technical component was also his. But that's not why he became a pilot. It was just that at that time, UAVs [unmanned aerial vehicles] were gaining momentum.

She was working now in Pokrovsk, but when she was on leave, I met her again in Kyiv. At the beginning of 2024, the war was dragging on – and not in Ukraine's favour. We were in Kupyansk, near Kharkiv. Roman, our army officer, had fought since 2014 and had cheated death so many times that he had become numb to danger. The road to the front line, barely more than a kilometre away from Russian positions, was more a muddy dirt track than anything resembling infrastructure.

The Russians were attacking in force in many places on the front line. They had recently captured Avdiivka, a fortress city on the front line that had been a suburb of Donetsk. As soon as we got near the positions, our car lights were cut and Roman wound down the window, navigating with a tiny redlight hand torch. Working this close to the Russians required as little light or noise as possible. We piled out of the car as quickly as possible and tiptoed over to a clearing next to a farmhouse. There, in the blackest hour of night, we saw the drone, its chassis and six rotors illuminated by the narrow beam of a red headtorch. The soldiers quickly strapped various explosives to a contraption that looked like a large metallic spider. Many of these explosives were made in local armouries in people's garages and backyards.

Necessity had been the mother of invention in this case. After the Republican-held US Congress had refused to pass a supplementary bill for aid to Ukraine in October 2023, Ukraine had found itself dangerously short of artillery ammunition. It was rationing shells all throughout the front. Avdiivka's defenders complained that the reason their fortress fell was not because they lost the will to fight but because they ran out of ammunition. In desperation, the Ukrainians had turned to drone technology. Drones had originally been meant for hobbyists taking photos of weddings and natural wonders, but here they were fashioned into the deadliest tools of war on the battlefield. They were extremely cheap, often going for a few hundred dollars.

The soldiers here were not exactly booming with fervour, but they were at least confident they could hold their positions. Yet it was the doldrums of Ukraine's war effort. The counteroffensive had been a miserable failure, and the Russians were already clawing back the meagre enough Ukrainian gains in Zaporizhzhia and Donetsk that had cost so much blood and treasure. From his workshop in a secret location in the eastern city of Kharkiv, Sergiy, a 45-year-old former IT technician, and his colleagues produce dozens of drones. 'I lost many of my friends and siblings in this war, so I want to save as many people on the front lines as I can,' he says. His only job is to work towards a Ukrainian victory.

They import cheap parts, including rotor blades, batteries and cameras, usually from China, then assemble them and strap them with explosives to turn them into deadly weapons. The FPV drone – the same as those that can be purchased on Amazon for less than £1,000 – have become some of the war's most omnipresent and deadly weapons for both sides. For Ukraine, as western aid has dropped and supplies of rockets and ammunition have slowed, Sergiy says these drones have become a crucial weapon in stopping the renewed Russian advances. Dozens of these 'do it yourself' arms production initiatives have been set up by tech-savvy Ukrainian civilians looking to plug the gaps in military aid and Ukraine's own industrial capacity. Vadim Adamov, the young man who had sent me his documentary on Bakhmut, had helped fight the Russian advance near Avdiivka, ran out of metal casings while preparing munitions for his drones, so packed explosives into a Pringles can and used it to blow up a Russian armoured vehicle. 'I don't need your fucking American shells,' he told me he'd whispered under his breath. Now he was helping make films and design drones. He yearned to get back into the fight. He asked me if I knew anyone at a brigade who would take him back. I protested. 'You've done your time; Ukraine needs talented young people like you!' I said. This war had enough dead heroes, and I didn't want him to be one of them. But he was crystal clear in his aims. I'd noticed this from many soldiers who had returned. Some were bored, cynical of civilian life; others felt guilty for leaving their brothers in arms on the front line. Even if they had served years with bravery, in their hearts they felt like deserters. Vadim's expertise in drones was becoming invaluable.

A 155mm artillery shell costs between $3,000 and $8,500 to produce, without considering the transport and logistics costs to get them to the battlefield. A locally produced drone can be in the hands of an operator within hours. Sergiy and his friends produce FPV drones for as little as a few hundred dollars. Even the more expensive, professional drones such as the Vampire that can drop individual explosives on Russian positions and return to be re-equipped costs around $30,000, compared to the millions that each artillery gun costs. A Ukrainian minister said that during the battle for Avdiivka alone, FPV drones had destroyed seventy-three Russian tanks in one week. They are also one of Ukraine's most potent weapons to strike logistics targets inside Russia and its own occupied territories, including fuel depots and storage warehouses. Last week, footage published by a Ukrainian drone production volunteer unit showed them destroying several Russian tanks in a warehouse in southern Ukraine. These tanks would have individually cost more than $1 million each and would have been destroyed for a few hundred dollars.

Between civilian and military industry, Ukraine said it planned to produce as many as 2 million by the end of 2024, a target it hit and wants to smash past in 2025, and Ukraine now has an entirely new branch of its armed forces devoted to unmanned systems. But soldiers still say that drones, while becoming crucial on the battlefield, are not yet a magic bullet to replace traditional artillery. As one soldier told the *Kyiv Independent*: 'There is a reason that to this day, our infantry calls for artillery support, not FPV support.' Drones take time to reach their target and still lack the explosive punch of an artillery shell.

Even here, civilian industry has found ways to innovate. 'I joke with some of my friends in the defence industry that we're going to put them out of business,' Yuriy Sokolianskiy, forty-seven, tells me, as he shows me around his garage. 'We just fired it off… and nailed a trench, thanks Yuri!' a Ukrainian soldier on the other end of the phone says from one of Ukraine's front lines. 'It was great, hardly shook at all, accuracy was perfect!' we hear him say on speakerphone. Our companion laughs and hangs up, excited at a job well done. We are standing in a makeshift car garage in the southern city of Zaporizhzhia, a few dozen kilometres from Russian forces. Yuriy and his nineteen-year-old son Maxim have been hard at work in this garage producing weapons to help the Ukrainian Army's effort to hold off the Russians in the region. Yuri and Maxim, and the half-dozen or so workers at their factory, specialise in makeshift artillery, like the mobile rocket launcher that received such a rave review.

Their effort requires almost no special equipment, instead being made nearly entirely from civilian parts. They take a large automobile – the Ford F-250 pickup truck being ideal – remove the backing and then weld a tripod on top of the ring for the rocket tubes to sit on. Their method gives the artillery 360-degree rotation to direct its fire, using a hand crank that was originally for a gate to lift the entrance into a parking lot.

The whole process is surprisingly cheap – buying the right vehicle costs between $4,000 and $6,000, and the metal and tools needed to convert the car are between $2,000 and $2,300, depending on how many rockets it should carry. The tubes themselves are salvaged from the battlefield, either from Ukrainian spares or from an abandoned Russian kit. So, for under $10,000, the Ukrainian Army can have an effective mobile rocket launcher that mimics the job of a professionally made piece.

In his office in Kharkiv, Ihor Yefimenko hands me a cup of coffee with one hand and a grenade with the other. The building hums with the clicking and whirring of printers – he has dozens of these. 'We use our 3D printers to print these,' he says and unscrews the grenade to show me how they pack them with explosives and then give them to drone operators.

Yefimenko also ran a car repair business before the war, but now his factory runs full-time producing anything that the Ukrainian Army can use. His warehouse is stacked with examples – drone munitions, body armour, guns, specialist shoes for de-miners.

'In other locations we produce… other things the military needs as well,' he says but declines to give details. Much of this industry is shrouded in secrecy, as the Russians regularly shoot missiles at Kharkiv and Zaporizhzhia hoping to hit such locations, which are close to active front lines. With the US leaving Ukraine to fend for itself, these citizen-led initiatives could end up saving the country from a Russian takeover.

KILLING FRENZY

POKROVSK, DONETSK OBLAST, AUGUST 2024

It was an eerie and depressing sight. Civilians, usually elderly, in raggedy clothes with unwashed hair, carrying a precious handful of bags that contained their entire worldly possessions. I don't know whether School Number Two in Pokrovsk had seen better days, but if so, they were long ago. The ugly grey concrete was full of cracks and in some places, the material had faded away so much that you could see the building's foundations.

In the park was a children's playground, with dodgems, swings and slides, completely empty and silent, except for the familiar sounds of war. The last of the summer flowers were still blooming, and the thick green grass remained well kept, only just beginning to overgrow.

The shots rang out in the distance, as they always do. At one point, an artillery barrage – likely coming from a nearby Ukrainian rocket system – went off so close as to shake the windows of the evacuation bus. A few people cried, some shouted or argued. Most stayed silent, their glum, pale and gaunt faces telling the only story that was needed. Police cars drove around the city with loudspeakers desperately calling for people to evacuate. It is only going to get worse, officials warned. Evacuate now, before it is too late.

Meanwhile, American-donated weapons were starting to lose their lustre, as the Russians invented countermeasures, particularly electronic jamming. Near Vovchansk, I met a Ukrainian artillery unit using a US-donated M777. The M777s had their own special type of advanced ammunition that was initially used to great effect: 'Excalibur' GPS-guided shells, which relied on a satellite, positioned shells directly over an enemy target. US changes to policy allowing Ukraine to strike inside Russia with this weapon have also helped. Vitaly Sarantsev, a Ukrainian military spokesperson, commented: 'It gave us the chance to hold [the Russians] and slow their advance. They don't feel comfortable on border territories, so they can't collect troops [together] without big problems. Basically, it gives us an opportunity to destroy them deeply into their territory, so they can't properly prepare.'

However, these heady days of Ukrainian technological superiority are mostly over. Russian electronic warfare systems have vastly improved, and they are now able to jam much advanced western technology. One of the Ukrainian officers on the scene noted:

> Excalibur has to have a satellite connection to hit the spot, without it becomes just... a metal that is firing into the sky ... [Our unit] used to work with them but now try not to use them ...

because of [Russian] electric defence ... It is firing, but it is not exploding, like the connection is not getting there. So, it lands, and it is like a dud.

These shells cost up to $100,000 apiece, but jamming turns them into a large chunk of metal, useless even compared to the millions of old shells that the Russians are getting from North Korea. The wider significance of this is that it ended western assumptions about technological superiority being a panacea for battlefield victories.

However, the soldiers claim that there are still many advantages to artillery over drones. Artillery can hit targets much more quickly and have a larger explosive power to take down a vehicle that is well shielded. In addition, a hail of artillery is – as I have experienced in these battlefields – utterly terrifying. It has a profoundly shocking effect on enemy morale and psychology that drones cannot yet match.

While the Ukrainians had stabilised the front lines near Kharkiv, the Russians were on the march elsewhere. They have recently made small but significant territorial gains in the Donetsk region and have pushed close to Pokrovsk. They were taking town after town: Avdiivka, Vuhledar, Velyka Novosilka, Kurakhove. The Russians had increased the tempo of their advances compared to any time during the war since June 2022. Yet their casualties were going through the roof, and many expectations of their continued success turned out to be pessimistic. When I visited Pokrovsk in August 2022, locals and volunteers working there reckoned the city would fall within two to four weeks, noting that the Russians were less than ten kilometres from the city gates. More than six months later, the Russians are yet to even enter a street in the city.

Meanwhile, casualties for the Russians continued to increase. Reliable estimates suggested that they suffered around 500 casualties a day, including wounded and missing, during 2022. This rose to 1,000 a day in 2023, peaking during the Battle of Bakhmut, and by the end of 2024 were frequently reaching 1,500 per day. Russian casualties for the month of January 2025 were an absolutely extraordinary 48,000, more in those four weeks than in the entire ten-year Soviet invasion of Afghanistan, which itself helped precipitate the fall of the Soviet Union.

None of these Ukrainian soldiers are yet ready to countenance a peace deal that cedes Ukrainian territory to Russia – or at least none will admit to it. A poll from the Kyiv International Institute of Sociology showed that more than 30 per cent of Ukrainians were now willing to consider giving Ukrainian territory to Russia for an end to the fighting. Roman's soldiers were contemptuous of this idea. When I asked one of his soldiers what he thought of people who suggested ceding territory for peace, he grinned and said, 'I want to punch those people in the face.'

Here was the price of the Ukrainian high command's failure to properly prepare this area. The Russian war aims had been to capture the entirety of the Donbas region, and this in many ways suited the Ukrainians fine. Their strategy to win in this region, such as it was, was that the Russians would bash their heads against a succession of fortress cities in a row – Bakhmut, Chasiv Yar, Kostyantynivka – before finally reaching the fortress agglomeration of Kramatorsk and Slovyansk. Here, the Ukrainians predicted that this defensive line would prove too much. They trusted that their other fortified cities, like Avdiivka, Vuhledar and Lyman, would hold. But the Russians had exploited the six-month delay in funding from the US Congress to punch a hole in the defences in Avdiivka. The

Ukrainians had neglected to fortify the space behind it, and the Russians eventually broke through. Now they were at the gates of the city of Pokrovsk. Behind it lay the flat steppe of Dnipropetrovsk Oblast, leading to Ukraine's third biggest city. Taking this shabby town would leave a soft underbelly of Ukrainian defence.

Most of those fleeing said that they hoped to return home one day – one said she didn't particularly care who won the war, only that the shooting stopped. For them, the Kursk incursion meant nothing. The only hint of normality was a group of four young people playing volleyball in a court next to an empty park. The thump as they hit the ball contrasted with the crack of artillery in the distance.

When we arrived back at Dnipro, Alina Frolova, a coordinator of the local volunteer centre, took me on a tour of a shelter for internally displaced people on the left bank of the river. The volunteers had moved mountains with an ever-diminishing pool of funds, yet nothing they could offer could make up for the comforts of home.

We opened the door to one room, to see an elderly woman sitting on a dorm bed, staring at the floor in nothing but a nightdress. She had no family with her, no possession that couldn't fit under the thin bedframe. 'This is her life now,' Alina said. 'Her whole life...' Despite the work that the volunteers did here, they could understand perfectly why someone would not want to evacuate. They were giving up the apartment where they had lived, often for their whole lives, in a familiar city, for an indefinite stay in a hostel dorm room with dozens of strangers in the same position as them. It was life, but it lacked home comforts or dignity. Many had left only after family members had begged them to do so. So, some chose the risk of death by staying. The food, a bland meal of buckwheat and spam, tasted like prison gruel. The coffee was particularly awful, oily and weak enough that I would have risked going to Pokrovsk if it meant having a decent cup.

I finally understood what Hanna Demidova, from nearby Kostyantynivka, had said to me:

It took so long to convince my parents to leave. I'm [a] completely different mentality, I know my parents and I know what they say. People there almost never travelled; the idea of going out of the country wasn't as common as in Kyiv or other parts of Ukraine. It was normal to stay [your] whole life and never travel abroad. My grandma used to have ground, planted potatoes, corn, had their garden and so it was a really nice time when I think about it. They didn't travel, but they had different things to enjoy. Their house and their land and their family gatherings.

Outside their home towns, they would have nothing.

One young boy, Maxim, was ten years old and looked as if he had been abandoned. He was extraordinarily underweight and every time I saw him was wearing the same threadbare red Bournemouth FC football shirt. He would always come over and keep asking to take photos on his smartphone. We humoured him and to his credit, he emerged with a few nice shots of Jay and me.

Still, I didn't expect 'Dasha' to be among those staying. When I walked through the empty park in Pokrovsk, I was stunned to find a tennis court, and four young people warming up for an afternoon of volleyball practice. I asked Dasha what on earth she was doing there. She wouldn't even give me her real first name, nor let me take a photo – I only got her age, twenty-four. 'This is my home, why would I leave?' she asked. 'The Russian Army hasn't been here.' She seemed rather cheerful, with the gleam in her eyes of a schoolchild who had been told that it was going to be the school holidays for ever. She said she didn't mind the danger, and I entirely believed her.

It was normal to see these frontline cities populated by the elderly or the infirm. Much stranger to see four young, good-looking people in the prime of their lives hanging out without a care in the world. We all liked pontificating on why Ukrainians made the decisions they made. Here, I came up blank. 'Well, have a good day, we're starting,' she told me, winked and smiled and she jogged off before giving the ball a powerful hit to her friend on the other side of the net.

One woman, from the small and recently occupied town of Ukrainsk, had a story worse than many I'd heard before. She said she had been hiding in a basement with a bunch of townsfolk when five Russians turned up, forced their way inside to use it as a hideout. They then would not let the civilians leave. There were twenty-two civilians, and five Russian soldiers who used them as effectively human shields. Then they got into a fight with Ukrainian troops in the area. The basement got set on fire; it was full of flammable material (coal bags, old mattresses) and she said fifteen of them died of smoke inhalation. This woman was in this basement, survived, crawled out and was picked up by a volunteer evacuation team. That town is now occupied.

It was getting more and more difficult to hide the truth of the war from young men as well. On a sunny day in Chernihiv, with its picturesque ancient churches and carefully manicured gardens, it would be easy to forget the war exists. Women, old men and children wander around the parks and cobbled streets. But stay long enough and you notice that the only young men you see are those in military uniform. A group of three soldiers in green and black fatigues, with light blue armbands, eventually find their target. A tattered-looking middle-aged man with a beer bottle standing on the main square is an ideal target, and they quickly surround him, check his documents and take him away. On a different trip, my journalist colleague Joshua was stopped as he was boarding a train from the city back to Kyiv by a soldier who tried to serve him papers, only letting him go when he produced a Canadian passport.

It is a sight familiar to most major cities in Ukraine. On the day of Russia's full-scale invasion, men between eighteen and sixty were banned from leaving the country, with certain exceptions. Now, they are being called, often unwillingly, to fight on the world's most dangerous front lines. Kyiv is an outlier, with the watchful eyes of its international press corps and the large aid worker sector which gives the men here some protection. You can still find bars, clubs and cafes with a reasonable presence of young men. Press-ganging men into military service, however justified, is not a great look for a country supposedly fighting to defend liberal democracy. With Russia resorting to a partial mobilisation, Ukraine had to follow suit and introduce much more heavy-handed measures than originally intended. One videographer in Odesa, when contacted to ask if he would be willing to work on a story in the region, said, 'I can't go these days. There is a chance to receive a mobilisation ticket for Ukrainian men on the block-post at the entrance to the city... don't want to risk it!'

Despite clean-up efforts, including the sacking of the Defence Minister and various military recruitment officials, corruption remains entrenched in the country, and many of those who were rich or well-connected could still find a way to get out of service. Many other young men spent all their time indoors, terrified of being spotted by mobilisation units.

'I just came from my family home Vyshhorod [a small town near Kyiv], to see my brother, but he almost never comes out of the house anymore,' said a friend living in London who was on a short visit back to Ukraine. 'He is terrified that the recruiters will catch him and send him to the army. He is a sensitive guy, not a warrior – he doesn't belong there.' According to Ukrainian law, men of fighting age and in good health can be served recruitment papers at any time, in a similar fashion to how a court would serve a subpoena, that obliges them to appear for military duty. As Ukraine becomes more desperate for troops, the list of those who can escape military service has dwindled. A recent decree allows the drafting of men with hepatitis, cured tuberculosis or HIV in remission.

Ukraine began to struggle with a large desertion problem; it was seen as the only way that men could leave the front lines. Because the military leave system was so onerous, many began leaving the front lines to take a break and recuperate or join another unit. This was unofficially tolerated in some sections of the military, as well as by society at large. It was easy to do as well. Taxi drivers working near the front lines were absolute daredevils and would happily drive within a few kilometres to pick up soldiers, and no one would ask too many questions.

The desertion numbers were even higher than those for Russia. Russian troops spoke a distinct dialect and often looked and sounded very different from local Ukrainians in the territories they occupied. AWOL Ukrainian soldiers could easily blend into their home environments, and even if someone did discover their status, it was unlikely they would report them. Everyone knew how difficult the situation on the front line could be, and any judgement on those who left could be rendered much harder on those who had never fought to begin with. Because of this, there was a general amnesty for deserters who returned, and many did.

For those determined to flee all chance of military service, the trip across the border became more difficult and dangerous as the war ground on and the rules and crossing points became harsher. Kateryna, however, somewhat unexpectedly considering her long military service, was sanguine about the young men enjoying themselves in Kyiv. She had no ill will against them. Ukrainian freedom fighters, she said, had been a small part of the country historically. 'The whole nation cannot fight,' she said with a shrug.

> This is normal. All wars, all centuries have been like this. In order not to feel anger, irritation, I understand that there has always been a relatively small group that changed history, that fought for independence. Even a society without war, civil society cannot be the whole nation. An active group, it is always not numerous. This is normal. And I understand that it would be unconstructive now to feel anger, hatred, resentment, apathy. Because it will not motivate me to do my job in the service. I have my goals and objectives, struggle, my brothers. And in order not to waste my life energy, I try not to be distracted by this, not to think that while I give my young years to the struggle, someone is simply trying to sit out, wait out the war. If the war drags on, in my opinion, most of us will help in one way or another. And the time will come for everyone if the war drags on. Therefore, it is everyone's business, I cannot condemn them. I have my own goals, I fulfil them, I am focused on them. On the other hand, I am glad that Kyiv is standing, I am glad that Kyiv is not burned down like Pokrovsk.

She sighed. 'My brothers and sisters died, so that there would be peace and tranquillity here. Such is the price.'

As for the numbers of Russian dead, they began to climb and climb, incinerated mostly by drones but also artillery, mines and machine-gun fire if they got close enough. Kateryna continued:

> I do not believe that this death is in vain, if all of Ukraine as of now is not burned down, not destroyed, not occupied. That is, the fact that there is no front line here is an achievement of the people who are fighting now, and those people who gave their lives.

HEROYAM SLAVA

'People in Donbas, they were never our people. They never believed in Ukraine … and I also believe most people in Crimea voted to leave Ukraine.' I was shocked that the passenger sitting next to me on the plane to Kraków, en route to Kyiv, would say something that has been unthinkable to express in Ukrainian society. I was even more shocked to find that he had been a minister in a previous Ukrainian government. Now an important businessman in Ukraine, he said that in the business community, most people would gladly accept a ceasefire along current lines of control that allows Ukraine to return to some sort of normality. He explains that all workplaces now suffer from labour shortages, and it is exceedingly difficult to attract foreign investment into the country at war. He claims his views have spread even to the front lines:

> I have one close friend in the military, he has been fighting in the south, in Mykolaiv, Kherson regions. Even last year, he was still

saying that Ukraine had to fight to a victory where we reclaimed all our territories. But when I called him this year, he had accepted that we will never get them back.

Even Ukrainian soldiers were beginning to be fed up. They deeply resented people who were not on the front line. 'Young men partying in Kyiv disgusts me,' one said. A video posted on Ukrainian social media of young people partying at a nightclub caused anger and disgrace. There is a growing divide in Ukraine between those who have fought in the war and those who have not. When Russia invaded Ukraine in February 2022, Matthew enlisted in the Ukrainian Army, while his best friend paid a bribe to flee the country. 'He's dead to me,' Matthew, a soldier with Ukraine's Third Assault Brigade, told me while we waited near a field hospital near Kostyantynivka in eastern Ukraine. 'My friends are all here now.' The road leads to the cities of Bakhmut and Chasiv Yar – the former destroyed and the ruins occupied, the latter under heavy Russian bombardment.

'Let's be honest, I would not join the military in 2024,' Alina Sarnatska, a former Ukrainian soldier, posted on X. 'Military personnel have the fewest rights in Ukraine ... Most expected to be in military status temporarily or to be demobilized in a year and a half ... The military now openly say that there are only two ways out of the army – injury or death.'

A recruitment poster on the road we pass leading to Kharkiv reads: 'Father, what did you do in the war?' Others feature the faces of Ukrainian soldiers fallen in battle, with taglines like 'He gave his life so you can live' and 'He died for your freedom'. All have contact numbers and links for potential recruits interested in signing up. But, as all frontline troops will tell you, anyone who wanted to join the army did so a long time ago. When Ukraine was consistently liberating territory and was well supplied with western weaponry, joining the military seemed a better deal. Now, with stories of soldiers holding the lines for two years with no respite and a well-known ammunition shortage, service in the Ukrainian military no longer looks like an attractive prospect. More than 600,000 men have fled overseas according to a BBC Ukraine report, despite a ban on men between the ages of eighteen and sixty leaving the country.

Not everyone in Kyiv is ignoring the war effort – many are finding their own unique ways to contribute their knowledge. In central Kyiv in February 2025, I attended a conference held by an organisation called BraveOne. It was full of the most extraordinary designs for drones, including some clever novel uses of them. Sasha Rubina, a Kharkiv-born tech designer for Ukrainian Unmanned Technologies, was showing off an unmanned ground vehicle, a mobile platform with wheels that could be piloted remotely. It could carry a huge load of food or ammunition on its back to soldiers on the front line. Sasha told me: 'The idea is that the person controlling it is in a safe place. The fewer soldiers used on the battlefield itself... the more lives we save, and we protect our medical personnel.'

Since 2023, Ukraine and Russia have been locked in an endless arms race. The first great innovation was the drone jammer, which interrupted the communication between the drone and its operator. So, the operators found ways to switch frequencies or fool the jammers. Then, someone realised that you couldn't jam a drone with no signal, so they started sending the drones on tiny fibre optic cables that couldn't be intercepted. Now, fields in Donbas are covered with tiny cords the size of a human hair.

Others would leave a drone on the road, its camera on but battery off, so it wouldn't be detected, then it would explode when a target came nearby, acting effectively as a remote-controlled mine. Much of the ammunition they use is now produced with 3D printers.

With no end to the war in sight, some Ukrainians see military service as, at worst, a death sentence, at best an endless trench nightmare. It is the same on other parts of the front. One brigade in the Zaporizhzhia region that had been involved in the liberation of Robotyne was then forced to defend the town from Russian counterattacks for nearly six months before a fresh brigade came in to replace them.

KURSK REDUX

Then, in August 2024, the Ukrainians launched a surprise raid into Kursk Oblast, in Russia. It was a smoothly executed plan that took the Russians almost completely by surprise, quickly capturing nearly 1,000 square kilometres of territory. It was intended both to divert troops from Russia's crushing assault in the Donbas and to grab a piece of territory that Ukraine could potentially hold and trade in any negotiations with Russia to end the war.

The troops that were used, including the 80th Air Assault Brigade, were some of Ukraine's best.

Many observers questioned the utility of using Ukraine's best troops here when their lines were threatening to buckle on the battlefield elsewhere. Podolyak, by then one of Zelensky's top aides, disagreed, defending the operation as a major psychological blow against Russia that was helping force them to the negotiating table:

> After the Second World War, Russia acts like she had some guarantees that the war could be somewhere else but not in her country. Sort of the red lines never would be crossed. Russia plays a

game on fear, and that is why Europe has a fear. She can start a war in Georgia, in Ukraine, in Syria, anywhere, understanding that the war would only be somewhere far, and that is the idea that the Russians like. They enjoy sitting in front of the TV and watching when Russian special forces kill someone, cut off their heads, rape somewhere, but in other territories. But as soon as the war is on their backyards – the fear begins to reign in them. Putin is afraid. Why is he ready to talk about negotiations today? Because he is afraid that there will be a scaled-up military influence on the territory of Russia.

In the meantime, Ukrainian drones began to make huge inroads into hitting not just the Russians on the front line but also ammunition depots and oil and gas facilities with long-range missiles and drones deep within Russia itself.

The Kursk incursion was not without its own losses. Serhiy Pixel, Kateryna's boyfriend, was killed fighting there shortly after he crossed the border. 'His battalion was one of the first to enter the Kursk region,' she told me when I met her in Kyiv recently.

They stormed a checkpoint, and then his drone captured seventy Russians at this checkpoint. He was killed on 21 December, when there was an offensive by the Koreans, these Korean assaults, when about a hundred Muscovites were sent to the front line from three directions. Well, the Koreans did. He was performing a combat mission, sortie after sortie, and at that time the enemy FPV ... During the combat mission, they worked to the last, held off the enemy to the last and repelled these Korean assaults in such huge numbers. It was very difficult there. I think it was harder than working in the Pokrovsk direction at that time.

She told me:

> No one in their unit lost their self-control. They methodically destroyed the enemy to the last. This is important. He did not go on vacation. He was at his positions almost all the time. People cannot work that much. I don't know where he got so much strength from.
>
> I was sure he would have a long and happy life. Paradoxically, although I was at the front for two years, I saw a lot of people who later died. There is a certain correlation that those who are the most courageous are, in principle, more likely to die.

Serhiy Pixel was killed in Kursk, likely while fighting North Korean soldiers. 'He held his duty to the end; he never surrendered or stopped his duty,' Kateryna told me. Just before Serhiy was killed, he sent Kateryna a recording of a poem he had written. 'You are my inspiration,' he wrote. 'You are my mirror.' That was when he disappeared for ten days after crossing the Kursk border. Then there was no contact. Kateryna said:

> Well, I prayed every day and really wanted him to come back. I was very scared that I could lose him … He was an ideal person. I was amazed by him. He was extremely motivated, kind, bright. He was all about life. Well, it seemed to me that there were no such people. He never shouted. He never offended people; he seemed to have no negative traits. And it seemed to me that he could not die. He simply could not. Although I know that the best die, yes. But I did not allow that he could die.
>
> It can be said more clearly that since we were military, every military man who went voluntarily, a motivated military man,

accepts that he could die. This is a possible development option. But we understood that the struggle is more important, and victory is more important than specifically, well, my life, for example. I am ready to sacrifice my life for the victory of Ukraine. And he is the same. And this is the price for an independent Ukraine for centuries. And a motivated volunteer is ready for this. He understands the risk.

So many of Ukraine's young, brilliant and beautiful people have paid the ultimate price, and more will before the end. I just checked Vadim Adamov's profile – he found a new brigade to join and is back on the front line. Now, Kateryna was preparing to take up her dead fiancé's sword and shield – or his drone and armour. She described the work of a drone with the dark grace of a ballet dancer. I thought of Natalie Portman in *Black Swan*, as Kateryna flicked her wrist slowly to represent the drone dropping its deadly payload on the target below.

EPILOGUE

TRAGEDY THEN FARCE: THE SECOND MUNICH BETRAYAL

'I knew the world would not be the same ... I remembered the line from the Hindu scripture, the Bhagavad Gita ... "Now I am become Death, the destroyer of worlds."'
– J. Robert Oppenheimer

'For the second time in our history, a British Prime Minister has returned from Germany bringing peace with honour ... Go home and get a nice quiet sleep.'
– Neville Chamberlain

MUNICH, GERMANY, FEBRUARY 2025

'You are lucky your country's so far away from Russia,' Volodymyr Zelensky smiled as he looked me in the eye across the small wooden table in a musty room of the Bayerischer Hof Hotel, and the room erupted into laughter. I'd introduced myself as being from New Zealand, and he'd interjected halfway through my question with a line that had brought the house down. Despite the years of war, he remained quick-witted, with a charisma and easy charm that dominated a room without seeming to expend any effort.

The truth was that most people in my home country had forgotten about the war. I wanted a way to convince them to care. 'I have a lot of connections with Australian leaders and New Zealand leaders, and I always say to them: Let's take the element of North Korea. Is that more dangerous for us or for your country!' The North Koreans, he said, would be bringing advanced missile and drone technology back to their home country, and they could use it to wreak havoc if not stopped. He made a veiled reference to other potential actors who could stir conflict in the region; likely referring to the possibility of China launching a military campaign against Taiwan but not wanting to cause a further diplomatic incident when his country already had enough problems on the world stage.

'Wars are no longer a matter of distance.' There was nowhere that you could hide; it was an implicit swipe at the Biden administration, which had stressed the importance of keeping the battlefield confined to Ukraine. But with North Korean troops now seen on the battlefield for the first time, how could this still be the case? A new world disorder was coming, and the war in Ukraine was just heralding it, Zelensky told me. Considering that this Munich Security Conference was being heralded as the end of the post-war era of American leadership, I thought the Ukrainian President in excellent spirits. Stress and pressure seemed to invigorate him, not tire him. After months of Zelensky, the world's most famous war leader, hanging over my work like a shadow, I was pleasantly surprised to find he lived up to the hype in person.

Donald Trump had just arrived in the White House, and his Vice-President J. D. Vance had given a speech at Munich castigating all European countries for what he saw as their lack of commitment to freedom of speech. The largest European land war since 1945, currently raging at full tilt a few hundred miles to our east, seemed uninteresting to him. Instead, US officials had attempted to

EPILOGUE

coerce Zelensky into signing a deal that would give up $500 billion of Ukraine's rare earth minerals. Neville Chamberlain had gone to Munich for his fateful meeting with Hitler at least genuinely desiring peace. The current US administration was behaving like a low-rent mobster shaking their war-torn ally down for protection money. I tweeted what I suspected, based on what I'd seen – 'Trump might have finally overplayed his hand here. Zelensky isn't some career Washington pol he can troll with a funny nickname. He's the world's most admired war leader, popular at home and abroad. That is respect that none of Trump's power or Musk's billions can buy' – and attached a photo I'd taken of Zelensky looking into my camera two years ago in Kherson. My message struck the mood – in just over a day, it had over 4 million views, 15,000 retweets and 90,000 likes, by far my most popular post.

The Ukrainian President was not to disappoint and was soon involved in one of the most spectacular diplomatic rows of all time when he went to Washington DC and, during a press conference, got into a public row with Trump and Vance over aid to Ukraine. The three men began shouting over each other, and the meeting broke up with rancour as years' worth of personal resentments poured out. Despite a public pledge to end the war 'within twenty-four hours', the United States began cutting off all aid, both military and humanitarian, and quitting intelligence sharing. It seemed shocking to Ukraine and confirmed some of the worst of the whispers that some had about the US effort. That it was convenient while they could use it to bleed Russia, but once they were bored of the conflict, they would cut their losses and move on. Much like how Russia used the Donbas merely to destroy and control Ukraine, the US had used Ukraine as a battering ram against Russia, with no thought for the well-being of the country itself. It was also a great wake-up call for

Europe that there was no longer any prospect of considering the US a reliable ally. It was to Zelensky's credit, I thought, that he was standing up for himself and his country's dignity on the world stage. He was facing pressure from Trump and Musk to resign, taking all the slander that their troll armies could throw at him, while still dodging missiles and shells from Putin's real army.

I thought of the comparison of Zelensky's courage with that of Secretary of State Marco Rubio, who was watching on, his facial expression suggesting he wanted to be swallowed by the couch. It was barely ten years ago that he'd given a barnstorming speech on the Senate floor calling for military aid to Ukraine after Putin's annexation of Crimea. 'This challenge is truly bigger than our partisan divides,' he had said to thunderous applause.

Michael Kofman, who was at Munich at the same time as me, had also just visited the Ukrainian front line. 'Morale was worse in Munich than it was at the front!' he said. The war in Ukraine was far from settled, he said, and there was still much to play for.

> Wars are fundamentally contests of wills. It isn't just the balance on the ledger territory gained or casualties suffered. It is who ends up imposing their will upon whom. This war will not be determined by the next thirty or forty kilometres of Donetsk. That's not what this war is about. It is about Russia imposing its will on Ukraine. In order for the war to end on acceptable terms, it can't be the imposition of Russian will that is so unjust that it negates the point of having fought the war in the first place. It has to pass this moral and emotional test; what did we fight this war, make all these sacrifices for?

European leaders were shellshocked, and their fears about America abandoning them had finally come true. In some ways, they only had themselves to blame. Ben Wallace had been scathing to me about the lack of preparation for serious conflict in Europe: 'I can speak for my own and some others in Europe, it looks good at the front – but under the bonnet, ammunition stocks, maintenance, availability, reliability of our equipment and the readiness of our soldiers to go anywhere has been hollowed out for decades.' Vance had hit out Zelensky for ingratitude, saying, 'Have you even said thank you once?' on this trip. For many Ukrainians, the thanks should be the other way around. They had given up their nuclear weapons in the 1990s to make the world a safer place.

For Mikhailo Podolyak, this war is proof of concept that might can make right, and the only way to stand up to an aggressor is with force and bravery. The rules-based international order just won't cut it anymore:

> Russia will pay for its crimes, but only if you are ready to go through to the end. Our example of bravery showed that it is possible to stand up against such giants as Russia. Ukraine proves that if you have a comparable number of weapons, you will effectively fight back and win. Ukraine proves that the value of life is a value, but if your children and your families are behind you, well, you have no choice. At last, in the twenty-first century, you also need to be able to defend yourself. If you don't know how to do this, then someone will always come to rob, rape, kill or deport you or your kids, take away everything you had in seconds.

No one had told the Ukrainians of their expected impending demise, however. After the brief cut-off of US aid and intelligence in March 2025, they continued fighting as normal and held back the

Russians; although Ukrainian military sources claim that this was a contributing factor to them losing the town of Sudzha in Kursk, which I had visited the previous year.

As of writing, in March 2025, the score of this war was a stalemate, a draw. Ukraine had beaten back the Russian advances early on and reclaimed more than 50 per cent of the territory it lost in the early weeks of the invasion. But it had still lost 20 per cent of its country overall, around 10 million of a shrinking population, to death, flight or occupation. Vast swathes of the country have been depopulated. Ukrainian sovereignty has been mostly preserved yet at an utterly awful price. We should note what Ukraine has kept that many countries under these circumstances would not. There is still freedom of expression, and media outlets frequently publish articles criticising the political leadership or military strategy. There is no cult of personality of Zelensky – he appears frequently in the media and fields all types of difficult questions, but I've never once seen a poster of him.

The Russians had their international credibility as a military power destroyed. They preserved a land bridge to Crimea for hundreds of thousands of bodies and countless billions of pounds in expenditure, as well as causing a huge capital flight of young and talented people from Russia. The Kremlin had supposedly fought this war to keep Ukraine out of NATO and stop the west from breaching its borders. By December 2024, NATO missiles began flying at Russian logistics targets in Belgorod and Kursk regions. NATO Leopard tanks were patrolling across the fields of Kursk again, in an eerie throwback to the great tank battle of 1943. Any peace deal, if signed, is likely to have NATO members the UK and France providing troops to patrol a premeditated zone. Ukraine really will be an 'anti-Russia', armed to the teeth on Russia's borders. Just like Ukraine's desire to reorient away from Russia and join NATO, which had been formed after the invasion of Crimea and Donbas in 2014, the Russians had brought this situation entirely upon themselves.

The Russian mobilisation was enough to stem the bleeding and to begin to slowly take more territory from Ukraine. But it was never enough to win the war. Likewise, the west's impressive-sounding but in reality delayed and piecemeal support for Ukraine was enough to keep it in the fight but never sufficient to strike a killing blow. If wars are fundamentally 'contests of will', then the Ukrainians wanted it the most, followed by the Russians, followed far behind by the west. Was this the time Europe would finally step up for its own security?

To make this point, one Ukrainian started a crowdfunder for Ukraine to buy a nuclear weapon, raising over $500,000 almost instantly. Some senior figures want to put the missiles back in their silos, ready to fire at anyone who would dare threaten Ukraine again. Oliksiy Honcharenko, a senior Ukrainian parliamentarian, told a panel:

> Ukraine sacrificed its security for the sake of non-proliferation, and everyone can see how that ended up for us. Ukraine's choice [for] survival is clear. The ideal option is to become a member of NATO and get a nuclear umbrella. If we are not accepted, then I see no other way than restoring our own nuclear capabilities.

A document from Ukraine's National Institute for Strategic Studies, which reports to the President's office, made the case that Ukraine could produce tactical nuclear weapons within months.

In February 2025, I took another trip to the nuclear missile museum. Now, with Ukraine betrayed again, the talk was of resurrecting the sleeping devils here.

'I felt bad when we had to give up our nuclear weapons,' said

Valeriy Kuznetsov, a 71-year-old former Soviet officer who spent most of his life working here. 'It was a crime by the leaders of the countries that forced us to sign the memorandum, and our own leaders who agreed to do it. For sure, yes, I'd like Ukraine to have nuclear weapons again.'

It is not only Ukraine that is looking at a nuclear deterrent. Soon after Trump cut off aid and intelligence to Ukraine, the Polish Prime Minister Donald Tusk announced that his country could no longer rely on US protection. He ordered that all young men must report for compulsory military training and hugely increased investment in his country's already formidable military.

This will be one of the great repercussions of this war; no country will ever make the same mistake Ukraine did in 1994 and trust international alliances and the rules-based international order to protect them. Only hard force will be a real deterrent. What autocrat like the Korean Kim family or the Iranian ayatollahs would give up a nuclear deterrent after looking at the fate of Muammar Gaddafi, the Libyan dictator who abandoned his nuclear programme only to be stabbed to death with a bayonet? What British Prime Minister or French President could convince their voters to peacefully eliminate the country's nuclear weapons programme after seeing the photos of Bucha and Mariupol? This is a brave new world, the implications of which we have not yet come close to grasping.

There is hope in Ukraine, and it lies in the ordinary men and women, Ukrainian and foreign, who have risked or given their lives to fight for the values of the democratic and liberal order, even as those values themselves erode worldwide: Kateryna picking up her dead fiancé's drone, injured Serhiy's desire to return to the front line and the mad dash of volunteers and journalists to support survivors and to report on the carnage that remains every day.

EPILOGUE

Some of the harshest criticism of Trump's decisions came in fact from family members of his officials, many of whom had served Ukraine in various ways. Nate Vance, cousin of J. D. Vance who fought in the Ukrainian armed forces, called Trump and Elon Musk 'Putin's useful idiots'. Then there was Meaghan Mobbs, the daughter of US Special Envoy Keith Kellogg who had been a great disappointment to Ukraine. She gave a speech at the Kyiv War Museum about the folly of her home country's policy of pushing a peace that was a barely disguised Ukrainian surrender:

> Peace at any cost is not peace – it is surrender, dressed in the false guise of virtue. In many of our societies, we have allowed comfort to become our guiding star and the pursuit of ease our mission ... It is a dangerous lie ... When we believe there is nothing worth defending, we lose the very essence of what it means to be free.

It was an extraordinary demonstration that not everyone in America had abandoned its founding ideals.

She continued her grand remonstrance by saying:

> We do not fight merely against what stands before us; we fight for what stands behind us – our families, our homes, our faith, our way of life ... We do so not because we are warmongers but because we understand the greatest sacrifice we can make is to die for what we believe.

In doing so, she became one of the ordinary people who the war in Ukraine had turned into a hero.

War, I said at the start of this book, changes the nature of all those who go through it.

AFTERWORD: THE THINNING OF THE VEIL

PRAGUE, CZECH REPUBLIC, OCTOBER 2024

The ashes of Mariupol were still pressed into Helga's face more than three years after, the red vessels of her bloodshot eyes a mirror reflecting the torrents of blood that she had seen pouring through the streets.

She was there with her husband, who had left around the same time – as a carer for his mother, he was allowed to cross the borders. They had found safety in Prague but not a home in the way they had in Mariupol. 'We will never go home again; it doesn't exist now,' Helga told me. Nor did the rest of Ukraine hold much appeal; they would forever be strangers in a strange land. The confident, airy hopes of victory had long since faded, and they now wanted a ceasefire at any cost and the chance to begin to rebuild the country.

After I left Prague, I received a final note from Helga, who was ready at last to share the final page of her diary, the night before she left Mariupol:

That night will stay with me for ever, a haunting reminder of how deeply fear can penetrate the soul ... We lay together on a single mattress, covered with whatever we could find, but it wasn't enough to keep the cold at bay. Sleep came in short, restless bursts. Every sound made us wake up and listen, tense and alert. At around 2 or 3 a.m., I heard a sound so chilling that the already biting cold felt even sharper. It echoed, deep and oppressive, as if it came straight from Hell. My first thought was, 'God, it sounds like thousands of the dead screaming in agony, begging for help.' It was a long, drawn-out 'Aaaa...' not from one voice but from hundreds, maybe thousands, woven into a single tormented

EPILOGUE

chorus. The sound travelled through the floors, reverberating in waves. At times, it grew louder, crashing down on us like a tidal wave, only to recede, fading as if it were moving away. This eerie rhythm made the experience even more terrifying – it felt alive, creeping through the dark corridors of our building. Immediately, I began doubting myself. Was I really hearing this, or was my stressed, exhausted mind playing tricks on me?

To make sure I wasn't imagining it, I cautiously whispered to my husband, 'Do you hear that too?' Without hesitation, he whispered back, 'Yes.' We lay there, frozen in fear, gripping each other tightly, barely breathing. Even the sound of swallowing felt deafening, as though we might give ourselves away to whatever was causing that dreadful noise. The tormenting sound lasted all night. I can't recall exactly when it stopped. Perhaps it dissolved with the first light of dawn, or maybe it vanished like a nightmare when you finally manage to wake up. All I remember is waking my brother, who was sleeping not far from us, and whispering, 'Do you hear that?' He turned over sleepily, barely awake, and replied calmly, 'No.' His indifference only deepened our terror. Why could he not hear what was so unmistakably real to us? Perhaps the sound existed only for us, born from our fear, cold and utter helplessness.

Or maybe it was real – but audible only to those on the thin, fragile boundary between life and death, where reality becomes elusive and the cold of the night consumes everything else ... We heard the sound of Hell, as thousands of tormented souls were calling for help. These sounds continued all night.

Before I sink into sleep, I realise that after what I've seen in Ukraine, while I'm not sure I believe in God, I do believe in the Devil. I wonder if Helga's husk of a city is the black mirror of that serene Carpathian peak forsaken by God and a thin place where the violence and trauma of the slaughter has rent asunder the veil between the earth and Hell while the great Satan lying on the empty fields of Ukraine prepares to awaken all his legions.

Many in Ukraine have retained an extraordinary faith in God's presence in the land, so deeply written in the monasteries and churches throughout the country, many erected when Moscow was swampland. Meaghan Mobbs's words portend a biblical struggle between the forces of light and darkness, saying, 'Christ himself laid down his life, not for his own comfort but for the salvation of others [because] to fight for those we love, for the values that sustain us, is to honour the very meaning of life itself.' While this great battle rages, the ghosts of the innocent dead are trapped in limbo and will never rest while the dogs of Mariupol still stalk through the shattered city scavenging for scraps.

ACKNOWLEDGEMENTS AND THE WRITING OF THIS BOOK

My journey in Ukraine took me to every corner of the country, from the snowcapped Carpathian peaks of the west to the shell-cratered battlefields of the east. I spent endless hours on trains and squashed in cars between Lviv, Kyiv, Kharkiv, Kramatorsk and countless other cities, travelling with motley crews of reporters from countries as varied as Greece, Argentina and Saudi Arabia. I even made it inside the Russian Federation itself, with a squad of Ukrainian soldiers who had just captured a town in the Kursk region. All these experiences gave me a deep appreciation for the depth of history, the rich and varied cultural traditions and the extraordinary inventiveness of a people and a nation that for years was seen in the view of so many foreigners, and even many Ukrainians themselves, as a 'Little Russia'. The war challenged many myths about the somewhat patronisingly called 'post-Soviet region'. The idea of Russia as a great military and economic power was destroyed for ever, as was the idea of a hopelessly weak and dysfunctional Ukraine. For sure, the war united Ukrainians as never before, but it made people realise that much of these shared values and unity in the country had always existed.

It also saw a renaissance of war zone reporting. Every generation has a 'freelancer war', a conflict like Bosnia or Libya, where an ambitious young scribe or snapper can turn up with little more than a camera, notebook and now a smartphone to make a name for themselves. The last conflict that dominated global attention was the war in Syria, where government forces and jihadists alike saw western reporters as explicit targets. The risk-reward calculation became untenable for all but the bravest or most foolhardy. Ukraine, on the other hand, provided easy access and opportunities for a new generation of up-and-coming hacks. I woke up in Kyiv in a daze on 24 February 2022, towards the end of what had been planned originally as a two-week trip. It turned into spending the best part of three years here. Along with my comrades, I fell in love and had my heart broken, came within whiskers of violent death and watched colleagues and friends lose their lives.

Researching this book has been a far stranger experience than I anticipated. On the one hand, it is almost certainly the most videoed, documented and commented war in history. On the other hand, I am shocked to find that this book will be the first full-length narrative account of the war to date in English. There has been a huge amount of high-quality analysis of various episodes or themes in the war, but no single, concise account that follows the conflict from its opening to the present. This book has drawn from these earlier accounts, including traditional sources of research – other books, including those in Ukrainian and Russian that are not available in English, unpublished diaries, newspaper and magazine articles and my own research trips and interviews. But the rapid expansion of social media has meant that the historian of this conflict must look at a dizzying array of content in various forms. I've also had to scour YouTube playlists, partisan Telegram channels, X threads

ACKNOWLEDGEMENTS AND THE WRITING OF THIS BOOK

from niche internet personalities, dense military podcasts, Open-Source Intelligence analysis, the list goes on. This search led to some odd and amusing discoveries. The most helpful documentary that explains why Putin launched his invasion is not by a professional documentarian or aired on prestige TV but a four-part YouTube series by an anonymous internet researcher who calls himself Sarcasmitron. The most incisive analysis of the invasion's failure from the Russian perspective comes from a Russian former ultra-nationalist named Anatoly Karlin, who became so disillusioned with the war that he decided the only way for Russia to save itself was to accept its status as an American vassal and signify this by throwing the world's largest Gay Pride parade down the centre of Moscow. Conversely, the best analysis of the failure of Ukraine's own offensive is a jargon-filled technical analysis from a British think tank. The information available is endless and collating it into a coherent narrative has been the real challenge. I am being as transparent as possible about the sourcing for this book, unless doing so would jeopardise the safety or security of an individual or their family. This is an honour but also a great responsibility. The book is also necessarily provisional. We are surely getting near the endgame, but a lot will only be revealed when passions have cooled and archives are opened.

They say the real treasure is the friends we made along the way. One of the most rewarding parts of this type of journalism is the chance to meet an extraordinary collection of colleagues from all across the world. You travel together, laugh, cry and fight but build some of the most important connections of your lives. So thanks to all of you. Ann Movchan has been very dear and deserves thanks for putting up with my rapid departures and uneven schedule and remaining supportive. I wish desperately I could convey my thanks to Arman Soldin for his support and encouragement, and I hope he can read this from above.

Often the unsung heroes of reporting work are the local fixers and producers we rely on to keep us safe and help us navigate these uncomfortable war zones. They suffer the privations of living the war every day, watching their friends and family suffer and die, yet continue to produce essential journalism in their own right. I'm particularly indebted to Borys Shelahurov in Kharkiv, Tetiana Drobotia in Kyiv and Zaporizhzhia, Nikoletta Stoyanova and Svetlana Horieva in Kherson and Oleksiy Ovchynnykov in Donbas. I commend Andrii Titok for his help in getting Patron to talk. Outside of Ukraine, Olena Stachko and Lelia Katalnikova spared no effort in helping me with translations and interviews, and this book owes a great deal to their efforts. Many thanks also to Daryna Puhach and Yana Ovcharenko for their translation work.

Yevhenii Pavlosky is thanked for the informative maps of Ukraine at the front of this book.

There are many friends and colleagues in Ukraine whose help sustained me – of those not mentioned in the text, Michaela Marcy, Melissa Martin, Natalie Vikhrov, Guillaume Ptak, Ashley Chan, Tomas Davidov, Matej Sulc, Zach Anders, Charles McBryde, Collin Mayfield, Fin de Pencier, Daniil Ukhorskiy and John Sweeney stand out.

Military analysts perform a different but equally important job to journalists, and there are several who have both provided essential coverage of Ukraine and been generous with their time during both my reporting in Ukraine and the writing of this book. I must especially thank Justin Bronk and Jack Watling of the Royal United

ACKNOWLEDGEMENTS AND THE WRITING OF THIS BOOK

Services Institute, Michael Kofman of the CNA, Rob Lee of King's College London and John Helin, for his help with early drafts.

A good editor is absolutely vital to supporting and encouraging freelance journalists in their often unrewarded effort to cover Ukraine. I have had a number who trusted me immensely over the years, and my greatest thanks go to Peter Jukes of *Byline Times*, Katie Strick of the *London Evening Standard*, Alanah Eriksen of the *New Zealand Herald*, Nico Hines and Noor Ibrahim of the *Daily Beast*, Jon Simkins and Kimberly Dozier of *Military Times*, Felix Forbes of TalkTV, Markus Bernath and Gordana Milchuk of *NZZ am Sonntag*, Mike Weiss then of *New Lines Magazine* and Courtney Linder of *Popular Mechanics*.

This book wouldn't have been possible without the team at Biteback. Many thanks to my painstaking, patient and diligent editor Ella Boardman for remaining cheerful through my constant requests for a few extra days here and a flurry of last-minute changes there. Thanks also to James Stephens and Olivia Beattie for taking a chance on a first-time author's ambitious proposal.

My great thanks to Michael Ashcroft for agreeing to review and pass on the proposal to Biteback – he had reason not to, and I'll be forever grateful that he did.

Above all, thank you to my parents, Carol Mutch and Ralph Brown, for putting up with the scares and the shakes during my years in Ukraine. I'm more grateful than you'll ever know, and thanks for believing in and keeping faith with me. I hope this book is something of a repayment for your trust and support.

SELECT BIBLIOGRAPHY AND NOTES ON SOURCES

The struggle for the historian of the Russian invasion of Ukraine is not a lack of sources. This is the most filmed and documented war in history, and sources appear everywhere. It is making sense of them as a thematic whole that is the challenge, situating them in their historical context in a midst of claim and counterclaim, propaganda and debunking.

The cliché that journalists love is that they write the first draft of history. With this book, that seems to be literally true. Despite the huge amount of analysis and argument spent on various aspects of the war in Ukraine, I believe this to be the first full-length account of the war to date in English.

There will be many who do the job of historian better than I do. I am writing as an observer and participant while the war is still raging, and I also lack the fluency in Russian or Ukrainian to properly exploit original sources in those languages. The unpublished work I have quoted has mostly been translated by those working for me, who are thanked in the acknowledgements.

GENERAL

Very few people have attempted to trace the history of the full-scale invasion in a narrative arc. One of the few who has is Michael Kofman, in his chapter 'The Russia–Ukraine War: Military Operations and Battlefield Dynamics', in *War in Ukraine: Conflict, Strategy, and the Return of a Fractured World* edited by Hal Brands (Johns Hopkins University Press, 2024), which looks at how or why particular battles unfolded as they did over time. As I'm broadly in agreement with his thesis, his structure has influenced my own. An interesting companion piece to this is Neil Hauer's article for War on the Rocks, 'Ukraine's War of Narratives', 18 January 2024, which tracks the swing from triumphalism to defeatism of Ukraine, their western allies and the Russians themselves.

There are a number of other memoirs of the war that do not fit neatly into the sections below but still influenced me in style and content. Special mention to Jen Stout's *Night Train to Odesa: Covering the Human Cost of Russia's War* (Polygon, 2024). Serhii Plokhy's *The Russo–Ukrainian War* (Penguin, 2023) is the first historical analysis of the war to date, although it ends in early 2023.

PROLOGUE

The story of Novopetrivka and the Russian occupation there is expanded from my dispatch filed there for *Byline Times*, 23 November 2022, 'How Russians Tormented One Occupied Ukrainian Village'. Neil Hauer, who I travelled with, translated the diary of the disillusioned Russian soldier for us, which he also published in *Military Times*, 3 January 2023, 'An unexpected glimpse of disillusionment in Russia's trenches'.

CHAPTER ONE

My account of the Strategic Missile Forces Museum is from two

SELECT BIBLIOGRAPHY AND NOTES ON SOURCES

visits I took there, first as a tourist in 2021, and second on a trip with my colleagues Caolan Robertson and Colin Freeman, whose article 'How a nuclear-armed Ukraine could become "Europe's Israel"', *Daily Telegraph*, 24 February 2025, I used as reference for my own work.

The standard reference account of Ukraine's history, especially before the Soviet era, is Plokhy's magisterial *The Gates of Europe: A History of Ukraine* (Penguin, 2016), which I drew on heavily for my account of Ukraine's early history. Another excellent companion work is Eugene Finkel's *Intent to Destroy: Russia's Two-Hundred-Year Quest to Dominate Ukraine* (Basic Books, 2024), a detailed and deeply persuasive case that Russia is waging a genocidal war against Ukraine, which he roots in the history of Russian imperialism. It deeply influenced my thinking on Russo–Ukrainian relations. Isaac Deutscher's perceptive article on Russo–Ukrainian relations 'Changes in the Ukraine: Three-Hundredth Anniversary of Union with Russia' ran in *The Times*, 15 January 1954.

Well-informed observers remain split on whether Ukraine could have kept a nuclear deterrent after the fall of the Soviet Union. Finkel, in *Intent to Destroy*, argues it was impossible, as the missile codes were stored in Moscow and Ukraine lacked the funds for upkeep. Robert Kelley, a US Department of Energy nuclear engineer, argues that Ukraine could have repurposed its stocks of fissile material to build a functioning deterrent in a different form than it inherited. See 'Should Ukraine have kept its nuclear weapons? We asked an expert', *Kyiv Independent*, 4 December 2024. The only book-length work on the subject, Mariana Budjeryn's *Inheriting the Bomb: The Collapse of the USSR and the Nuclear Disarmament of Ukraine* (Johns Hopkins University Press, 2022), claims that Ukraine could have taken several different courses of action, including keeping conventionally armed bombers and cruise missiles. I'm inclined to the view that it could have, especially as Ukraine had the scientific, manufacturing and existing nuclear refinement facilities to reconstruct a deterrent, but it is an open question.

On my second trip, my guide Olena argued it was unrealistic to maintain nuclear weapons, while Major Kuznetsov is sure that Ukraine should and could have kept them. John Mearsheimer's prescient argument 'The Case for a Ukrainian Nuclear Deterrent' in *Foreign Affairs*, Summer 1993, is curious in the context of later history, as Mearsheimer would go on to take the view that the Russian invasion of Ukraine was caused by the west and Ukraine, as seen in 'Why the Ukraine Crisis is the West's Fault: The Liberal Delusions that Provoked Putin', *Foreign Affairs*, September/October 2014. I strongly disagree, but it is a perspective that any scholar of these events must engage with.

The most powerful and vivid account of the Maidan Revolution in English is unquestionably that of Chris Miller, in his book *The War Came to Us: Life and Death in Ukraine* (Bloomsbury, 2023). I also drew on Illia Ponomarenko's recollections in *I Will Show You How It Was: The Story of Wartime Kyiv* (Bloomsbury, 2024), which is very insightful on the situation in Mariupol. I thank Illia and Bloomsbury Publishing for their kind permission to quote from the book. Mustafa Nayyem was kind enough to grant me an interview and share his recollections on his role in sparking the uprising.

Miller's book is also excellent on the hot phase of the first war in Donbas in 2014/15. My account of the first Donbas war is drawn from several first-hand accounts, including my first ever report from Ukraine in 2018, which became part of *White Flag? An Examination of the UK's Defence Capability* (Biteback, 2018).

My own account of the diplomacy surrounding the build-up to

SELECT BIBLIOGRAPHY AND NOTES ON SOURCES

the war is very brief, as it is one of the parts of the war that has been covered in detail, best in Owen Matthews's *Overreach: The Inside Story of Putin and Russia's War Against Ukraine* (Mudlark, 2022). I also drew on 'Road to war: US struggled to convince allies, and Zelensky, of risk of invasion' in the *Washington Post*, 16 April 2022, and 'The Spy War: How the CIA Secretly Helps Ukraine Fight Putin' in the *New York Times*, 25 February 2024.

For Kyiv and Mariupol before the war, I drew on a brace of dispatches written for *Byline Times*, 'The West Will Fight Russia. To the Last Drop of Ukrainian Blood!', 12 February 2022, and 'Ukraine Under Siege: "We've Been at War Here for Eight Years Already!"', 18 February 2022, as well as my explainer for openDemocracy 'What you need to know about the Russia–Ukraine crisis', written with Polina Aronson and Thomas Rowley. I also drew on Neil Hauer's account of the calm in Mariupol, 'In port city of Mariupol, Ukrainians see few signs of government preparing for Russian invasion', CBC News, 15 February 2022.

CHAPTER TWO

The battle for Kyiv has been covered in exhaustive detail. Essential reading is Michael Kofman, Liam Collins and John Spencer's 'The Battle of Hostomel Airport: A Key Moment in Russia's Defeat in Kyiv', War on the Rocks, 10 August 2023; Luke Mogelson's 'How Ukrainians Saved their Capital', *New Yorker*, 2 May 2022; and Paul Sonne et al.'s 'Battle for Kyiv: Ukrainian valor, Russian blunders combined to save the capital', *Washington Post*, 24 August 2022. Oz Katerji's account that he related to me is expanded upon in his dispatch for *Rolling Stone*, 'How Ukraine Won the Battle for Kyiv', June/July 2022, and his subsequent film *The Battle for Kyiv*,

BylineTV, 2024. Thanks to Anthony Loyd for allowing me to use his words from *My War Gone By, I Miss It So*, one of the classics of war reporting, as the epigraph for this chapter.

The battles in northern Ukraine outside Kyiv are much less well documented. Joshua Yaffa's 'The Siege of Chernihiv', *New Yorker*, 15 April 2022, is a good early dispatch on a battle that was arguably just as important as that for Ukraine's capital. But the best account of the battle is that of Andrii Titok and his colleagues at Suspilne Chernihiv, whose three-part documentary *Battle for Chernihiv* vividly documents all the most important events in the fight for their home city. It is essential watching and is dubbed into English on their YouTube channel. Titok took me around Chernihiv so I could see the sights in his film for myself, for which I am very grateful. Yuri Vietkin's self-published 2024 memoir *Chas Che* was an extraordinary find, and I'm grateful for his permission to share it more widely.

Similarly little-known is the Ukrainian defence of Sumy. Isobel Koshiw's 'How Sumy residents kept Russian forces out of their city', *The Guardian*, 2 January 2023, is essential reading here, as is Michael G. Anderson's Modern War Institute at West Point's report 'How Ukraine's Roving Teams of Light Infantry Helped Win the Battle of Sumy: Lessons for the US Army', 17 August 2022.

The killings in Bucha and other areas of northern Ukraine live in infamy and are meticulously documented in the United Nations Human Rights report 'Killings of civilians: summary executions and attacks on individual civilians in Kyiv, Chernihiv, and Sumy regions in the context of the Russian Federation's armed attack against Ukraine'. Thank you to Mykhailo Podolyak for his interview with me describing the situation here, as well as the difficulties negotiating with Russia in Istanbul. For this, I also drew heavily on Samuel

SELECT BIBLIOGRAPHY AND NOTES ON SOURCES

Charap and Sergey Radchenko's 'The Talks That Could Have Ended the War in Ukraine', *Foreign Affairs*, 16 April 2024. More definitive proof, as if it was needed, of Russian crimes here is documented in the *New York Times*' 'Caught on Camera, Traced by Phone: The Russian Military Unit That Killed Dozens in Bucha'. I was extremely lucky to get a personal sit-down with Kyiv's mayor for a first-hand account of the battle for Kyiv, much of which was first published in *Men's Health*: 'As a Former Fighter, It's the Biggest Mistake to Say That Size and Power Are Everything', 13 April 2023.

My account of my travels during and after the battle for Kyiv are based on a number of dispatches for the *Daily Beast*, including 'Ukrainians Want to Know Why They Were Not Prepped for War', 25 February 2022; 'Ukrainians Are Heroic – but Putin's Ready to Unleash Hell', 6 March 2022; 'Putin's "Bastards in Rusty Tanks" Torched a Legendary Church', 11 March 2022; and 'Putin's Depraved Secrets Exposed in New Trail of Horrors', 15 April 2022. Platon and Barbara's touching story first appeared in *New Lines Magazine*, 'Love Survives Russia's Onslaught in Kyiv's Underground', 27 February 2022. I explored the wider fates of Kyiv's residents in a piece for the *London Evening Standard*: 'Dispatch from Kyiv: "Our neighbours, our friends, are bombing us – it breaks my heart"', 1 March 2022.

I also published wider reflections for *Byline Times*: '"War Is War, But You Need to Carry on Living": The Beginning of the Rebuilding of Ukraine', 29 April 2022; and '100 Days of Tragedy and Triumph', 3 June 2022. My diary of the first week in Ukraine was published by the *New Zealand Herald* under the title 'Ukraine: Kiwi journalist Tom Mutch's diary from a war', 5 March 2022.

Michael Kofman and Rob Lee cover the more general problems with Moscow's key political and military assumptions, as well as force structure and employment issues in 'Not Built for Purpose:

The Russian Military's Ill-Fated Force Design', War on the Rocks, 2 June 2022. I am grateful to Kofman for granting me a long and enlightening interview to explain these concepts. Thanks to Atlas Obscura for taking an interest in the museum sector and allowing me to explore how Ukraine was telling the story of the Russian invasion in 'How Ukraine's Museum Curators Are Risking Life and Limb to Document the War', 11 January 2024.

CHAPTER THREE

My account of the road of death trip to Lysychansk is based on my dispatch for the *Daily Beast*, 'The Do or Die Battle That Putin Could Actually Win', 20 May 2022. The best dispatch any of us wrote from Donbas was Danny Gold's 'Where the Shelling Never Stops: Near the "Zero Line" With Ukrainian Soldiers Trying to Maintain in Donbas' in *Rolling Stone*, 19 June 2022. I reported Ukraine's desperate ammunition shortages for *New Lines Magazine* in 'Under Russian Artillery Fire, Ukrainians Wait on Western Arms', 14 June 2022. I first introduced Stanislav, Oksana and Oksen in the *London Evening Standard*'s 'Postcard from Donbas: trenches, shelling and families living by candlelight – it feels like WWI', 14 June 2022. I'm very grateful to Oksen Lisovyi for taking time out of his ministerial schedule for a long interview on his service in the war.

I'm extremely grateful that Helga Ihnatieva allowed me to publish her riveting and harrowing diary of her *Twenty Days in Mariupol* – not to be confused with Mstyslav Chernov's Oscar-winning film of the same name, which is also essential viewing. Just expect to be emotionally wrecked at the end. Shaun Pinner's memoir *Live. Fight. Survive: One Soldier's Extraordinary Story of the War Against Russia* (Penguin, 2023) is a fantastic account of the Russian invasion of Ukraine and the Battle of Mariupol. Thanks to Pinner for taking an entire afternoon to lay out his story for me, including his account of torture in Russian captivity and mental resilience that I drew on for *Men's Health*, 'Ukraine War PoWs Share How They Survived Captivity: "Every Day We Were Beaten"', 23 May 2024.

Thanks to the Ukrainian pilots who allowed me to document what are normally secret missions such as those into Azovstal, which first ran in the *Daily Beast*, 'Ukraine Pulled Off Death-Defying Raids Right Under Putin's Nose', 23 December 2023.

Amnesty International's controversial and misleading mini-report 'Ukraine: Ukrainian fighting tactics endanger civilians', 4 August 2022, fell apart under scrutiny that many observers provided, including myself in *Byline Times*, 'Why did Amnesty International Ignore My Warnings about their Ukraine Investigation?', 8 August 2022. Charlie Savage at the *New York Times* reported on Amnesty's critical independent review in 'Unreleased Report Finds Faults in Amnesty International's Criticism of Ukraine', 27 April 2023. A good account of the controversy is that by Cathy Young in *The Bulwark*, 'What's Behind Amnesty International's Victim-Blaming in Ukraine?', 11 August 2022.

CHAPTER FOUR

My account of the horror and absurdities of the Russian torture system in Kharkiv are from a series of dispatches, including 'Shocking Torture Methods Revealed in Russian Horror Chamber', *Daily Beast*, 24 September 2022; and 'War in Ukraine: "The Hardest Part is Leaving"', *Byline Times*, 11 January 2023.

My initial impressions of Kharkiv and its metros were published in *New Lines Magazine*, 'In Kharkiv's Rubble, Hatred for Russia

Is Strong', 22 March 2022 and 'Despite Liberation, Kharkiv Is in for Long-Term Misery', 30 May 2022. For the *Daily Beast*, I profiled Kharkiv's despairing priest in 'Bitter Putin Unleashes Hell on the City That Humiliated Him', 28 April 2022, and travelled with Ukrainian troops during their first offensive in 'Town Makes Mockery of Putin's Troops and His Sh*tty Arsenal', 11 May 2022. Kharkiv's Mayor Ihor Terekhov generously gave me an interview to tell me about the early defence of the city.

Nick Fisher, AKA Indigo Traveller, has come very far since his first piece of reportage from Ukraine, seven years ago, 'Tourist Eats Ukraine Food'. His six-part series from Ukraine in 2022, which I helped produce, from 'Walking Ukraine's Destroyed Streets in War (beyond words)' to 'Caught in Bombing on Ukraine Front Line (beyond extreme)', is one of the most deeply human and empathetic looks at the lives of Ukrainian civilians. With just under 10 million views in total, it proves there is still a huge audience for long-form journalism. I was delighted to profile him and tell the story of us reuniting for the *New Zealand Herald* in 'Ukraine war: They grew up together in NZ and reunited 20 years later on battlefield', 28 May 2022.

The account of the counteroffensives in Kharkiv in Yaroslav Trofimov's book *Our Enemies Will Vanish: The Russian Invasion and Ukraine's War of Independence* is my favourite of any that I've read. I draw on his account, where we crossed paths, significantly in my telling of the story. It is from here that I draw his claim about it being Ukraine's chance to win. The *Washington Post*'s 'Inside the Ukrainian counteroffensive that shocked Putin and reshaped the war', 29 December 2022, is an extraordinarily detailed report.

Michael Kofman and Rob Lee's work, such as their analysis for the Foreign Policy Research Institute, 'How the Battle for the Donbas

SELECT BIBLIOGRAPHY AND NOTES ON SOURCES

Shaped Ukraine's Success', 23 December 2022, informed my analysis of the reasons for the success of the Kharkiv offensive.

The embed with Leshy's battalion was first published in *Byline Times* as 'Inside the Trenches in Ukraine Where Exhausted Soldiers Fight to Hold the Line as Ammunition Runs Out', 27 March 2024. Olya Filipskaya kindly provided much of her time, as well as her diary, to inform the section on civilian life in this city.

CHAPTER FIVE

I reported both Zelensky's triumphal entrance into Kherson and the horrific flooding of the city for the *London Evening Standard*: 'Signed flags, sunflowers and tears of joy – but Ukrainians in liberated Kherson are not out of danger yet', 22 November 2022; and 'Postcard from a drowned city – corpses, floating land mines and rockets in the canals of Kherson', 14 June 2023.

Ukrainska Pravda's 'The battle for Kherson: the defenders that stood firm to the end', 8 March 2023, corrects the record about the city's early fall, and I use it generously. I draw from Neil Hauer's account, which bests my own, of our meeting with Vitali Kim in 'Tension high in Mykolaiv, southern Ukrainian city at centre of one of the most crucial battles in war', CBC News, 12 March 2022. I used the version of Serhii Vodotyka's notes from Kherson's occupation published in *Ukraina Moderna* as 'The City That Did Not Fear: Kherson in The First Months of Russian Occupation', 10 September 2024.

I first published a redacted and anonymised version of Denys Tsurkunov's torture and resistance to occupation in *New Lines Magazine*, 'From Kherson, Ukrainians Report of Russian Atrocities and Propaganda', 13 April 2022. Now that the city is liberated, he can speak freely. I reported the upcoming difficulties with the campaign for Kherson also for *New Lines Magazine*, in 'A Deadlocked War for Ukraine and Russia', 29 August 2022. Awkwardly timed for it was published just as the wildly successful Kharkiv counteroffensive was gaining steam, it has held up better in retrospect.

I drew much my history of the Kherson offensive from the work of Jack Watling and Michael Kofman, particularly War on the Rocks' *The Russia Contingency* podcast discussion 'Lessons From Ukraine's Offensive Operations With Jack Watling, Part 1', 26 July 2024. They disagree over whether Ukraine's success in Kherson was due to the introduction of HIMARS – Watling arguing for, Kofman against. I don't have the technical expertise to judge, but the wider consensus seems to say that it was. It is notable that Ukraine's major offensive successes correlated closely with the period when HIMARS were just introduced and there were no effective countermeasures.

Strelkov's rant is taken from his '39 Questions' that the Club of Angry Patriots asked about the war and was translated and summarised by Anatoly Karlin on X.

I wrote a portrait of the Ukrainian special forces' operation for the *Daily Beast*, 'Miracle Boats Secretly Snatch Families Putin Left to Drown', 15 June 2023. Zarina Zabrisky and Paul Conroy were the first to publicise the concept of the 'drone safari' in Kherson, mostly for *Byline Times*, in 'Kherson on the Verge of Ruin as Russia's Scorched Earth Offensive Rages on', 4 October 2023. Caolan Robertson's viral film *Hunted in Kherson* blew the issue into wider perception of the war, and most major media outlets have followed up the story.

The rebirth of Posad-Pokrovske and its contrast with Kherson first ran in *WhoWhatWhy*, 'While Kherson Drowns, Another Ukrainian

SELECT BIBLIOGRAPHY AND NOTES ON SOURCES

Town is Resurrected', 6 June 2023, while Mustafa Nayyem expanded my understanding of Ukrainian reconstruction in an interview.

CHAPTER SIX

I first ran with Katyerna Petrenko's story for *Military Times*, in 'Holding the Line, Ahead of Ukraine's Counteroffensive', 22 May 2023. I drew much of her story from an interview she did with Ukraine's Armyinform news service, '"I had tickets to France, but I went to an interview in Borova": the story of journalist Kateryna Petrenko, who voluntarily joined the Armed Forces of Ukraine', and a follow-up interview I did with her in Kyiv when she returned from the front.

The early chapters in Chris Miller's *The War Came to Us* are a touching description of a beautiful and charming small city teeming with life, before its name became a byword for 21st-century industrial bloodbath.

The documentary that features Vadim Adamov, *Bloodshed in Bakhmut: Fearless Fighters in Ukraine's Deadliest Meat Grinder*, 8 March 2024, produced by my colleague Ibrahim Nader for Welt, is a haunting look into the talented young people killed in this city of horrors.

There is no article on the history of Ukraine that describes the dull monotonous banality that is trench life like Luke Mogelson's *New Yorker* article 'Two Weeks at the Front in Ukraine', 22 May 2023, where the Wagner fighters first appeared.

My most difficult piece of reporting in the war remains 'I met the British volunteers killed in Ukraine – they were brave but ill-prepared', *London Evening Standard*, 25 January 2023, which received a polarising reception. I didn't write the title, which I'm uneasy with, and I still wrestle with the piece's implications.

I have mixed feelings about *The Quiet Hero: The extraordinary life and death of a Kiwi aid worker in Ukraine* (Allen and Unwin, 2023), Philip Matthews's biography of Andrew Bagshaw. I was never given a chance to reply to the facts or arguments he raised against my article, which included simple errors – he got the newspaper I wrote the article in wrong and misstated the locations where I reported the piece.

On its other merits, the book is a genuinely moving portrait not just of Bagshaw but of the community of men and women who risk their lives for no money or any other worldly rewards. I can't deny it contains valuable material, even if I'll never love it.

I reported our run-in with the saboteurs for the *Daily Beast*, 'The Traitorous Spooks Helping Putin Crush Their Own People', 16 January 2023.

Mediazona's article 'The price of Bakhmut. We reveal the staggering toll of Russia's bloodiest battle since WW2 and Wagner's inmates recruited to fight it', 10 June 2024, was the source for the statistics about the endless meat fed into the grinder of the city by Russia. Matthews's worries about collaborators make an appearance in my piece for *WhoWhatWhy*, 'Divided Loyalties in Ukraine', 3 December 2023.

I drew on Oskar Hallgrimsson's description of Bakhmut in *Heimildin*, 'Life in the most dangerous place in the world', 4 February 2023, as well as Francis Farrell's piece in the *Kyiv Independent*, 'One night in Bakhmut: Civilians wait for the end as Russia draws closer', 4 February 2023. I wrote on Dmytro Kotsubailo's death, and Rob Lee's doubts, for *Byline Times*: 'Bakhmut: Ukraine Fights to the Death while Observers are Split on Withdrawal', 31 March 2023.

SELECT BIBLIOGRAPHY AND NOTES ON SOURCES

I can't trace the origin of the line 'we see our friend groups more regularly at funerals than at weddings', but I saw it online several times.

The Institute for the Study of War was a useful source, both for reliable information on the progress of the Battle of Bakhmut and a less sure grasp on the meaning of those facts. I have quoted from their article 'The Kremlin's Pyrrhic Victory in Bakhmut: A Retrospective on the Battle for Bakhmut', 24 May 2023.

CHAPTER SEVEN

The epigraph which begins this chapter is from Lara Marlowe's *How Good It Is I Have No Fear of Dying: Lieutenant Yulia Mykytenko's Fight for Ukraine* (Apollo, 2024), an extraordinary memoir which explores the melancholy relationship between soldiers who float between love and war. My chapter is based on the spirit of this work.

I draw much of Rosa's story from my conversations with her, as well as an interview she did for *Mission*, 'Images of War: A Civilian Story by Mella Rosa', 2022. I first wrote more widely about the extraordinary rebirth of Kyiv and its uneasy state of war and peace for the *London Evening Standard*; my dispatch 'Postcard from Kyiv: tulips blooming, wine bars re-opening and people starting to return', 9 May 2022, is one of the pieces I am most proud of. My later report 'Missile strikes, nuclear blackmail and a return to the bomb shelters – it's déjà vu in Ukraine', 12 October 2022, is less cheery. My series on Kyiv concluded with 'Christmas in Ukraine: doves, military deliveries and a change of date amid the darkest December yet', 20 December 2022.

I first wrote about the experiences of women returning home from abroad, including Marta's poem on loneliness and shame, in

WhoWhatWhy, 'The War in Ukraine Isn't Over, but Many Refugees Are Coming Home', 17 July 2023.

CHAPTER EIGHT

I reported from Suzdha for the *Daily Beast*, 'The Uncensored Truth That Humiliated Putin Wants to Hide', 24 August 2024.

I consulted many weird and wonderful sources for this chapter. On the start of the war in Donbas, Alexander Zhuchovsky's independently published *85 Days in Slavyansk*, translated by Peter Nimitz, is an interesting read and an insight into the Russian mindset in Ukraine.

Anatoly Karlin's insane but brilliant essay 'The Z of History' is one of the most extraordinary insights into Russian thinking, both at the political and intellectual level, about the war. It also provides a Russian perspective on why things went so poorly. A pseudonymous blog, full of odd but fascinating conspiracy theories, published excerpts and commentary from a copy of a book called *Why the SMO?*, which is an in-depth look into Russian failings from a perspective aligned with the Wagner Group.

Polina Ivanova's *Financial Times Magazine* article, 'How Putin's war destroyed a golden age of Russian culture', 15 March 2023, was helpful.

Access to the front line on the Russian side is vanishingly rare for western media. The controversial documentary *Russians at War* that followed a correspondent embedded on the Russian front line is one of the few sources on this. Alas, the producer agreed to allow me to view the film and then retracted the offer, 'having now taken the time to review your work and socials'. So, I am yet to judge their offering.

SELECT BIBLIOGRAPHY AND NOTES ON SOURCES

CHAPTER NINE

I rode along with Kiwi ambulances for the *New Zealand Herald* feature 'Russia–Ukraine War: Kiwi ambulances act as the "Ubers for the wounded"', 28 October 2023. I published my piece on Kiwi troops training Ukraine also with the *New Zealand Herald*, 'Meet the Kiwi soldiers training Ukrainians for the frontline', 16 December 2022.

I placed my interview with Defence Secretary Ben Wallace in the *Daily Beast*, 'Russia Risks Knockout Blow in War as Putin Hits Rock Bottom', 24 November 2022.

Michael Kofman and Rob Lee's *Foreign Affairs* article 'Beyond Ukraine's Offensive: The West Needs to Prepare the Country's Military for a Long War', 14 May 2024, was early to raise doubts about how easy it would be for the offensive to succeed or the idea that it would be a miracle blow that would knock Putin's forces out of Ukraine. They later described the difficulties the offensive was running into in 'Perseverance and Adaptation: Ukraine's Counteroffensive at Three Months', 4 September 2023.

The best postmortem on the counteroffensive is a detailed report by Jack Watling, Oleksandr Danylyuk and Nick Reynolds for the Royal United Services Institute, 'Preliminary Lessons from Ukraine's Offensive Operations, 2022–23', which I used to formulate my own description of the offensive.

The soldiers in Velika Novosilka revealed their frustrations to me about western aid in my piece for *Military Times*, 'Even with aid arriving, training still needed for Ukraine triumph', 22 May 2024.

CHAPTER TEN

Adam Entous's epic 'The Partnership: The Secret History of the

War in Ukraine', *New York Times*, 29 March 2025, is essential for the backstory of American involvement in the war in Ukraine. Michael Kofman and Rob Lee's 'Ukraine's Gamble: The Risks and Rewards of the Offensive into Russia's Kursk Region', *Foreign Affairs*, 2 September 2024, gives an interesting view into Ukraine's strategic movements here.

My reports from Kursk and Pokrovsk ran together in a feature for the *New Zealand Herald*: 'Russia–Ukraine war: Kiwi photojournalist Tom Mutch, banned from Russia, sneaks in with Ukrainian troops', 15 September 2024. Asami Terajima wrote a thorough piece on the fall of Ukraine's defences in Donbas for the *Kyiv Independent*: 'With all eyes on Kharkiv, Russian troops take one Donbas village after another', 4 June 2024.

The descriptions of the rapid developments in drone technology come from Michael Kofman and Rob Lee's discussions on War on the Rocks' *The Russia Contingency* podcast, 'Tech, Tactics and Innovation at the front', 17 March 2025.

I've never been more shocked by a film than Conal Kearney's, aka Cocobongo666's, film for UNITED24, 'Surrounded by the Russians: Paratroopers & United 24 Journalists Under Assault', available on their YouTube channel, where he got caught in the middle of a large-scale Russian trench assault. That level of access to the true face of war is vanishingly rare and for good reason – he is incredibly fortunate to have escaped.

I published my pieces on medics at stabilisation points originally for *Military Times*, 'Only Ukraine's guardian angel docs know the true toll of Ukraine's counteroffensive', 29 September 2023.